Governance and Financial Performance

Current Trends and Perspectives

Governance and Financial Performance

Current Trends and Perspectives

Editors

Emilios Galariotis
Alexandros Garefalakis
Christos Lemonakis
Marios Menexiadis
Constantin Zopounidis

NEW JERSEY • LONDON • SINGAPORE • BEIJING • SHANGHAI • HONG KONG • TAIPEI • CHENNAI • TOKYO

Published by

World Scientific Publishing Co. Pte. Ltd.

5 Toh Tuck Link, Singapore 596224

USA office: 27 Warren Street, Suite 401-402, Hackensack, NJ 07601

UK office: 57 Shelton Street, Covent Garden, London WC2H 9HE

Library of Congress Cataloging-in-Publication Data

Names: Galariotis, Emilios, editor. | Garefalakis, Alexandros, editor. | Lemonakis, Christos, editor.

Title: Governance and financial performance : current trends and perspectives / editors, Emilios Galariotis (Audencia Business School, France), Alexandros Garefalakis (Hellenic Mediterranean University, Greece), Christos Lemonakis (Hellenic Mediterranean University, Greece), Marios Menexiadis (Aegean Airlines, Greece) and Constantin Zopounidis (Technical University of Crete, Greece)

Description: Hackensack, NJ : World Scientific, [2023] | Includes bibliographical references and index.

Identifiers: LCCN 2022022515 | ISBN 9789811259579 (hardcover) | ISBN 9789811260506 (ebook) | ISBN 9789811260513 (ebook other)

Subjects: LCSH: Corporate governance. | Corporations--Finance.

Classification: LCC HD2741 .G6859 2023 | DDC 338.7--dc23/eng/20220712

LC record available at https://lccn.loc.gov/2022022515

British Library Cataloguing-in-Publication Data

A catalogue record for this book is available from the British Library.

For any available supplementary material, please visit
https://www.worldscientific.com/worldscibooks/10.1142/12926#t=suppl

Desk Editors: Soundararajan Raghuraman/Lum Pui Yee

Typeset by Stallion Press
Email: enquiries@stallionpress.com

https://doi.org/10.1142/9789811260506_fmatter

Editorial

1. Editors

Prof. Emilios Galariotis PhD, *Audencia Business School, Department of Finance, Atlantic Campus, Nantes, France, Email: egalariotis@audencia.com*

Assist. Prof. Alexandros Garefalakis, *Department of Business Administration and Tourism, Hellenic Mediterranean University, Heraklion, Crete, Greece, Email: agarefalakis@hmu.gr*

Assoc. Prof. Christos Lemonakis, *Department of Management Science and Technology, Hellenic Mediterranean University, Agios Nikolaos, Crete, Greece, Email: lemonakis@hmu.gr*

Dr. Marios Menexiadis, *Group Internal Audit Director, Aegean Airlines, Email: m.menexiadis@outlook.com*

Prof. Constantin Zopounidis, (1) *Technical University of Crete, School of Production Engineering and Management, University Campus, Chania, Greece,* (2) *Audencia Business School, France, Email: kzopounidis@tuc.gr*

2. Scope of the book

Good governance is not only important for corporations but also for the society. To begin with, good corporate governance improves the public's faith and confidence in its corporate leaders. Legislative processes were designed to protect societies from known threats and to keep problems from occurring or reoccurring. Recent corporate scandals shed light on the effect that corporations have on social responsibility. The new focus on corporate governance framework increases corporations' responsibility and accountability to their stakeholders and provide though a solid framework for firms' increased performance.

As a result, we are seeing corporations increasingly placing pressure on themselves to improve best practices for corporate governance with the goal of enhancing their relationships with stakeholders. The largest attraction for corporations to direct some of their attention on better performance is that it ultimately improves corporations' ability to thrive and prosper.

This book proposes a novel framework for combining the Corporate Governance Framework (CGF) with up-to-date corporate finance topics arising within the Contemporary Business Environment (CBE) and their cointegration in the today's business needs. It seeks to underscore whether corporate governance characteristics regarding ownership, board of directors' composition, shareholders' rights, etc., do influence and to what extent the financial performance of firms. We provide solid descriptions and references on the question of whether corporate governance structures worldwide are used as determinants of differences in economic performance. We look also at the identities of owners, monitoring boards, and legal systems and search for Corporate Governance (CG) structures that give rise to differences in performance.

Moreover, we extend the current public debate on CG and the globalization of financial markets, if any. Furthermore, we use a variety of methodologies to compare the CG implementation within a corporation with plethora of financial performance indicators, e.g. ROA, ROE, Price to Book ratio and P/E to find out any relationship between them. Concisely, this book identifies methodological aspects revealing the deployment of the functioning of CG with firm characteristics and operating performance.

Also, the book will perform a significant role in improvising understanding of the Contemporary Environment to a great extent. Both researchers and practitioners working in field of Corporate Governance will highly benefit from it. This book is a good collection of state-of-the-art approaches for CG aspects to various firm-performance fields. It will be particularly beneficial for new researchers and practitioners working in the field and help them to quickly grasp the current status on CG and Corporate Financial Performance. This book will be very useful because there is a limited number of books in the market that provide a good collection of state-of-the-art references on prosperous Investment Decisions regarding the CG environment, Agency Problems, Corporate Performance Measurement and Efficient Markets and Behavioral Finance while considering issues that are important to all stakeholders, such as gender quality, fraud, responsibility, and ESG.

Keywords: Corporate governance system, agency theory, return on assets, stock return, firm performance, responsible management, ESG

3. Topics of Interest

The purpose of this book is to report the latest advances and developments in the field of Corporate Governance and Financial Performance. Mainly the book will be in the following three parts. More details of the coverage and contents are discussed in the following section.

Table of Contents

An initial table of contents is as follows (CG is the abbreviation of Corporate Governance).

Part I: CG and the Performance Process

Chapter 1: Corporate Governance's Characteristics and Financial Performance in the Innovative SMEs

This chapter focuses on the relationship between corporate governance and financial performance over the period 2015–2019 on a dataset of Italian Innovative Small and Medium-sized Enterprises (SMEs). The characteristics of corporate governance are investigated with respect to three main aspects: Workers' education attainment, ownership of software or patent and prevalence of women, young and foreigners in the corporate board. In order to deal respectively with time-invariant corporate variables and the endogeneity issue related to past firm performance, Hausman–Taylor (HT) model and two System Generalized Method of Moments (Sys-GMM) have been employed for the examination of the aforementioned relationship in both static and dynamic terms. Results show that most of the considered corporate governance variables, affect innovative SMEs' profitability except for the ownership of software or patent.

Chapter 2: Ownership and Governance of State-Owned Enterprises: A Compendium of National Practices

This chapter focuses on efforts to create a more effective corporate governance framework in the Hellenic Republic (Greece). Recent efforts to modernize and improve the governance regime began in 1999, with the publication of the Corporate Governance Principles in Greece, and continued with the regulation of the Capital Market Commission which covers transparency, market behavior, and acquisitions of listed companies. In 2002, a regulation was introduced that emphasizes the structure and conduct of the board.

New laws and regulations that have introduced a series of new ideas — including requirements for independent board members, internal control services, faster dissemination of information, and new measures to protect against the use of confidential information — stimulate a trend toward a more efficient corporate governance system in Greece. The new rules of behavior of listed companies have also improved accountability, transparency and disclosure of information, with severe punishment for violations, although the existing laws provide a fair degree of flexibility. The expected implementation of the proposed new laws will address the issue of market abuse, including both price manipulation and the use of confidential information.

Nonetheless, despite these initiatives, many businesses are still falling below the levels best suited to Europe and the US. Implementation of governance practices remains in many cases more of a result of mandatory compliance than a conscious effort by corporate boards to be more accountable.

Chapter 3: New Corporate Governance Law in Greece: Key Elements and Analysis

The interest of this chapter focuses on corporate governance issues and current relevant developments in the international and Greek landscape. For this reason, the relevant issues are examined at both the theoretical and practical levels. The objective of this chapter is to examine and evaluate the new legal framework of corporate governance in Greece and to identify the main functions it integrates into corporate practice. The aim of this work is to study the practices that are applied in the application of the new law and differentiate them in relation to the Environment-Social-Governance (ESG) framework. Through this analysis, there is a scope to clarify the possible interventions of the law at the different levels of its interference in corporate practices. As part of the above, literature review on corporate governance issues and the main trends emerging in academic research is also carried out.

Chapter 4: Corporate Governance and Agency Problems
In this chapter, the *principal–agent* problem is addressed. The agency problem is explained along with real cases used as examples that have been analytically described. The different types of the *principal–agent* problem, are presented and analyzed, along with ways of mitigating the problem.

Chapter 5: Corporate Governance Gender Equality and Firm Financial Performance: The Case of Euronext 100 Index
This chapter analyzes how financial performance indicators and gender equality of large cap stocks impact on governance scores. In particular, we examine how the return on equity, reinvestment rate, price to book value, market capitalization and gender equality of large cap firms in Europe are related to their governance pillars scores. Based on the Euronext 100 index we conduct a multiple regression analysis for the period 2010–2020. As regard the above financial indicators, we find that return on equity and market cap have a significant positive impact on governance scores. In addition, we conclude that reinvestment rate and price to book value have a negative and significant effect on governance scores. Finally, the low percentage of female board membership is confirmed by the non-effect of gender inequality on governance score. Our empirical investigation provides evidence in support of the moderate governance score in European companies. However, European companies should consider the benefits of good governance practices and apply sustainable strategies.

Part II: CG and the Corporate Debt

Chapter 6: A Bibliometric Overview of the State-of-the-Art in Bankruptcy Prediction Methods and Applications
This chapter aims to help future researchers and practitioners explore different statistical methods (discriminant analysis, logistic regression,

probit analysis) and modern analytical methods (support vector machines, artificial intelligence, neural networks) to provide improved predictions. It is also intended to facilitate their research by providing a clear overview of their interests and finding relevant information for further research.

Over the past decades, the topic of bankruptcy prediction methods has developed significantly, becoming a relevant research area in many disciplines, including business economics, computer science, operations research, finance and accounting. Motivated by the severe impact that the 2007–2009 financial crisis and the recent COVID-19 global health crisis have had on companies of all sizes, and subsequently the need to develop new methodologies for predicting corporate failures, this chapter provides a systematic literature review, based on bibliometric analysis of 993 reviewed articles, and an in-depth review of 103 articles published on bankruptcy prediction methods over the period 1997–2019.

Chapter 7: CG and Viable Corporate Debt

This chapter presents a basic level explanation about corporate debt and its viability. Also, it presents basic corporate governance types and their relationship with corporate debt and its manifestations worldwide.

It is an indisputable fact that corporate governance is increasingly appearing on the world stage. How listed companies are controlled and managed has begun to concern the firm environment in its totality, such as the board of directors, senior executives, shareholders, employees and those who present a relative interest in that company. After the pressure of the collapse of many large companies, the supervisory authorities of almost all economies began to look for systems to deal with and solve the problems of protecting shareholders and creditors of stock exchange-listed companies. The main objective of corporate governance systems is the fully transparent and effective management of a company, which will maximize its financial value and protect shareholders and creditors. A large part of corporate governance concerns the financial viability of businesses, and that is where loans and corporate debts, in general, come in. Corporate debts in the modern economy have skyrocketed and are now determining the economic scene worldwide.

Chapter 8: Corporate Governance and Financial Fraud Detection

Corporate governance (CG) includes principles such as rules, processes or laws, according to which a company should operate and be controlled.

CG affects all stakeholders' interests, including shareholders, customers, vendors and management. Within a firm, the principles of good CG involve all top-level management committees, including the board, the audit committee and the CG committee.

Although the principles of CG are now well established and widely accepted, the number of cases of corporate fraud is growing, raising the need to thoroughly investigate factors that can be used as early-warning signals. Among the various types of corporate fraud, financial fraud is among the most important ones. The auditors' weakness to detect financial scandals renders the usage of specific audit methods and tools necessary (Lin *et al.*, 2003). A plethora of academic researchers (Dechow *et al.*, 2011; Price *et al.*, 2011) have proposed various methods to detect financial fraud, often based on information derived from financial statements (Ngai, 2011). Nowadays, even if the audits are intensive, the fraudsters can override them, and auditors cannot detect the scams on time. Thus, it is imperative to approach the detection of frauds studying the motivation, the opportunity, the pressure and the ability of a fraudster to conduct fraudulent actions.

These four elements constitute the fraud diamond theory, which this chapter adopts for the application of a machine learning approach. The results show a high accuracy (overall accuracy over 83%), thus setting a basis to investigate more variables which are from fraud diamond theory and more generally, are corporate governance elements.

Part III: CG and Externalities

Chapter 9: Governance and Corporate Control around the World
This chapter presents basic corporate control types and their influences on their formation by cultural and other factors. In addition, this chapter also presents basic corporate governance types and their relationship with corporate control types at various countries around the world, based on 2019 recent studies by OECD.

Corporate control, within the context of capitalism, could take many forms that might make communication among various groups, such as academics, public authorities or employees of any level, difficult and complicated. In the US and other developed countries, capitalism is formed through a large number of corporations of any size who compete each other, while monopolies are prohibited. Owners of those corporations, the shareholders, especially the minor ones, are usually disorganized and powerless, while other corporations or even state-owned corporations act as shareholders of other corporations and promote their interests through active participation in management with, among others, the selection and the influence of Board members. CEOs, as the heads of management of such corporations, even audited and controlled by many mechanisms in place, could affect decision-making of those corporations by incorporating their personal beliefs and mindsets, cultural influences and political beliefs in their decision making process. In less-developed countries, capitalism is formed through the creation of corporations by wealthy families, with a limited number of shareholders, and there are many cases that members of the family possess the vast majority of shareholders' voting rights. The owners of such corporations might sometimes have the power to affect governments' decision-making in order to gain advantage over their competitors, so even though monopolies are prohibited, the actual situation is far away from the terms of perfect competition.

Within this economic context, historically, the evolution of corporate governance has been affected by several factors and events that took place during financial history. Those factors and events not only contributed to the evolution of corporate governance but also differentiated its content among countries with different corporate control types, different cultures, economic power, etc. Emergency events at countries' history like wars, changes in political systems, etc., along with major economic crises due to corporate collapses led corporate governance to emerge and to evolve. Reinforcement of concentration of corporations by wealthy families in some countries, along with the decline of power of some wealthy families in other countries and the corresponding corporate failures, created discrepancies among countries to the applicable legislation for corporate governance. The formation of big business groups, through mergers, acquisitions and the creation of new corporations as a response to cope with competition, created new risks for shareholders and stakeholders that had to deal with effectively by legislative authorities, within the context of corporate governance and the established mechanisms of corporate control. The rapid evolution of technology in recent years that had massive impact on privacy issues led to the creation of relevant legislation that also had an impact on the governance model of corporations and on elements of control of corporations. Legislation itself, is a factor that not only is affected by the evolution of corporate governance, but also affects and triggers its revolution. Capital markets legislation, for example, affects the behavior of shareholders, especially of controlling shareholders who might set up their strategy extending from passive block holders to active participants with diversified portfolios of investments.

Chapter 10: Event Study Methods in Corporate Governance Studies
This chapter essentially has two main parts. The first part is on the techniques for testing the price changes (more precisely, abnormal return) in the short run (i.e. days) around the time of the event. The second part describes the methods for analyzing price movements during a longer period (e.g. 5 years) following the event. The first part of this chapter is largely self-contained so that the second part is optional to those who need to examine only short-term abnormal return. However, it is advisable that those with the research objective of examining long-term abnormal return first familiarize themselves with the tests of short-term abnormal returns in order to install an understanding of the rationale underlying an event study. Such an understanding is essential because the tests of long-term abnormal return are fundamentally an outgrowth of the methodology fundamentally designed for a short window.

Chapter 11: CG and Prosperous Investment Decisions — The Paradigm of Mergers and Acquisitions
Mergers and acquisitions are business transaction that if they occur they have a pervasive effect both to the seller and the buyer and they can derive in substantial benefits or failures. The chapter aims to approach mergers and acquisitions in a spherical way, synthesizing business reasons driving to M&As, the risks, the challenges, the financial aspects and the accounting treatment based on the IFRS's.

https://doi.org/10.1142/9789811260506_fmatter

About the Editors

Emilios Galariotis is full Professor of Finance at Audencia Business School (EQUIS, AMBA, AACSB), France and Associate Dean for research. He also sits on the management board of the Independent Authority for Public Revenue (IARP) of the Hellenic Republic. He has occupied several high impact administrative posts in the academia, and he is also a member of the Board of Directors of the Financial Engineering and Banking Society, the Hellenic Association for Energy Economics, the French Finance Association (Affi) where he has also served in the past as President. His research is mainly on the efficiency of financial, banking and energy markets and on behavioral finance issues, and it has been published in more than 60 articles in leading journals, while he has edited and contributed to several books including for the Frank J. Fabozzi Series and the *Wiley Encyclopaedia of Management*.

Alexandros Garefalakis is Certified Internal Controls Auditor (CICA), Certified Public Accountant (Fellow of CPA), Certified Management Accountant (CMA), Certified Controls Specialists (CCS) and Business Consultant in numerous companies, organizations and European programs from 2006. Also, he is an Assistant Professor at the Department of Business Administration and

Tourism at Hellenic Mediterranean University (HMU) in Greece. He holds a degree in Financial Applications, a master's degree in Accounting and Finance from University of Southampton and PhD in Accounting from Hellenic Open University.

He has coauthored 10 books on Audit Accounting and Management Accounting issues. He has more than 100 publications in peer-reviewed journals and has participated in more than 30 national and international conferences. He has also been awarded first prize in an innovation competition "Young Businessman" for the Intelligent Qualitative Analysis Database (AIQAD) and the Ma.Co.I index that he developed in 2003.

He also has 12 years of academic teaching experience (in undergraduate and postgraduate programs) and his areas of research interest include the Disclosure Narrative Information, ESG, Management Commentary Index (Ma.Co.I), Accounting and Operation Research and Auditing.

Christos Lemonakis is a Certified Public Accountant (Fellow of CPA), Certified Management Accountant (CMA), and Certified Risk and Compliance Officer (CRCO). He is also an Associate Professor of Business Administration in Small and Medium Enterprise (SME) Management at the Faculty of Management Sciences and Technology of the Hellenic Mediterranean University (HMU) in Greece.

He holds a Diploma in Production Engineering and Management, a bachelor's degree in Economics, and a PhD in Banking and SME Management. His research interests include banking efficiency, corporate governance and SME management.

Marios Menexiadis is an economist specializing in Internal Audit. He is the Group Internal Audit Director and Data Protection Officer of Aegean Airlines. Prior to joining the aviation industry in 2009, he offered his services as Director of Internal Audit in the chemical as well as food and beverage industry, while his professional career started within the "Big 5".

He offers his expertise as Chairman of Audit Committees of BoDs and has been member of the

Audit Committee of the Hellenic Institute of Internal Auditors. He is a Senior Council Member and Chairman of the Educational Committee at the Association of Certified Public Accountants International.

Menexiadis is an affiliate professor on a series of postgraduate programs and a co-author in a series of books.

He holds a Post-doctorate research degree from NKUA, a PhD degree in Internal Audit and Best Practices from NKUA, an MSc in Internal Audit from City University and an MAcc in International Accounting and Financial Management from Glasgow University. He is a fellow CPA member and CRSO from ACPAI and a fellow member from AICPA, while he has been awarded the professional titles of CICA, CCS and GRC.

He is an affiliate Professor in the universities of BSBI, NKUA, Piraeus, Hellenic Open University, Escem (France) and Patras and Technical University of Chania.

Constantin Zopounidis is Professor of Financial Engineering and Operations Research, at Technical University of Crete (Greece), Distinguished Research Professor in Audencia Business School (France) and Senior Academician of both the Royal Academy of Doctors and the Royal Academy of Economics and Financial Sciences of Spain. He is member of the Editorial Board of the New Mathematics and Natural Computation (World Scientific). He is also elected President since early 2012 of the Financial Engineering and Banking Society (FEBS).

In recognition of his scientific work, he has received several awards from international research societies. In 2012, he was the recipient of the Long-lasting Research Contribution Award in the field of Financial Engineering & Decision Making by ESCP Europe. In 2013, he received the Edgeworth-Pareto prestigious Award from the International Society of Multicriteria Decision Making and in 2015 he received the Award for Outstanding Contribution to Research in Management Science and Decision Making by Audencia Business School. In 2018, the Aristotle University of Thessaloniki awarded him the title of Honorary Doctor.

He has edited and authored 100 books with international publishers and more than 500 research papers in scientific journals, edited volumes, conference proceedings and encyclopedias in the areas of finance, accounting, operations research and management science.

https://doi.org/10.1142/9789811260506_fmatter

Contents

Part I

CG and the Performance Process

https://doi.org/10.1142/9789811260506_0001

Chapter 1

Corporate Governance's Characteristics and Financial Performance in the Innovative SMEs

Silvia Angilella*, **Sebastiano Mazzù**†, **and Maria Rosaria Pappalardo**‡

Department of Economics and Business, University of Catania, Corso Italia 55, Catania, Italy

**silvia.angilella@unict.it*

†*sebastiano.mazzu@unict.it*

‡*mariarosaria.pappalardo@unipa.it*

Abstract

This chapter focuses on the relationship between corporate governance and financial performance over the period 2015–2019 on a dataset of Italian Innovative Small and Medium-sized Enterprises (SMEs). The characteristics of corporate governance are investigated with respect to three main aspects: workers' education attainment, ownership of software or patent and prevalence of women, young and foreigners in the corporate board. In order to deal respectively with time-invariant corporate variables and the endogeneity issue related to past firm performance, Hausman–Taylor (HT) model and two System Generalized Method of Moments (Sys-GMM) have been employed for the examination of the aforementioned relationship in both static and dynamic terms. Results show that most of the considered corporate governance variables, affect innovative SMEs' profitability except for the ownership of software or patent.

Keywords: Corporate governance, small and medium-sized enterprises (SMEs), firm performance, innovative firms

1. Introduction

Corporate governance characteristics play a fundamental role in the management of companies, since they influence their financial performance. For this reason, the relationship between corporate governance features and company performance has aroused the interest of many scholars, whose results are not always concordant. The literature review has considered many aspects of corporate governance that have a significant influence on corporate profitability as measured by return on assets (ROA).

Among them, the most debated ones concern board size, female board representation, the education, and experience level of board members and the presence of independent outside directors. This study is part of this stream of research, but differs from previous studies in that since it analyzes the influence of corporate governance characteristics on the performance of innovative firms.

Since such SMEs are characterized by high risks related to the implementation of the innovative project, which are not comparable to those of traditional firms, some features of corporate governance may be relevant. Indeed, the characteristics of corporate governance affect the innovativeness of firms and thus their ability to be profitable. In addition, these firms often encounter financing of their activity through bank loans with finance gap effects that impact on the realization of innovative projects.

Following these research assumptions, we explore how corporate profitability of innovative SMEs is influenced by the following aspects: (a) workers' education attainment; (b) ownership of software or patent; (c) prevalence of women, young members and foreigners in the board composition.

We test our research hypotheses through the application of different static and dynamic model estimators. Results are reported for a sample of 1,604 Italian companies over the period 2015–2019, obtaining in total a strongly balanced panel of 8,020 firm-year observations.

Since the firms analyzed are not listed and belong to the category of small and medium-sized firms, we have considered ROA as an indicator for measuring the profitability of firms. Instead, ROA, being computed as net income over total assets, represents a true profitability measure of business performance (Hagel *et al.*, 2013). It is well suitable especially in three situations: when similar companies have to be compared, when a company has to be compared to its past performances or when company's debts have to be considered into the analysis.

Moreover, a set of control variables has been added to this analysis, as determinants of board structure. They account for company's size, growth opportunities and leverage as well as company's age, sector and legal form.

The rest of the chapter is organized as follows. Section 2 presents the main literature review about the impact of corporate governance's characteristics on companies' performance. Sections 3 and 4 describe, respectively, the static and the dynamic panel estimators, by highlighting the main pros and cons to deal with the issue of time invariant corporate variables and the endogeneity issue related to past firm performance. Section 5 provides some preliminary and post-estimation tests to verify whether the used estimators are correctly specified. Section 6 describes the data used to analyze the aforementioned relationship. Section 7 discusses the model specification by implementing three different steps and summarizes the main findings. Finally, Section 8 concludes the study.

2. Literature Review

Several studies have investigated how the structure of corporate governance plays a role in the value of the company, the share price and how the independence of the board, the skills developed, the relationships with shareholders and the stock ownership of board members, influences the profitability and competitiveness of the company (Black, 2001; Joh, 2003; Klapper and Love, 2004; Bhagat and Bolton, 2008; O'connell and Cramer, 2010; Arora and Sharma, 2016). Most of these studies are based on large firms and do not include SMEs. Few studies, however, have investigated the relationship between governance characteristics and the profitability of innovative enterprises and in particular the importance of individual workers' features. In this respect, Ayyagari *et al.* (2011) analyzed a large sample of firms with patents and R&D expenditure located in 47 countries. They find that the level of education of both managers and the workforce is significantly related to the extent of innovation of a firm and that the more innovative firms are younger, but larger. Likewise, a higher level of education of board members and workers is correlated with a higher level of innovation in the company, as well as being determinants of earnings management and positively associated with strategic decision-making (Hambrick and Mason, 1984; Wally and Baum, 1994; Leiponen, 2005; Graham *et al.*, 2013; Kouaib and Jarboui, 2016). In contrast, Bolli *et al.* (2018), find that diversity in formal education degrees of workers is insignificantly related with process innovation and the intensive margins of R&D and product innovations. The authors argue that experience rather than level of education is more important. In this regard, Grinza and Quatraro (2019) argue that experienced workers are a crucial asset for innovative companies because they are repositories of knowledge and organizational routines.

The ability of firms to produce patents is not always recognized as an important element of firm growth and profitability (Sher and Yang, 2005).

There is a conflicting empirical evidence in this regard. Artz *et al.* (2010) find that there is a negative relationship between patents, ROA and sales growth. They argue that patents have value as devices to protect proprietary technologies and limit that rival firms can encroach on the firm's business area. Conversely, there seems to be an increasing return for R&D spending compared to patents, because the firm can immediately take advantage of producing and bringing new products to market. Likewise, Guo *et al.* (2012) show that R&D expenditures become a significant positive factor in firm profitability. Patents, on the other hand, have an insignificant impact on accounting or market returns. This may be because patents need more time to produce its value and increase firms' earnings. On the other hand, Cheng *et al.* (2010) have demonstrated that the contribution of patents to a company's profitability measured in terms of ROA depends on the quality of the patent and its citations in the scientific field. When the patent concerns an important invention there is a direct and positive impact on a company's profit-earning ability. This usually occurs in large companies that have more resources to invest in innovation.

Regarding the relationship between board characteristics and performance, scholars have shown different effects depending on the types of diversity (gender, age, foreign nationals). Using ROA as the measure of accounting performance, Darmadi (2011) finds that none of the proportions of women, foreign nationals and young members have significant influence on firm performance. The relationship between the presence of women and improved firm performance is highly debated (Maravelaki *et al.*, 2019). Rose (2007) argues that female representation does not influence firm performance measured by Tobin's Q. In accordance, Fernández-Temprano and Tejerina-Gaite (2020) did not observe any positive effect on ROA related to the presence of women on the board for a sample of Spanish non-financial firms in the period 2005–2015. On the contrary, Perryman *et al.* (2016) find that increases in gender diversity not only reduce firm risk and improve firm performance, but also reduce the wage gap at the top executive level. Quiroz-Rojas and Teruel, (2020) show, instead, that female contributions on firm growth is higher in non-innovative firms in comparison with their contribution to innovative firms. This is due to the conservative approach to risk taken by women compared to men. Therefore, the contribution of women in the development of innovative enterprises is lower.

Since innovation is a feature of new firms, in most cases the presence of young people is one of the characteristics of the organization. On this aspect, Ouimet and Zarutskie (2014) find that younger have more recent education and they have more current technical skills. The authors find that the greater risk tolerance of young people allows for the development of innovations and firm growth. By the way, this characteristic in some sectors favors an increase in the failure rate of innovative firms. Empirical evidence show, however, that in innovative firms the ability to grow and achieve performance depends on the specificities of human capital (Aubert *et al.*, 2006; Coad, 2018). In this view, young members have a strong aptitude for creativity and novelty and therefore represent the most important strength for innovative firms. While age diversity on the board generates positive effects on firm performance due to the mix of knowledge, cultures and approach to risk (Kim and Lim, 2010; Mahadeo *et al.*, 2012; Fernández-Temprano and Tejerina-Gaite, 2020), the presence of young members is associated with strategic change and the tendency to innovate (Ahn and Walker, 2007). However, while younger board members are more inclined to technology and its application in business processes, on the contrary, their presence generates positive effects on company performance when there is adequate experience. In this regard, Daveri and Parisi (2015) using a sample of Italian firms compare the effect of board managerial experience expressed in terms of age on firm performance of a sample of innovative and non-innovative Italian firms. They find that the presence of older board members has a negative effect on innovation and productivity, while in non-innovative firms, there is no such effect.

The empirical evidence on the ability of innovative firms to improve their performance in the presence of foreign board members is different. Makkonen *et al.* (2018) find there is there is a positive association between foreign board members and firm innovativeness, while Carter, D'Souza *et al.* (2010) and Masulis *et al.* (2012) find no systematic evidence that foreign corporate governance affect positively financial performance of major US firms. Expanding the studies not only to board members but also to those of foreign workers in innovative firms, the literature has shown that the contribution of foreign members is not always significant. Ozgen and de Graaff (2013) show that nationality diversity generates positive effects on product innovation but no also on firms' process innovations. In general, however, the positive impact of worker nationality diversity on innovation is quantitatively modest.

3. Static Panel Models

3.1 *Static pooled OLS model*

The simplest econometric model for panel data estimates is Pooled OLS. It is based on the Ordinary Least Square estimator and it is one of the most applied method for empirical researches. Although it is unsuitable for most of cases, it provides a guideline of comparison with more complex models.

The following equation describes the pooled OLS model:

$$Y_{it} = \beta X_{it} + u_{it} \tag{1}$$

with $i = 1, 2, \ldots, N$ and $t = 1, 2, \ldots, T$; where i and t represent the indices, respectively, for individuals and time, Y_{it} the dependent variable, X_{it} the vector $1 \times k$ of independent variables or regressors, β the vector $k \times 1$ of coefficients for the independent variables, and μ_{it} the random error term.

The pooled OLS model is based on several assumptions. The most important one is that regressors X_{it} have to be uncorrelated with the unobserved effect (i.e. $E(X_{it}, \alpha_{it}) = 0$); otherwise pooled OLS is an inconsistent and biased estimator since no time constant variable is included in the model (Wooldridge, 2016).

Regardless of potential biases, Pooled OLS estimates are used in this paper as a starting point to compare other estimates, as is usually done by similar empirical studies.

3.2 *Fixed and Random effects model*

Fixed Effects (FE) and Random Effects (RE) models are feasible generalized least square techniques, which are asymptotically more efficient than Pooled OLS when time constant attributes are present. The error term can be decomposed in two components, and:

$$u_{it} = \alpha_i + \varepsilon_{it} \tag{2}$$

and the previous OLS Equation (1) can be rewritten as:

$$Y_{it} = \beta X_{it} + \alpha_i + \varepsilon_{it} \tag{3}$$

for $i = 1, 2, \ldots, N$ and $t = 1, 2, \ldots, T$, where α_i is the unobserved time-invariant individual effect and ε_{it} is the random or idiosyncratic error term.

Assumptions on error term μ_{it} allow distinguishing between fixed or random effects. More specifically, if u_{it} is assumed to vary non-stochastically over *i* and *t*, we have a fixed effects model; while, if μ_{it} is assumed to vary stochastically over *i* and *t*, we have a random effects model. In this latter, unobserved individual effects α_i are not treated as fixed parameters (as in FE), but as realizations of a random variable not correlated with regressors (hence the name RE).

3.3 *Hausman–Taylor model*

The FE and RE models provide consistent estimates. However, it is possible that some individual specific unobservable effect is correlated with some explanatory variables, making FE and RE inconsistent. In order to deal with the endogeneity issue, the Hausman and Taylor model has been proposed (Hausman and Taylor, 1981). It is an instrumental variable estimator that allows estimates also for time-invariant variables, which otherwise would be dropped from the FE model.

The HT model is expressed through the following formula:

$$Y_{it} = \beta_0 + \beta_1 X_{1,it} + \beta_2 X_{2,it} + \gamma_1 Z_{1,i} + \gamma_2 Z_{2,i} + \alpha_i + \varepsilon_{it} \tag{4}$$

for $i = 1, 2, \ldots, N$ and $t = 1, 2, \ldots, T$, where: X_1 and X_2 are two vectors of time varying variables and Z_1 and Z_2 are two vectors of time invariant variables. More specifically, X_1 and Z_1 are exogenous variables in the sense of being uncorrelated with the individual effect α_i, whereas X_2 and Z_2 are endogenous variables and therefore correlated with α_i. All the explanatory variables are assumed to be uncorrelated with the error term ε_{it}.

To eliminate the potential correlation issue between α_i and the endogenous variables (X_2 and Z_2), this model does not require to search for external instruments as the FE model, but instruments are derived internally.

For instance, the two internal instruments of time-varying endogenous variables (X_2) are made by:

(a) the deviations from group mean of the time-varying exogenous variables $(X_{1,it} - \overline{X_{1,it}})$ and
(b) the deviations from group means of the time-varying endogenous variables $(X_{2,it} - \overline{X_{2,it}})$.

While, the two internal instruments of time invariant endogenous variables Z_2 are made by:

(c) the means of the time varying exogenous variables $(\overline{X_{1,it}})$ and
(d) the time invariant variables (Z_i).

These instruments are used in HT model with the following two steps procedure. Initially the coefficients β are estimated through the FE estimator and residuals are obtained. Then these residuals are regressed on Z_i by using the internal instruments (a)–(d), and getting intermediate estimates of γ. Overall and within residuals are achieved and used to estimate the components of variance of the dependent variable. Finally, the estimated variance components are employed to perform a General Least Square transform on each variable in the second stage.

4. Dynamic Panel Models

Dynamic panel models are characterized by the inclusion of lagged dependent variable values as regressors. This means that the dependent variable could be affected by its past history.

The simplest linear dynamic panel model includes one lag of the dependent variable generating the following equation:

$$Y_{it} = \rho Y_{it-1} + \beta X_{it} + \alpha_i + \varepsilon_{it} \tag{5}$$

with $|\rho| < 1$; $i = 1, 2, \ldots, N$ and $t = 1, 2, \ldots, T$, where Y_{it} is the dependent variable, $Y_{i,t-1}$ one lagged dependent variable, X_{it} the vector of explanatory variables, α_i the unobserved individual effect and ε_{it} the error term.

In a dynamic panel model, when the lagged dependent variable is introduced as regressor, strict exogeneity of independent variables is not held and correlation between $Y_{i,t-1}$ and both α_i and ε_{it} arises (Baltagi, 2008). Therefore, estimating Equation (5) with OLS and FE leads to biased and inconsistent estimates. Indeed, OLS ignores the data's panel structure by omitting the fixed effects α_i and generates a biased-upward coefficient estimate for the lagged dependent variable (Bond, 2002); while the FE considers the data's panel structure but ignores the correlation between the lagged dependent variable and the error term, generating a biased-downward coefficient estimate for the lagged dependent variable (Nickell, 1981).

4.1 *System generalized method of moment*

To overcome the biases associated with OLS and FE, other econometric techniques have been developed. Among the most efficient ones in short sample periods ($T < N$), the traditional instrumental variables approaches formulated by Arellano and Bond (1991), Arellano and Bover (1995) and Blundell and Bond (1998). Among these, the System Generalized Method of Moment (GMM-sys) has been proved to be asymptotically more efficient than Difference GMM since it explores much more moment conditions.

However, when time invariant regressors are included in the aforementioned models, the strong orthogonality assumptions on which they are based in order to find valid instruments, could fail and also the estimated time varying coefficients could be biased and inconsistent. Thus, the paper of Kripfganz and Schwarz (2019) suggests applying a *two-stage system GMM* to properly estimate time invariant coefficients. It is a two-stage estimation procedure, which allows time varying variables, to be not influenced by the estimation results of the time invariant ones.

It is a sort of dynamic Hausman–Taylor model defined by the following equation:

$$Y_{it} = \beta_0 + \rho Y_{it-1} + \beta_1 X_{1,it} + \beta_2 X_{2,it} + \gamma_1 Z_{1,i} + \gamma_2 Z_{2,i} + \alpha_i + \varepsilon_{it} \quad (6)$$

with $|\rho| < 1$; $i = 1, 2, \ldots, N$ and $t = 1, 2, \ldots, T$, where Y_{it} is the dependent variable, $Y_{i,t-1}$ one lagged dependent variable, $X_{1,it}$ the vector of time-varying exogenous variables, $X_{2,it}$ the vector of time-varying endogenous variables, $Z_{1,i}$ the vector of time-invariant exogenous variables, $Z_{2,i}$ the vector of time-invariant endogenous variables, α_i the unobserved individual effect and ε_{it} the error term.

The two-stage system GMM is a sequential approach that works in the following way. At the first stage, the dependent variable is regressed only on time varying variables and residuals are stored; at the second-stage, residuals of first-stage are regressed on time invariant variables.

In order to achieve consistent estimates, instruments for endogenous variables can be used at both stages.

5. Tests on Models

In order to assess the goodness of fit of a specific model, several tests have to be performed on the aforementioned estimators. They are implemented to different aims: to evaluate the goodness of fit of a single model, to compare one estimator over another and to validate the model suitability as post-estimation test.

In this section, we distinguish these tests according to their application on the static or the dynamic panel models described before.

5.1 *Tests performed on static panel models*

The main tests performed on the static panel models are:

- **F-test (OLS/FE):** It compares the Pooled OLS against the Fixed effect model in order to assess how the FE model enhances the general goodness of fit. It tests the null hypothesis (H_0) that the fixed effects α_i are equal for all companies. If H_0 is rejected ($p < 0.05$), than FE is valid and Pooled OLS is not suitable to analyze the relationship;

- **Breush–Pagan Lagrange Multiplier test (LM) (OLS/RE):** It compares the Pooled OLS against the Random effect model in order to evaluate how the RE model enhances the goodness of fit. It tests the null hypothesis H_0 that the variance of unobserved effects across companies α_i is null. If H_0 is rejected ($p < 0.05$), then there is a significant random effect into the dataset;
- **First Hausman test (FE/RE):** It compares the fixed effect against the random effect model. It tests the null hypothesis (H_0) that the individual effects α_i are not correlated with any explanatory variables of the model. If H_0 is rejected ($p < 0.05$), then individual effects are significantly correlated with at least one regressor. Therefore, RE model is problematic to implement and FE model is preferred (Hausman, 1978);
- **Second Hausman test (FE/HT):** It compares the fixed effect model against the Hausman–Taylor model. It tests the null hypothesis (H_0) of no systematic difference between FE and HT estimates. If H_0 is rejected ($p < 0.05$), then FE model is preferred, otherwise the Hausman Taylor model has to be implemented ($p > 0.05$);

5.2 *Tests performed on dynamic panel models*

The tests implemented for dynamic panel models, are usually post estimation tests, which evaluate from one side the validity of instruments used in the model and from the other side the correlation between regressors and the error terms. The most applied post estimation tests are:

- **Sargan/Hansen J-tests:** They check for over identifying restrictions, i.e. for the model and instruments validity. They test the null hypothesis (H_0) that instruments used in the model are exogenous and thus correctly specified. If H_0 is rejected ($p < 0.05$), then the model or the instruments used in the estimation model have to be reformulated;
- **Arellano–Bond tests:** They check for first order autocorrelation (AR(1)) and second order serial-correlation (AR(2)) in idiosyncratic errors.

AR(1) tests the null hypothesis (H_0) of no first order autocorrelation in the differenced residuals; if the null hypothesis (H_0) is rejected, there is strong evidence that the lagged dependent variable is correlated with the error term.

AR(2) tests the null hypothesis (H_0) that the error term ε_{it} of the differenced equation is not serially correlated at the second order; if the null hypothesis (H_0) is not rejected, it indicates the absence of serial correlation in disturbances.

Therefore, to have valid GMM estimates, the expected result for Arellano–Bond tests is to reject H_0 for AR(1) ($p < 0.05$) and not to reject H_0 for AR(2) ($p > 0.05$).

6. Data

The data covers corporate governance and financial information of a sample of innovative Italian Small and Medium Enterprises (SMEs) over the period 2015–2019. The dataset was constructed by merging two datasets. The first one is the Italian Ministry of Economic Development dataset, which identifies innovative companies compliant with Law 33/2015 and contains qualitative information of the companies (age, workers, education of team, organization composition). The second dataset is AIDA by Bureau vanDijk from which the financial information of the firms included in the first dataset was taken. Under the Italian law 33/2015, the main requirements of SMEs innovative to be formed are:

- Not listed in a regulated market and with a certified statement of the accounts, with latest published audited financial statements;
- At least 2 out of 3:

(1) expenses in R&D and innovation are at least 3% of either its turnover or its production value (the largest value is considered);
(2) highly qualified personnel (at least one-fifth PhD holders and students, or researchers, or at least one-third Master's graduates);
(3) owner, depositary or licensee of a registered patent, or the owner of a registered software.

The original sample includes 1,768 innovative companies belonging to five different industrial sectors such as agriculture and fishing, commerce, industry or trade, services and tourism. The original sample has been cleaned up of all missing values for which the corporate governance and financial data were not available for at least 2 years of the sample period considered. Instead, those financial data that were not available for just 1 year have been filled according to the following strategy:

- If the missing financial value was in the boundary range of the considered years (i.e. 2015 or 2019), it has been filled with the closest financial value observed (i.e. the financial value of 2016 for the missing value of 2015 or the financial value of 2018 for the missing value of 2019);
- If the missing financial value was within the range of the considered years (i.e. for 2016, 2017 or 2018), it has been filled with the average of the observed company's financial values in the whole-time span considered.

Hence, the final panel consists of 1,604 companies over the sample period of 5 years, obtaining in total a strongly balanced panel of 8,020 firm-year observations.

The resulting panel includes both time varying financial variables and time-invariant corporate governance indicators that will be carefully described in next section.

Moreover, the presence of outliers in the considered financial variables has been treated with the winsorization method by truncating their values to their 95th and 5th percentiles and by setting these values to the highest or lowest value within the specified range.

6.1 *Variables and descriptive statistics*

6.1.1 *Dependent variable*

In this study, Return on Asset (ROA) has been used to measure the performance of innovative SMEs and thus as dependent variable to analyze the aforementioned relationship.

The reasons that lead us to this choice are different. Firstly, ROA, represents a profitability indicator that highlights better than others how well a company uses its assets. Secondly, because performance indicators such as Tobin's Q (Q), profit rate (PR), total return (TR), return on equity (ROE), return on investments (ROI) and return on sales (ROS) present some problems of interpretation or application.

Therefore, ROA is the most suitable performance indicator among all of these. However, it presents the disadvantage to reduce its usefulness when it is used to compare companies belonging to different sectors. To overcome to this problem, in this research the Industry-Adjusted ROA (InAdROA) has been employed as dependent variables and computed as the firm's ROA less the median ROA of each sector (Wintoki *et al.*, 2011).

In this way, it is possible to take into account the heterogeneity value of ROA for different sectors.

6.1.2 *Corporate governance variables*

The effects of the current financial performances have been considered on a set of five time-invariant corporate variables: workers' education (EDUC), patent or software ownership (INNOVATION), prevalence of women (WOMEN), young (YOUNG) and foreigners (FOREIGN) on corporate boards, which have been defined as follows:

- **EDUC:** It is a dummy variable that takes the value 1 if one of these conditions occurs: one-third of workers owns a Master's degree, one-fifth are PhD students or own a PhD qualification, one-fifth are graduated with three years of experience in certified research activities. It takes the value 0 otherwise;
- **WOMEN, YOUNG, FOREIGN:** These are categorical variables that take four different values each one, from 1 to 4, according to whether the prevalence of women/young/foreign on corporate boards is null (1), majoritarian (2), strong (3) or exclusive (4) with respect to some thresholds. More specifically, the prevalence of woman/young/foreign on corporate boards has been computed as half of the sum between the percentage of share capital and the percentage of women/young/foreign managers. If this last value is less than or equal to 50%, the prevalence of women/young/foreign is null (1); if it ranges between 50% and 66%, the prevalence is majoritarian (2); if it ranges between 66% and 100%, the prevalence is strong (3); if it is equal to 100%, the prevalence is exclusive (4);
- **INNOVATION:** It is a dummy variable that takes the value 1 if the company is depositary/licensee of industrial property rights or registered software owner; 0 otherwise.

6.1.3 *Control variables*

Control variables are often considered in similar analysis as determinants of board structure. Among these, the most used are company's size, age, growth opportunities and leverage. In this study, in order to take into account these main aspects, LogASSET, REVCHANGE and AssEqRATIO have been considered as time varying control variables, respectively, for company's size, growth opportunities and leverage; while AGECON, SECTOR and SOCIETY have been considered as time-invariant control variables for company's maturity, sector and legal form.

- **LogASSET:** It is the logarithm of the company's total assets;
- **AGECON:** It represents the firm's age, from its constitution until now. It is computed as difference between the current year (2021) and the year of incorporation as society;
- **REVCHANGE:** It is the percentage change on sales revenues between two consecutive years and it denotes the growth opportunities of a certain company. It is computed according to the formula $\left(\frac{R_t - R_{t-1}}{R_t} \cdot 100\right)$ where R_t and R_{t-1} indicate the company's return on sales respectively in the period t and in the previous one $t-1$. It has to be pointed out that when a certain R_t observation is equal to 0, the ratio is impossible to compute. In order to allow for this computation, the zero values have been replaced with a small value equal to 0.01;
- **AssEqRATIO:** It is the asset to equity ratio and it is computed as the ratio between the company's total assets and shareholders' equity. It suggests if the company's leverage used to finance the firm is geared more on debt or equity. The higher the ratio, the greater the debt the company holds;
- **SECTOR:** It is a categorical variable that takes five different values according to the sector in which the innovative company operates. For instance, if the company operates in agriculture and fishing sector it takes the value 1; similarly, if the company operates in commerce (2), industry/trade (3), services (4) and tourism (5) sector;
- **SOCIETY:** It is a categorical variable that takes four different values according to the legal form adopted by each company. For instance, if the company adopts a cooperative form, it takes the value 1; similarly, if it adopts a consortium (2), a limited liability (3) and a public limited (4) legal form.

Table 1 provides a short description of the performance, governance and control variables employed in this study while Table 2 shows their descriptive statistics. The mean value for our key corporate governance dummy variable EDUC is almost 1.7 meaning that most of innovative companies (67%) have workers that satisfies the characteristics of high educational levels (master's degree, PhD or 3-years of experience in

Table 1: Definition of variables.

Variable Name	Definition	Type of Variable	Time Varying/ Invariant
Dependent variable			
— Industry adjusted return on asset (InAdROA)	The firm's ROA less the median ROA of each sector	Continuous	Time varying
Corporate governance variables			
— Workers' education (EDUC)	1 if 1/3 of workers own a master's degree, 1/5 are PhD or 1/5 are graduate with 3 years of experience in research activities; 0 otherwise	Dummy	Time invariant
— Patent or software owner (INNOVATION)	1 if the company is depositary/ licensee of industrial property rights or owns a registered software; 0 otherwise	Dummy	Time invariant
— Prevalence of women on corporate boards (WOMEN)	1 if the prevalence of women-young-foreign is null (≤ 50%); 2 if it is majoritarian (50%–66%); 3 if it is strong (66%–100%); 4 if it is exclusive (=100%). The prevalence is computed as (% share capital + % women-young-foreign managers)/2	Categorical	Time invariant
— Prevalence of young on corporate boards (YOUNG)		Categorical	Time invariant
— Prevalence of foreigners on corporate boards (FOREIGN)		Categorical	Time invariant
Firm-specific features/Control variables			
— Logarithm of total assets (LogASSET)	The logarithm of company's total assets	Continuous	Time varying
— Firm's age (AGECON)	The difference between the current year (2021) and the year in which the company's incorporation as society	Continuous	Time invariant

Table 1: (*Continued*)

Variable Name	Definition	Type of Variable	Time Varying/ Invariant
— Revenues change (REVCHANGE)	The percentage change on sales revenues between two consecutive years computed as $((R_t - R_{t-1})/R_t) \cdot 100$	Continuous	Time varying
— Asset Equity Ratio (AssEqRATIO)	The ratio between total assets and shareholders' equity	Continuous	Time varying
— Sector (SECTOR)	1 if the company operates in the agriculture and fishing sector; 2 commerce sector; 3 industry or trade sector; 4 services sector; 5 tourism sector	Categorical	Time invariant
— Society (SOCIETY)	1 if the company is a cooperative society; 2 if it is a consortium; 3 if it is a limited liability; 4 if it is a public limited society	Categorical	Time invariant

Source: Authors' elaboration.

Table 2: Summary statistics of performance, governance and control variables in the sample period considered (2015–2019).

Variables	Obs.	Mean	Std. Dev.	Min	Max
lnAdROA	8,020	−3.526	24.334	−151.15	59.61
EDUC	8,020	1.669	0.470	1	2
INNOVATION	8,020	1.635	0.481	1	2
WOMEN	8,020	3.844	0.562	1	4
YOUNG	8,020	3.928	0.381	1	4
FOREIGN	8,020	3.970	0.250	1	4
LogAsset	8,020	6.758	1.673	2.197	10.79
AGECON	8,020	12.388	8.446	1	95
REVCHANGE	6,416	7,357.825	68,894.41	−100	843,550
AssEqRATIO	8,020	5.300	10.335	−35.39	92.86
SECTOR	8,020	3.653	0.599	1	5
SOCIETY	8,020	3.806	0.474	1	4

Source: Authors' elaboration.

certified research activities). Likewise, the variable INNOVATION has a mean value equal to 1.635 meaning that most of companies (63.59%) are depositary/licensee of industrial property rights or owner of registered software. The average of our dependent variable InAdROA is negative and equal to −3.52 since the values of adjusted ROA vary significantly (between the minimum of −151.15 and the maximum of 59.61) according to the different sectors in which the companies operate.

In this sample, most of variables have 8,020 observations arising from 1,604 sample companies over 5 years. However, the variable REVCHANGE, accounts for 6,416 observations. This dissimilarity derives from its definition. Indeed, being defined as the percentage change on sales revenue between two consecutive years (t and t–1), it takes into consideration only the variations occurred in four periods rather than in five (2015–2016, 2016–2017, 2017–2018, 2018–2019), simply for the lack of 2014's observations needed to compute the 2014–2015 variation. Moreover, the mean and the standard deviation of this variable is very high since, as we suggested before, the R_t values equal to 0 have been replaced with a very small quantity, allowing for the ratio computation from one side but for very high variable values from the other side.

7. Model Specification and Estimation Results

In this section, we analyze the relation between firm performance and some significant corporate governance indicators over the period 2015–2019. For this purpose, firstly we apply the four static model estimators of Section 3 (pooled OLS, FE, RE and HT). Then, we perform the first and the second Hausman test (see Section 5.1 in order to choose the most suitable static model among these latter. Finally, we implement the dynamic panel model estimator of Section 4.1 on the same dataset (the two-stage system GMM), since the pooled OLS with the lagged independent variables highlights high significant coefficients also for the previous 2 years.

7.1 *Step 0. Correlation of variables and variance inflation factor analysis*

Before applying the static and dynamic models, a correlation analysis has to be performed to detect and eliminate possible collinearity problems between variables. Table 3 shows the Pearson correlation coefficients

Table 3: Pearson correlation coefficients among variables.

Variables	InAdROA	EDUC	INNOV	WOMEN	YOUNG	FOREIGN
InAdROA	1.0000					
EDUC	0.0381	1.0000				
INNOVATION	−0.0044	−0.5123	1.0000			
WOMEN	−0.0272	−0.0101	−0.0130	1.0000		
YOUNG	0.0041	0.0035	0.0277	0.0383	1.0000	
FOREIGN	−0.0015	−0.0257	0.0079	0.1044	−0.0029	1.0000
LogAsset	0.0858	−0.1155	0.1338	0.0886	0.1431	−0.0069
AGECON	0.1504	−0.0540	0.0931	−0.0007	0.1139	0.0232
REVCHANGE	−0.0335	0.0079	−0.0089	0.0110	0.0126	−0.0254
AssEqRATIO	0.0134	−0.0352	0.0144	−0.0281	−0.0262	−0.0055
SECTOR	0.0387	0.1932	−0.1978	0.0198	−0.0051	0.0015
SOCIETY	0.0181	−0.0105	−0.0225	−0.0053	−0.0321	−0.0384
Variables	**LogAsset**	**AGECON**	**REVCHANGE**	**AssEqRATIO**	**SECTOR**	**SOCIETY**
LogAsset	1.0000					
AGECON	0.4293	1.000				
REVCHANGE	0.0061	−0.0618	1.0000			
AssEqRATIO	0.0025	−0.0184	0.0093	1.0000		
SECTOR	−0.1614	−0.0762	−0.0081	−0.0171	1.0000	
SOCIETY	−0.3460	−0.1616	−0.0107	0.0018	0.0048	1.0000

Source: Authors' elaboration.

among variables from which it can be observed that most of correlations are not significant (below 0.42). A moderate negative correlation is displayed between EDUC and INNOVATION (−0.512); however, this correlation can be overlooked since it is lower than the conventional threshold value of 0.65.

In addition, the Variance Inflation Factors analysis (VIFs) has been implemented then, as second test of collinearity among independent variables specified in a regression model. A common rule of thumb suggests that if VIF exceeds the value of 5, regression coefficients are poorly estimated because of multi-collinearity issue and those variables have to be eliminated (Montgomery *et al.*, 2021).

However, the paper of Murray *et al.* (2012), recommends to researchers to be cautious in using this rule when dummy variables are involved in the analysis. In order to handle with this type of variables, they propose the application of VIFs on the set of continuous variables first, to check for collinearity without the influence of dummy variables, and to add then each dummy variable progressively to detect their effect on VIFs.

In this study, we follow this approach and the results of progressive VIFs are displayed in Table 4. More specifically, seven tests have been implemented gradually. Test (0) in which the VIFs has been performed on continuous variables only, and Tests (1)–(7) where the VIFs has been applied by adding progressively the dummy and the categorical variables EDUC, INNOVATION, WOMEN, YOUNG, FOREIGN, SECTOR and SOCIETY to the previous ones.

Until Test (4), no variable displays a significantly correlation except YOUNG in category 4 and denoted with * (VIFs = 5.20). However, this variable has been retained also in the subsequent tests (6) (7), since his VIF is not significantly high. Instead, from Test (5) it emerges that FOREIGN in category 4 shows a significantly high VIF (= 6.24), (from which we decided to eliminate this variable in next tests. Indeed Test (6) and Test (7) have been performed without FOREIGN and by adding respectively SECTOR and SOCIETY to the previous variables of Test (4). Both variables, SECTOR and SOCIETY, display a very high VIFs (> 10, denoted with**) for most of categories and therefore they have also been removed.

To summarize, three explanatory variables, FOREIGN, SECTOR and SOCIETY, have been eliminated from progressive VIFs tests; while the variable YOUNG has been retained since the VIFs value is not significantly high (=5.20).

Table 4: Variance Inflation Factors (VIFs) Analysis performed progressively by adding dummy and categorical variables.

	VIFs							
Variables	**(0)**	**(1)**	**(2)**	**(3)**	**(4)**	**(5)**	**(6)**	**(7)**
AGECON	1.23	1.23	1.24	1.24	1.24	1.24	1.25	1.25
LogAsset	1.23	1.24	1.25	1.26	1.27	1.28	1.31	1.59
REVCHANGE	1.01	1.01	1.01	1.01	1.01	1.01	1.01	1.01
AssEqRATIO	1.00	1.00	1.00	1.00	1.01	1.01	1.01	1.01
EDUCATION		1.01	1.36	1.36	1.36	1.37	1.39	1.37
INNOVATION			1.37	1.37	1.37	1.37	1.39	1.37
WOMEN								
2				2.84	2.84	2.86	2.84	2.84
3				2.37	2.38	2.40	2.39	2.39
4				4.12	4.13	4.17	4.13	4.14
YOUNG								
2					3.21	3.21	3.21	3.21
3					3.05	3.05	3.06	3.05
4					5.20*	5.20*	5.20*	5.21*
FOREIGN								
2						4.75		
3						2.52		
4						6.24*		
SECTOR								
2							28.51**	
3							98.34**	
4							113.46**	
5							4.33	
SOCIETY								
2								1.44
3								14.62**
4								14.50**
Mean VIF	1.12	1.10	1.20	1.84	2.34	2.78	17.05**	3.93

Note: *VIFs > 5; **VIFs > 10.

Source: Authors' elaboration.

Therefore, all variables of Test (4), i.e. AGECON, LogAsset, REVCHANGE, AssEqRATIO, EDUC, INNOVATION, WOMEN and YOUNG, have been considered to develop models of next sections. The low values of both VIFs and Mean VIF in this Test, prove that no collinearity exists among these variables.

7.2 *Step 1. The static panel models: Pooled OLS, Fixed effects and Random effects models*

In this study, the first step we perform is the static pooled OLS regression. Thanks to its wide application in the early governance-performance literature, this model allows from one side to analyze the direct effect of our corporate governance variables (EDUC, INNOVATION, WOMEN, YOUNG) on current companies' performances (InAdROA) and from the other side to provide a baseline approach to compare alternative methodologies.

The empirical results are presented in Table 5, Model (1). As we can observe, all the considered corporate variables are statistically significant at a very high percentage level (1%) which suggests that the current performance of firm is affected by most corporate governance indicators except INNOVATION. However, the signs of these correlations differ according to the variable under consideration. For instance, EDUC has a positive impact on the current firm performance as we expect, such that the higher the workers' education level, the higher the current company's performance. While the prevalence of WOMEN and YOUNG on corporate boards has a negative effect on the firm's performance no matter what kind of prevalence it is (null, majoritarian or strong); i.e. the higher the WOMEN/YOUNG prevalence on corporate boards, the lower the company's performance.

With regard to firm specific features, LogAsset and AGECON show a positive relationship with current adjusted ROA at high significant levels (5% and 1%), whereas REVCHANGE and AssEqRATIO are not statistically significant in determining current ROA.

However, a simple Pooled OLS regression is not suitable here, since the application of F-test and Breush–Pagan Lagrange Multiplier test (LM) confirm that Fixed Effects and Random Effects model present a higher goodness of fit compared to Pooled OLS. In F-test the null hypothesis that fixed effects are equal for all companies is rejected ($p = 0.000$), so that

Table 5: Empirical results of four static panel regression models: Pooled OLS (OLS), Fixed Effects (FE), Random Effects (RE) and Hausman–Taylor model (HT).

Static Panel Models				
Variables	**Model (1)**	**Model (2)**	**Model (3)**	**Model (4)**
lnAdROA	**OLS**	**FE**	**RE**	**HT**
EDUC (TIex)				
YES	2.6893***	0	3.0878***	4.1438***
	(0.7049)	—	(1.1653)	(1.3304)
INNOVATION (TIex)				
YES	0.2097	0	−0.1915	−1.2881
	(0.7166)	—	(1.1765)	(1.3288)
WOMEN (TIex)				
Strong	−6.3056***	0	−7.3772***	−9.9816***
	(1.9532)	—	(3.1177)	(3.5477)
Majoritarian	−7.3156***	0	−8.1513*	−10.3742**
	(2.6611)	—	(4.2744)	(4.6846)
Null	−6.7016***	0	−8.4015***	−12.8247***
	(1.6275)	—	(2.7325)	(3.0872)
YOUNG (TIex)				
Strong	−10.7273***	0	−10.0427	−8.0632
	(4.0872)	—	(6.5773)	(6.1932)
Majoritarian	−19.9966***	0	−20.1142***	−20.4642***
	(4.1048)	—	(6.1838)	(5.6258)
Null	−11.3384***	0	−12.6768**	−16.0722***
	(2.9326)	—	(4.9791)	(4.3217)
LogAsset (TVen)	0.5356***	7.5637***	2.4348***	7.5805***
	(0.2337)	(1.0239)	(0.4269)	(1.0314)
AGECON (TIex)	0.3843***	0	0.2428***	−0.1585*
	(0.0298)	—	(0.0501)	(0.0872)
REVCHANGE (TVen)	−9.12e-06	4.83e-06	3.30e-06	4.81e-06
	(6.02e-06)	(5.05e-06)	(5.09e-06)	(5.06e-06)
AssEqRATIO (TVex)	0.0388	0.0495	0.0531	0.0417
	(0.0294)	(0.0495)	(0.0393)	(0.0437)

(Continued)

Table 5: (*Continued*)

Static Panel Models				
Variables	**Model (1)**	**Model (2)**	**Model (3)**	**Model (4)**
InAdROA	**OLS**	**FE**	**RE**	**HT**
Constant	3.7873	−53.4870***	−4.1550	−25.2516***
	(3.5183)	(6.6732)	(5.8947)	(6.6509)
Observations	6,416	6,416	6,416	6,416
Number of firms	1,604	1,604	1,604	1,604
R-squared	0.0319	0.0075	0.0235	
F	20.51***	12.07***		
Chi 2			145.54***	153.97***
Sargan test (*p*-value)				0.5953

Note: *significant at the 10% level; **significant at the 5% level; ***significance at the 1% level. Robust Standard errors are in parentheses. Year dummies included.

TIex refers to Time Invariant exogenous; TVex refers to Time Varying exogenous; TVen refers to Time Varying endogenous in Hausman–Taylor model.

Source: Authors' elaboration.

there is a significant fixed effect into the model. Similarly, the LM test rejects the null hypothesis that the variance of unobserved effects across companies α_i is null ($p = 0.0000$) and thus there is a significant random effect into the panel (Breusch and Pagan, 1980).

Therefore, the Fixed-Effects (FE) and the Random-Effects (RE) model have been performed then, to control for unobservable heterogeneity across companies.

The estimation results for FE panel model are displayed in Model (2). However, since most of explanatory variables are time invariant, FE estimator omits these variables and estimates coefficients just for firm internal characteristics. For these latter, similarly to Pooled OLS, LogAsset improves the current performance of firm, while REVCHANGE and AssEqRATIO do not; conversely to OLS instead, nothing is possible to state for AGECON since the coefficient is omitted due to its time-invariant nature.

Hence, the Random-Effect panel model has been performed then, to include also time-invariant variables in the regression. Model (3) shows the empirical results of RE from which it is possible to observe that estimates are very similar to Model (1). Indeed, most of corporate governance characteristics have a strong impact on current firm performance, with the only exception of INNOVATION; the signs of these effects are equal to the previous ones, i.e. positive for EDUC and negative for WOMEN and YOUNG; the control variables LogAsset and AGECON affect positively the current level of ROA with high significant levels (1%).

7.3 *Step 2. The static panel model: The Hausman–Taylor model*

The estimations of the previous static panel models (OLS, FE and RE), are consistent under the strong assumption of exogeneity between regressors; when this assumption is relaxed, OLS, FE and RE parameters are biased and instrumental variables estimator (IV) has to be applied.

Hence, the second step of this analysis is to check for endogeneity and to implement a model based on IV estimator if endogeneity among explanatory variables occurs.

The most suitable model able to deal simultaneously with the endogeneity issue and the presence of explanatory variables that are time varying and time invariant, is the Hausman–Taylor (HT) model (See Section 3.3). It is an instrumental variable estimator (implemented in stata with *xthtaylor* command), which allows for some possible correlations between regressors and unobserved individuals effects.

Therefore, in this section the following two main phases have been performed:

(1) To check for endogeneity through the Mundlak model (Mundlak, 1978). It is a RE model based on the simultaneously estimation of all the explanatory variables along with the mean of each variable for which we suspect *a-priori* to be endogenous. If the estimated coefficients of the mean of the variables inserted in the model are statistically significant (at 1%, 5% or 10% level), then those variables are endogenous; otherwise they are exogenous;
(2) To perform the HT model if endogeneity exists.

However, in order to apply the HT model properly, the study of Baltagi *et al.* (2003) suggests performing a pre-test based on the application of two Hausman tests (Section 5.1. This preliminary test, composed by the following two sub-phases, has to be implemented before phase (2):

- SUB-PHASES 1: If the null hypothesis (H_0) of the traditional Hausman test (FE against RE) is not rejected, then a RE model has to be chosen;
- SUB-PHASES 2: If the null hypothesis (H_0) of the traditional Hausman test (FE against RE) is rejected, then a FE model has to be chosen;
  - If the null hypothesis (H_0) of the second Hausman test is not rejected (no systematic difference between FE and HT estimates), then HT model has to be applied;
  - If the null hypothesis (H_0) of the second Hausman test is rejected (no systematic difference between FE and HT estimates), then FE model has to be used.

To summarize, the following three conditions have to be carried out in order to apply the HT model properly:

(1) Endogeneity of time varying regressors (Mundlak model);
(2) H_0 of the traditional Hausman test (FE-RE) has to be rejected ($p < 0.05$);
(3) H_0 of the second Hausman test (FE-HT) should not to be rejected ($p < 0.05$).

Tables 6 and 7 report, respectively, the Mundlak model estimates and the Hausman tests results.

From Mundlak model estimates it emerges that LogAsset and REVCHANGE are endogenous variables since both their means are statistically significant (1%), whereas AssEqRATIO is exogenous since its mean is not significant. For the sake of clarity, the mean of the time-invariant regressors of Table 6 have been typed in bold.

With regard to the two Hausman tests, the first column of Table 7 shows that the first Hausman test rejects H_0 ($p < 0.05$) and thus FE estimator is strongly preferred to RE; while the second column of Table 7 displays that the second Hausman test does not rejects H_0 ($p > 0.05$) and thus HT estimator is superior to FE estimator.

Therefore, HT model has to be implemented in this study, since it represents the most suitable model to highlight the static relationship between current firm performance and corporate governance indicators.

More specifically, the HT model has been applied here with the two endogenous variables (LogAsset and REVCHANGE) highlighted from

Table 6: Empirical results of Mundlak model.

Variables	**Mundlak Model**
InAdROA	**RE**
EDUC	
Yes	2.6736**
	(1.1443)
INNOVATION	
Yes	0.2780
	(1.1478)
WOMEN	
Strong	−5.5259*
	(3.0504)
Majoritarian	−7.0021*
	(4.2263)
Null	−5.9973**
	(2.6583)
YOUNG	
Strong	−11.2974*
	(6.7939)
Majoritarian	−19.6653***
	(6.5257)
Null	−10.0743*
	(5.2310)
LogAsset	7.6099***
	(1.0016)
AGECON	0.4448***
	(0.05858)
REVCHANGE	4.80e-06
	(5.06e-06)
AssEqRATIO	0.0451
	(0.0485)
mean_LogAsset	**−7.6448***
	(1.0520)

(*Continued*)

Table 6: (*Continued*)

Variables	**Mundlak Model**
lnAdROA	**RE**
mean_REVCHANGE	**−0.00007******
	(0.00001)
mean_AssEqRATIO	**−0.0029**
	(0.0799)
Constant	2.0338
	6.0951
Observations	6,416
Number of firms	1,604
R-squared	0.0554
Chi 2	180.57***

Note: *significant at the 10% level; **significant at the 5% level; ***significance at the 1% level. Robust Standard errors are in parenthesis, Year dummies included, The mean of the Time-Invariant regressors are indicated in bold

Source: Authors' elaboration.

Table 7: The two Hausman tests.

	Hausman Tests	
	First FE-RE	**Second FE-HT**
Chi 2 (5)	= 151.88	0.84
Prob > Chi 2	= 0.0000	0.9323

Source: Authors' elaboration.

Mundlak model, and six exogenous variables (AssEqRATIO, EDUC, INNOVATION, YOUNG, WOMEN and AGECON).

Model (4) in Table 5, reports the estimation results for HT model. Once more, it emerges that most of corporate indicators affect current ROA except INNOVATION and the sign of this influence is positive for EDUC and negative for the remaining corporate regressors (YOUNG, WOMEN).

Moreover, with respect to the firm internal characteristics, LogAsset and AGECON have again a significant relationship with the current firm performance but of opposite sign (positive for LogAsset and negative for AGECON), whereas REVCHANGE and AssEqRATIO do not affect our dependent variable.

In addition, the Sargan–Hansen test, reported in the last line of Table 5 for Model (4), accepts the null hypothesis that the instruments used in HT model are valid ($p > 0.05$) and confirm the appropriateness of model specification with these instruments.

7.4 *Step 3. The dynamic panel model: The System Generalized Method of Moment*

Up to now, we performed and compared four different static panel models, where the lagged dependent variable (InAdROA) has not been included as explanatory variable.

However, several studies suggest that the relationship between firm financial performance and corporate governance indicators is dynamic, since past realization of firm performance could affect the current one.

This allows for OLS, FE and RE estimators to be biased and inconsistent (Wooldridge, 2016).

To highlight the endogeneity issue related to past firm performance, a dynamic OLS model has been applied here, by including two lags of our dependent variable as explanatory variables (InAdROA (−1) and InAdROA (−2)).

Estimates are shown in Table 8, Model (5). They provide evidence that past firm performance affects the current level of ROA in a highly significant way (1% level) for both year-1 and year-2. Therefore, the use of a dynamic panel model, which takes into account the endogeneity issue arising from explanatory variables correlated with the unobserved individual-effect (LogAsset and REVCHANGE) and past performances, is recommended for this study.

As suggested in Section 4.1 in literature, one of the most suitable dynamic models able to deal with the endogeneity concern is the Generalized Method of Moment (GMM) estimator. It controls for the three major sources of endogeneity such as unobserved heterogeneity, simultaneity endogeneity and dynamic endogeneity, by transforming the data and including lagged values of the dependent variable. Therefore, it provides more consistent and efficient estimates than simple OLS model for analyzing the relationship between firm performance and corporate governance.

Usually, the System GMM is implemented on Stata with *xtabond2* command. However, the traditional System GMM model is not suitable here since some regressors are time invariant and various statistical estimation issues may arise.

Therefore, in this study, the Two-Step System GMM proposed by Kripfganz and Schwarz (2015) has been implemented with the *xtseqreg* Stata command as follows:

- *In the first stage*, the dependent variable has been regressed on a set of regressors composed by time varying independent variables (LogAsset, REVCHANGE, AssEqRATIO) and the lagged dependent variable InAdROA (−1). This last variable has been used as internal instruments along with LogAsset and REVCHANGE; while AssEqRATIO has been used as external instrument since it is exogenous;
- *In the second stage*, the dependent variable has been regressed on the first stage's residuals and on the corporate time invariant variables (EDUC, INNOVATION, WOMEN, YOUNG); these latter have been used as internal instruments.

Estimations results are shown in Table 8, Model (6). It emerges that the coefficient of one-year lagged dependent variable is significantly positive (0.2397) and confirms what several similar studies suggest, that is the previous year's firm performance has a strong and positive relationship in determining the current firm performance.

Moreover, most of corporate governance indicators affect significantly the current firm performance, except INNOVATION and YOUNG in the strong specification. The sign of this relationship is positive for EDUC and negative for WOMEN and YOUNG. Hence, the higher the level of workers education, the more performing the company; instead, the higher the prevalence of WOMEN and YOUNG in the board size, the lower the firm performance.

With regard to firm internal characteristics, it is possible to observe that most of them affect the actual level of ROA with a positive (LogASSET, REVCHANGE) and negative sign (AGECON); instead, AssEqRATIO does not.

Table 8: Dynamic panel models estimates: Pooled OLS with two lagged dependent variables and System GMM performed in one and two stages.

Dynamic Panel Models			
Variables	**Model (5)**	**Model (6)**	**Model (7)**
InAdROA	**OLS**	**GMM-Sys (Two-Step)**	**GMM-Sys (One-step)**
InAdROA (−1)	0.4854***	0.2397***	0.2825***
	(0.0287)	(0.0466)	(0.0407)
InAdROA (−2)	0.1818***		
	(0.0252)		
EDUC (TIex)			
SI	0.6002	4.1755***	3.9501***
	(0.6216)	(1.3788)	(1.4064)
INNOVATION (TIex)			
YES	−0.1709	−2.1774	−2.5956*
	(0.6331)	(1.3288)	(1.3492)
WOMEN (TIex)			
Strong	−2.7843	−10.7664***	−10.5886***
	(1.8945)	(3.8104)	(3.9733)
Majoritarian	−2.1330	−10.6826**	−10.6093**
	(2.5954)	(4.5413)	(4.6275)
Null	−1.6081	−14.6860***	−14.1593***
	(1.4819)	(3.3657)	(3.4672)
YOUNG (TIex)			
Strong	−1.5753	−3.2031	−3.1496
	(3.2066)	(5.0785)	(4.9567)
Majoritarian	−4.7336	−15.867***	−15.2883***
	(3.8543)	(4.7503)	(4.7560)
Null	−3.6324	−16.0990***	−15.2503***
	(1.6835)	(3.3210)	(3.3008)
LogAsset (TVen)	0.3136	11.4086***	11.2961***
	(0.2352)	(1.5711)	(1.5329)
AGECON (TIex)	0.1344***	−0.5560***	−0.5940***
	(0.0223)	(0.1274)	(0.1252)

(*Continued*)

Table 8: (*Continued*)

Dynamic Panel Models			
Variables	**Model (5)**	**Model (6)**	**Model (7)**
lnAdROA	**OLS**	**GMM-Sys (Two-Step)**	**GMM-Sys (One-step)**
REVCHANGE (TVen)	2.20e-06	9.63e-06***	9.89e-06***
	(9.13e-06)	(3.67e-06)	(3.68e-06)
AssEqRATIO (TVex)	0.0581	0.0565	−0.0101
	(0.0289)	(0.0777)	(0.0319)
Constant	0.4741	−46.1920***	−49.1115***
	(2.5574)	(8.2911)	(8.4806)
Observations	4,812	6,416	6,416
Number of firms		1,604	1,604
R-squared	0.4180		
F	62.93***		
Chi 2			218.08***
AR (1) (p-value)		0.0000	0.0000
AR (2) (p-value)		0.3836	0.2891
Sargan/Hansen test (p-value)		0.2397	0.3348

Note: *significant at the 10% level; **significant at the 5% level; ***significance at the 1% level. Robust standard errors are in parentheses, Year dummies included.

TIex refers to Time Invariant exogenous; TVex to Time Varying exogenous; TVen to Time Varying endogenous.

TVex and TVen have been introduced in the first step of model (6), while TIex in the second step of model 6 together with the estimates of TVex and TVen obtained from first step.

TVen (LogAsset and REVCHANGE) have been used as instruments for model (7) together with lnAdROA (−1).

To prove that the Two-Stage System GMM estimator is valid for our analysis, the Hansen's J test and the Arellano-Bond post-estimation tests have been conducted.

The specification tests indicate that the model is well specified in terms of endogeneity and instruments validity. As shown in the last line of Table 8, Hansen's J test reports a p-value = 0.2397, meaning that the set of instruments used in two-stage System GMM are valid. Similarly, the

Arellano and Bond tests suggest no serial correlation since there is a high first order autocorrelation (*AR* (1) *p*-value = 0.0000) and no evidence for significant second-order serial correlation (*AR* (2) *p*-value = 0.3836).

Finally, to prove the robustness of two-stage System GMM estimates, the traditional one-stage System GMM estimator has been performed then, with the Stata command *xtdpd* and the option *hascons*, to allow for time-invariant estimates. Even in this case, the lagged dependent variable has been used as internal instruments along with LogAsset and REVCHANGE; while AssEqRATIO has been used as external instrument.

Estimates are shown in Model (7) and the previous results of two-stage System GMM model are confirmed in terms of significance, sign and coefficients estimated. Once again, most of corporate governance indicators affect significantly the current firm performance; however, compared to model (6), the current level of Adjusted ROA appears to be negatively affected also by INNOVATION with a low significance level (10%), that therefore can be overlooked by our analysis. In addition, Sargan and Arellano-Bond tests, confirm that the model is correctly specified since instruments are valid and no serial correlation is revealed in the first-differenced residuals.

To summarize, the two dynamic panel models implemented in this Section (GMM-Sys Two-step and GMM-Sys One-step) give us back the following main results on the three preliminary research hypotheses (see Section 1).

(a) Workers' education attainment (EDUC) affect positively the performance of innovative SMEs by increasing reasonably their profitability. This means that if workers own a master's degree, a PhD qualification, or three years of experience in certified research activities, they contribute to strengthen the company's value, confirming the results of that strand of literature suggesting the positive role of high education attainments in determining wider earnings and strategic decisions (Hambrick and Mason, 1984; Wally and Baum, 1994; Leiponen, 2005; Graham *et al.*, 2013; Kouaib and Jarboui, 2016);
(b) Ownership of software or patent (INNOVATION) impact only marginally on the SMEs' profitability and with a negative sign (just in the GMM-Sys One-step and with a low significance level). Therefore, as supported by the work of Sher and Yang (2005), it can be concluded

that the ownership of software or patent is not always recognized as a driving factor of firm growth;

(c) Prevalence of women and young in the corporate boards (WOMEN and YOUNG) affect strongly and negatively the adjusted ROA of innovative SMEs, suggesting that their presence within the corporate board decrease the SMEs' performance.

With respect to WOMEN, these results are in line with the study of Quiroz-Rojas and Teruel (2020), supporting the evidence of the conservative approach to risk taken by woman compared to men, more evident in innovative firms.

Instead, with regard to YOUNG, these results disagree with the empirical evidences of Ahn and Walker (2007) for which the presence of young in the corporate board fosters strategic change and the propensity to innovate and agree with the findings of Daveri and Parisi (2015), where SMEs' profitability increases only when young experienced as corporate members.

8. Conclusions

This chapter analyzes the relationship between corporate governance and company performance on a sample of Italian small and medium-sized innovative companies (SMEs), over the period 2015–2019. The reason of this choice is related to the fact that innovative SMEs' profitability might be affected differently than traditional companies by the features of corporate governance, because of high riskiness of innovative projects.

Three main research hypotheses have been tested: (a) workers' education attainment; (b) ownership of software or patent; (c) the prevalence of women, young and foreigners in the board size. However, this last variable (FOREIGN) has been eliminated from subsequent estimates because of its collinearity problems with other considered variables.

In order to deal with the problem of time-invariant corporate variables on one side and the issue related to past firm performance on the other side, different static and dynamic models have been applied in this study, highlighting the main pros and cons of each model estimator. The two suitable models to analyze the aforementioned relationship are the Hausman–Taylor (HT) and the System Generalized Method of Moment (Syst-GMM) respectively for static and dynamic estimation.

More specifically, two different System GMM models have been implemented here, to provide more robustness to the results: the Two-step System GMM proposed by Kripfganz and Schwarz (2019) and the One-step System GMM (with the Stata command *xtdpd*), to allow for time-invariant estimates. The performed Sargan and Arellano–Bond tests, confirm that both dynamic model estimators are correctly specified and the obtained results on corporate governance variables are aligned each other in terms of significance and sign.

Results show that: (a) higher workers' education attainment (EDUC) such as master's degree, PhD qualification or experiences in certified research activities, affect positively the performance of innovative SMEs by increasing reasonably their profitability, in line with what is claimed by the main strand of literature; (b) the ownership of software or patent (INNOVATION) impacts only marginally on the SMEs' profitability and with a negative sign, confirming the outcome of Sher and Yang (2005) for which the ownership of patent is not always recognized as a driving factor of firm growth; (c) the prevalence of women and young in the corporate board (WOMEN and YOUNG) affect strongly and negatively the adjusted ROA of innovative SMEs, confirming from one side the evidences found by Quiroz-Rojas and Teruel (2020), that is the conservative approach to risk taken by women compared to men, especially in innovative firms, and highlighting, from the other side, the idea of insufficient experience of young members for supporting the growth of innovative companies if young are corporate board members (Daveri and Parisi, 2015).

References

Ahn, S. and Walker, M.D. (2007). Corporate governance and spinoff decision, *Journal of Corporate Business Research*, 63(3), 284–291.

Arellano, M. and Bond, S. (1991). Some tests of specification for panel data: Monte Carlo evidence and an application to employment equations, *The Review of Economic Studies*, 58(2), 277–297.

Arellano, M. and Bover, O. (1995). Another look at the instrumental variable estimation of error–components models, *Journal of Econometrics*, 68(1), 29–51.

Arora, A. and Sharma, C. (2016). Corporate governance and firm performance in developing countries: Evidence from India, *Corporate Governance*, 16(2), 420–436.

Artz, K.W., Norman, P.M., Hatfield, D.E. and Cardinal, L.B. (2010). A longitudinal study of the impact of R&D, patents, and product innovation on firm performance, *Journal of Product Innovation Management*, 27(5), 725–740.

Aubert, P., Caroli, E. and Roger, M. (2006). New technologies, organisation and age: Firm-level evidence, *The Economic Journal*, 116(509), F73–F93.

Ayyagari, M., Demirgüç-Kunt, A. and Maksimovic, V. (2011). Firm innovation in emerging markets: The role of finance, governance, and competition, *Journal of Financial and Quantitative Analysis*, 46(6), 1545–1580.

Baltagi, B. H. (2008). *Econometric Analysis of Panel Data*. John Wiley and Sons: Hoboken.

Baltagi, B.H., Bresson, G. and Pirotte, A. (2003). Fixed effects, random effects or Hausman–Taylor? A pretest estimator, *Economics Letters*, 79(3), 361–369.

Bhagat, S. and Bolton, B. (2008). Corporate governance and firm performance, *Journal of Corporate Finance*, 14(3), 257–273.

Black, B. (2001). The corporate governance behavior and market value of Russian firms, *Emerging Markets Review*, 2(2), 89–108.

Blundell, R. and Bond, S. (1998). Initial conditions and moment restrictions in dynamic panel data models, *Journal of Econometrics*, 87(1), 115–143.

Bolli, T., Renold, U. and Wörter, M. (2018). Vertical educational diversity and innovation performance, *Economics of Innovation and New Technology*, 27(2), 107–131.

Bond, S.R. (2002). Dynamic panel data models: a guide to micro data methods and practice, *Portuguese Economic Journal*, 1(2), 141–162.

Breusch, T.S. and Pagan, A.R. (1980). The Lagrange multiplier test and its applications to model specification in econometrics, *The Review of Economic Studies*, 47(1), 239–253.

Carter, D.A., D'Souza, F., Simkins, B.J. and Simpson, W.G. (2010). The gender and ethnic diversity of US boards and board committees and firm financial performance, *Corporate Governance: An International Review*, 18(5), 396–414.

Cheng, Y.H., Kuan, F.Y., Chuang, S.C. and Ken, Y. (2010). Profitability decided by patent quality? An empirical study of the US semiconductor industry, *Scientometrics*, 82(1), 175–183.

Coad, A. (2018). Firm age: A survey, *Journal of Evolutionary Economics*, 28(1), 13–43.

Darmadi, S. (2011). Board diversity and firm performance: The Indonesian evidence, *Corporate Ownership and Control Journal*, 8.

Daveri, F. and Parisi, M.L. (2015). Experience, innovation and productivity: Empirical evidence from Italy's slowdown. *ILR Review*, 68(4), 889–915.

Fernández-Temprano, M. A. and Tejerina-Gaite, F. (2020). Types of director, board diversity and firm performance, *Corporate Governance: The International Journal of Business in Society*, 20(2), 324–342.

Graham, J.R., Harvey, C.R. and Puri, M. (2013). Managerial attitudes and corporate actions, *Journal of Financial Economics*, 109(1), 103–121.

Grinza, E. and Quatraro, F. (2019). Workers' replacements and firms' innovation dynamics: New evidence from Italian matched longitudinal data, *Research Policy*, 48(9), 103804.

Guo, W.C., Shiah–Hou, S.R. and Chien, W.J. (2012). A study on intellectual capital and firm performance in biotech companies, *Applied Economics Letters*, 19(16), 1603–1608.

Hagel, J., Brown, J.S., Samoylova, T., Lui, M., Damani, A. and Grames, C. (2013). Success or struggle: ROA as a true measure of business performance. *Report 3 of the 2013 Shift Index Series*.

Hambrick, D.C. and Mason, P. A. (1984). Upper echelons: The organization as a reflection of its top managers, *Academy of Management Review*, 9(2), 193–206.

Hausman, J.A. (1978). Specification tests in econometrics, *Econometrica: Journal of the Econometric Society*, 1251–1271.

Hausman, J.A. and Taylor W.E. (1981) Panel data and unobservable individual effect, *Econometrica*, 49(6), 1377–1398.

Joh, S.W. (2003). Corporate governance and firm profitability: Evidence from Korea before the economic crisis, *Journal of Financial Economics*, 68(2), 287–322.

Kim, H. and Lim, C. (2010). Diversity, outside directors and firm valuation: Korean evidence, *Journal of Business Research*, 63(3), 284–291.

Klapper, L.F. and Love, I. (2004). Corporate governance, investor protection, and performance in emerging markets, *Journal of Corporate Finance*, 10(5), 703–728.

Kouaib, A. and Jarboui, A. (2016). Real earnings management in innovative firms: Does CEO profile make a difference? *Journal of Behavioral and Experimental Finance*, 12, 40–54.

Kripfganz, S. and Schwarz, C. (2019). Estimation of linear dynamic panel data models with time-invariant regressors, *Journal of Applied Econometrics*, 34(4), 526–546.

Leiponen, A. (2005). Skills and innovation, *International Journal of Industrial Organization*, 23(5–6), 303–323.

Mahadeo, J.D., Soobaroyen, T. and Hanuman, V.O. (2012). Board composition and financial performance: Uncovering the effects of diversity in an emerging economy, *Journal of Business Ethics*, 105(3), 375–388.

Makkonen, T., Williams, A.M. and Habersetzer, A. (2018). Foreign board members and firm innovativeness: An exploratory analysis for setting a research agenda, *Corporate Governance: The International Journal of Business in Society*, 18(6), 1057–1073.

Maravelaki, A., Doumpos, M. and Zopounidis, C. (2019). Corporate governance, women's participation and firm performance: Empirical analysis using a non-parametric evaluation methodology, *INFOR: Information Systems and Operational Research*, 57(3), 394–410.

Masulis, R.W., Wang, C. and Xie, F. (2012). Globalizing the boardroom. The effects of foreign directors on corporate governance and firm performance, *Journal of Accounting and Economics*, 53(3), 527–554.

Montgomery, D.C., Peck, E.A. and Vining, G.G. (2021). *Introduction to Linear Regression Analysis*. John Wiley: New York.

Mundlak, Y. (1978). On the pooling of time series and cross section data, *Econometrica: Journal of the Econometric Society*, 69–85.

Murray, L., Nguyen, H., Lee, Y.F., Remmenga, M.D. and Smith, D.W. (2012). Variance inflation factors in regression models with dummy variables. Conference on Applied Statistics in Agriculture. https://doi.org/10.4148/2475-7772.1034

Nickell, S. (1981). Biases in dynamic models with fixed effects. *Econometrica: Journal of the econometric society*, 1417–1426.

O'connell, V. and Cramer, N. (2010). The relationship between firm performance and board characteristics in Ireland, *European Management Journal*, 28(5), 387–399.

Ouimet, P. and Zarutskie, R. (2014). Who works for startups? The relation between firm age, employee age, and growth, *Journal of Financial Economics*, 112(3), 386–407.

Ozgen, C. and de Graaff, T. (2013). Sorting out the impact of cultural diversity on innovative firms: An empirical analysis of Dutch micro-data. NORFACE Research Programme on Migration, Department of Economics, Univ. College London.

Perryman, A. A., Fernando, G. D. and Tripathy, A. (2016). Do gender differences persist? An examination of gender diversity on firm performance, risk, and executive compensation, *Journal of Business Research*, 69(2), 579–586.

Quiroz-Rojas, P. and Teruel, M. (2020). Does gender matter for innovative and non-innovative firms' growth? An empirical analysis of Chilean managers, *Innovation and Development*, 1–19.

Rose, C. (2007). Does female board representation influence firm performance? The Danish evidence, *Corporate Governance: An International Review*, 15(2), 404–413.

Sher, P.J. and Yang, P.Y. (2005). The effects of innovative capabilities and R&D clustering on firm performance: The evidence of Taiwan's semiconductor industry, *Technovation*, 25(1), 33–43.

Wally, S. and Baum, J.R. (1994). Personal and structural determinants of the pace of strategic decision-making, *Academy of Management Journal*, 37(4), 932–956.

Wintoki, M.B., Linck, J.S. and Netter, J.M. (2012). Endogeneity and the dynamics of internal corporate governance, *Journal of Financial Economics*, 105(3), 581–606.

Wooldridge, J.M. (2016). *Introductory Econometrics: A Modern Approach.* Nelson Education: Toronto.

https://doi.org/10.1142/9789811260506_0002

Chapter 2

Ownership and Governance of State-Owned Enterprises: A Compendium of National Practices

George Alexopoulos[*,¶], **Alexandros Garefalakis**[†,‡,||], **Eirini Stavropoulou**[§,**], **and Konstantinos Spinthiropoulos**[§,††]

[*]*Department of Business Administration, University of Patras, Greece*

[†]*Hellenic Mediterranean University, Department of Business Administration & Tourism, Operations Research and Management Audit Laboratory, Heraklion, Crete*

[‡]*Neapolis University Pafos, Cyprus*

[§]*University of West Macedonia, Department of Management Science & Technology*

[¶]*alexopoulos.ga@gmail.com*

[||]*agarefalakis@hmu.gr*

[**]*stavreirini@yahoo.gr*

[††]*kspinthiropoulos@uowm.gr*

Abstract

In this chapter, we focus on the analysis of the corporate governance framework in the Hellenic Republic (Greece) under the institution of the PCC (Private Capital Company). We analyze the main characteristics of this corporate form, highlighting the innovations it brings and the advantages it has over other corporate forms. We also address the adaptability of corporate governance to the specificities of social enterprises and the EU Directive/Communication on Corporate Governance.

Keywords: Corporate governance, state-owned Enterprises, market behavior, acquisitions of listed companies, literature review

1. Introduction

This chapter focuses on efforts to create a more effective corporate governance framework in the Hellenic Republic (Greece). Recent efforts to modernize and improve the governance regime began in 1999, with the publication of the Corporate Governance Principles in Greece, and continued with the regulation of the Capital Market Commission which covers transparency, market behavior and acquisitions of listed companies. In 2002, a regulation was introduced that emphasizes the structure and conduct of the board.

New laws and regulations that have introduced a series of new ideas — including requirements for independent board members, internal control services, faster dissemination of information and new measures to protect against the use of confidential information — stimulate a trend toward a more efficient corporate governance system in Greece. The new rules of behavior of listed companies have also improved accountability, transparency and disclosure of information, with severe punishment for violations, although the existing laws provide a fair degree of flexibility. The expected implementation of the proposed new laws will address the issue of market abuse, including both price manipulation and the use of confidential information.

Nonetheless, despite these initiatives, many businesses are still falling below the levels best suited to Europe and the US. Implementation of governance practices remains in many cases more of a result of mandatory compliance than a conscious effort by corporate boards to be more accountable.

2. The Evolution of Corporate Governance in the Greek decade of 1992–2002

The period of 10 years between 1992 and 2002 was characterized by certain shortcomings in the Greek capital markets, the most notable of which was the lack of a proper culture in corporate governance.

Table 1: Differences between Greek Accounting Standards and International Financial Reporting Standards (IFRS) for basic financial accounts.

Financial Accounts	**Greek Accounting Standards**	**IFRS**
Depreciation charges	Under the tax law	According to the life of the assets
Stock portfolio	They are valued on the basis of the lowest price between acquisition cost and market value. If the market value is greater than the cost of acquisition, the difference can be amortized (thus affecting profits) or deducted from equity	The equity portfolio is categorized as between its investment portfolio and its trading portfolio. Investment losses are deducted from equity, while the trading period losses affects earnings
Real estate assets	They are valued at acquisition cost and incorporated into each asset revaluation required by Greek law	They are valued either on the basis of the acquisition value or the market value. An independent consultant determines the purchase price of the asset
Surplus value	It is not treated as an asset. Removed directly from equity, does not affect earnings	It is treated as an asset. It expires in the long run, thus affecting profits

The need for corporate governance reforms in Greece became even more apparent after the high market stocks in 1999, which had devastating effects on the market. Rhetoric-based prices, coupled with market abuse, created a bubble effect and ultimately contributed to the fall (see Table 1). An increase in the number of IPOs by companies with outdated corporate structures, accompanied by the aging of the regulatory framework, had produced negative outcomes for investors, who often ignored the real situation of their holdings. The loss of investor confidence in the market was perhaps the most catastrophic long-term consequence, and since 2000 there has been a capital exit away from the Stock Exchange. By 2003, total annual transactions had fallen to €34.9 billion.

At an early stage by the Greek authorities to restore market confidence, the institutional and legal framework of the capital markets has been revised and updated. Efforts began in 1999 with the publication of the principles of Corporate Governance in Greece and continued with the regulations introduced by the Hellenic Capital Market Commission covering transparency and market behavior for listed companies. This was followed by the

Regulation of the Capital Market Commission 1/192/2000 setting the acquisitions. Law 3016/2002 followed and dealt with the structure and conduct of the board of directors. These, and other subsequent laws and regulations were the first major efforts to revise the 85-year corporate law. The combined effect of these laws attempted to separate the roles of shareholders, management and boards, and to increase the transparency, quality and dissemination of information to investors.

2.1 *Measures included*

Major measures are reviewed and end up in key parts of corporate governance such as:

- Mandatory independent directors. Although there has always been a distinction between the role of the management, the shareholders and the directors of the company, in fact, the main shareholder has appointed the members of the board of directors and ruled the shareholders' meetings in most cases. Decisions were often taken for the benefit of the main shareholder and used the assets of the company. This was not surprising, given the strong concentration of ownership in Greek listed companies. The introduction of independent executives was, therefore, a positive step, although concerns about the independence of the assignment process and the assignment were not addressed (L3016/02).
- Mandatory announcement prior to the purchase or sale of the company's inventory by management members or Board members prior to a major corporate event. There are, however, cases of violation, such as fines imposed by the authorities and low as opposed to potential profits (5/204/00 Capital Market Regulation).
- Improving the dissemination of information to investors. The introduction of investment relationships was a step toward better communication with investors. Not all companies take investor relations seriously, however, and dissemination of information is not always effective (L3016/02).
- Creating internal audit segments. Reporting to the board of directors, internal audit departments were created to help senior executives at work and its investors in decisions. This reform is particularly useful to independent members of the Board in the sense that they will be notified of irregularities (L3016/02).

Since these measures were imposed on the business community and were not readily accepted, many listed companies initially ignored the code.

3. Can the Legal Infrastructure of Greece Support Corporate Governance?

3.1 *Harmonization with EU directives*

Throughout the 1990s, the legal framework of the Greek capital market has undergone significant changes following the adoption of EU directives. Harmonization has focused on three areas:

- L2076/96 presents the second EU banking directive that provides for the liberalization of efficient banking services for foreign institutions in Greece and Greek institutions abroad.
- L2396/96 introduced free access to investment of EU institutions in Greece and Greek institutions in EU Member States.
- Law No. 1969/91 has complied with the EU on institutional investment practices.

3.2 *The establishment of the Information Structure*

3.2.1 *Adoption of International Financial Reporting Standards (IFRS)*

Since January 2005, listed companies in Greece are required to publish annual and interim financial statements in order to comply with IFRSs. The preparation and publication of financial statements in accordance with IFRSs will be made in accordance with the provisions of L3229/2004 (Government Gazette 38/10, February 2004) and L2190/1920. Article 13 of L3229/2004 states that, in 2005, listed companies should report the use of IFRS only for the financial year of 2005 or interim periods of the same year without providing financial accounts from the previous year or the period for comparison.

The new IFRS financial statements will be more extensive and more detailed than those published in accordance with the Greek Accounting Standards. According to IFRS, the financial statements of all Greek companies will be directly comparable to those of listed corporate entities in all other euro area countries.

It is too early to assess the precise qualitative and quantitative results for the financial accounts of Greek listed companies after the adoption of IFRS. According to market sources, it is most likely to be more prominent in banks, insurance companies, brokerage companies and leasing companies, and is more likely to be related to issues such as fair valuation of property, stocks, derivatives, economic treatment of M&As, treatment of leased assets, exchange differences and retirement benefits.

In addition to executive compensation, another mechanism used to mitigate the organization's problem is to strengthen the role of the Board. The Board of Directors is the second most important tool of the company that incorporates political power. The more independent the Board is, the greater is the power of monitoring. In addition to the degree of independence, the Boards should consist mainly of non-executive members. This will in part ensure even greater autonomy and compliance with decisions that are not detrimental to major shareholders (Jensen, 1993). The Board of Directors should also meet at such frequencies as to ensure maximum monitoring and control (Shivadasani and Zenner, 2004). Vafeas (1999) argues that the Council should judge the required frequency of meetings by balancing between the costs and the benefits derived from them. An additional feature of the Board's efficiency is its leadership structure, which cannot be ensured simply by increasing the number of non-executive members. Some degree of involvement of executive members is necessary and a strong nomination committee can ensure that only the most competent and committed people are part of it.

The size of these committees is a further aspect that the academic literature has explored, since small committees are not affected by internal wishes (Hermalin and Weisbach, 2003). On the contrary, larger committees are more prone to manipulation. Klein (2002) argues that the maximum independence of these committees is highly desirable so that efficient management practices are promoted in the day-to-day management of the institution. Greek laws require members of the Audit Committee to combine specialized knowledge in control functions, along with the generally accepted concept (Bedard, 2004). It is also argued that the frequency of committee meetings directly affects control quality and facilitates proactive action on potential mistakes.

In the second year of law enforcement requiring detailed information on corporate governance practices, our research finds that in some aspects companies do not deviate significantly from the minimum necessary practices, although they seem to have a greater understanding of the wishes and objectives of the Code. Non-executive members in the Council are one in two, while the ratio required by law is one in three. Independent members on the other hand are on average no more than two, which represents the minimum requirement. Companies tend not to give much information about the frequency of Council Meetings, compensation packages of Council members and official top executives or Audit Agency and practices. They carry out Audit Committees as required by law for the last 10 years, but only one in two is carrying out other specialized Committees such as Compensations and Nominees, although the requirements of the Code and its best practice proposals worldwide indicate that all said bodies should operate collectively. We emphasize the fact that the difference in compliance with nationally expected standards for corporate governance is enormous by comparing small and medium-sized companies with large corporations, with the latter showing, as expected, a greater insistence on the operation of corporate governance practices. This could be attributed to the fact that investors, who traditionally value high standards of corporate governance in companies, primarily lead their funds to large companies in the Greek market, given also the great economic crisis.

3.3 *Relationship between risk management and corporate governance*

Analysts have dealt with identifying the correlations between company value and financial management, particularly from the perspective of escalating economies. The implementation of financial management departments creates an incentive for economic growth as risk mitigation techniques support the accumulation of wealth. This relationship has been the subject of a survey of studies that have focused particularly on non-financial corporations since financial institutions entail particularities within the capital structure. There are several theories about the allocation of risk management to shareholder value. However, capital market imperfections — representation costs, transaction costs, taxes and rising costs of the foreign economy — represent the level at which the value of the company may increase to benefit from shareholders. Risk management tools represent support to maximize the value of the company and become essential in the context of capital market integration. Increasing the risk together with risk concentration can add vulnerability to the corporate sector. Hence, risk management strategies make a significant contribution to value creation.

3.4 *Revision of bibliography through corporate governance developments*

The economic structure of the company can be perceived as a recipient of various systems of factors arising from the level of the company and industry, institutional, legal, political and social context (Gietzmann and Ireland, 2005). In addition to these factors, the capital structure bears the signal of the directors' decision on the company's financial policy, being deeply linked to corporate governance. In the context of this idea, previous studies highlighted the impact of corporate governance on the capital structure (Hart, 1995; Fosberg, 2004; Andersonetal, 2007). This influence has proved to be particularly possible in the case of corporate trading as well as in the case of large companies. Most surveys have argued that the size and structure of the council, the duality of the CEO and compensation are core variables of corporate governance. Along with these findings, Bergeretal (1997) revealed that companies with a large board have low leverage. This is because the big board is likely to impose on directors less corporate debt to increase its profitability. Subsequent studies (Wen *et al.*, 2002; Abor, 2007) revealed the opposite findings, meaning that large councils encourage leverage and this leads to rigorous supervision of the company's directors. The latter restores the higher leverage, as it follows its policy of a positive correlation between debt and profitability. Anderson *et al.* (2004) stressed that it is cheaper for big board companies to attract external financial resources as lenders perceive these companies as having strictly monitored the financing decision. Wen *et al.* (2002) identified a negative relationship between the number of external directors on the board and leverage. The authors assume that external directors have the incentive to control directors very strictly, by fixing them to adopt a lower leverage in order to encourage a high stock purchase price. The duality of the Managing Director affects the capital structure of the company (Fama and Jensen, 1983; Fosberg, 2004). The bibliography revealed the importance of the two-tier leadership (inability for the same person to be at the same time as the board of directors and the CEO of the Board of Directors). It does not allow both the management of decision-making and the control of decisions to be taken jointly, and this helps to reduce the Agency's expenditure. Fosberg (2004) argued that firms that do not promote the duality of the Managing Director are more likely to adopt an optimal capital structure with a heavy debt burden on the economic mix. In addition, Anderson *et al.* (2004) argued that dual leadership violates the balance of power that affects the clear division of responsibilities into the company's manager. Shamsul (2004) states that the effectiveness of the Council's role is reduced in the case of dual leadership by one person who has the right to manage both business (as CEO) and internal control (as chairman of the board). Another key variable of corporate governance, which is likely to be correlated with the capital structure, is the CEO's Compensation Scheme. Bibliography revealed contradictory results as to the correlation between CEO's compensation and financial leverage. Stulz (1988), Milton and Raviv (1998) and Abor and Biekpe (2008) highlighted that companies promoting stable compensation schemes for CEOs adopt a lower leverage in order to reduce financial risk while Wen *et al.* (2002) brought a negative relationship to the fore. As for the CEO's term, the authors have emphasized that the long-term CEO prefers low leverage due to his goal of reducing potential shareholders' pressures in order to gain a certain level of profitability. This aspect is determined by the fact that shareholders usually perceive higher debt with a similar level of risk, requiring an equivalent reward, which gives incentives for significant pressure on the CEO.

3.5 *The European direction for the efficiency of corporate governance*

Although the development of a European-level voluntary code could add to general awareness and understanding of governance issues across the European Union, given the continuing variation in the legal frameworks of the member states, we believe that a code agreed by all member states could focus more on the basic principles of good governance than on the detailed recommendations of best practice. The OECD Principles on Corporate Governance (issued in 1999, following extensive consultation and participation from each Member State of the European Union) already include a coherent, thoughtful and agreed set of core principles of corporate governance. Achieving broad agreement on a more detailed set of best practices to suit the different legal frameworks of the Member States

Table 2: The main parts of corporate governance.

Rights of shareholders
Equal treatment of shareholders
The role of the parties concerned
Information and transparency
Responsibilities of the Board of Directors

Table 3: Rates for main parts of corporate governance.

Rights of shareholders	10%
Equal treatment of shareholders	15%
The role of the parties concerned	10%
Information and transparency	25%
Responsibilities of the Board of Directors	40%
Total quota allocation of the departments	100%

Table 4: Milestones for Corporate Governance implementation in Greece.

Date	Corporate Governance Activity
1998	The Athens Stock Exchange conducts a study on corporate governance
1999, April	The OECD Principles on Corporate Governance
1999, October	Corporate Governance Code from the Commission on Corporate Governance in Greece (under the direction of the Securities and Exchange Commission)
2000	The Ministry of National Economy and Development adopts a law on the establishment of a committee on corporate governance
2000, July	Capital Market Commission Rules: "Competition offers to the capital market to obtain insurance"
2000, November	Capital Market Commission Rules: "A Code of Conduct for listed companies in the Athens Stock Exchange and related parties"
2001, August	Principles of Corporate Governance by the Federation of Greek Industries
2002, March	A corporate evaluation system is presented by the Center for Economic Studies of the University of Athens (a program funded by the Athens Stock Exchange)
2000, May	Law 3016/2002: "On Corporate Governance, Board Compensation and Other Issues"
2000, July	The Athens Stock Exchange establishes quality criteria covering corporate governance, transparency and investor communication

will be difficult and can only succeed in the expression of the "lowest common denominator".

Future EU-level efforts on corporate governance will be more valuable if instead of focusing on the level of the code (best practice), they focus on the following:

- Reducing participation barriers that currently make it difficult for shareholders to participate in cross-border voting and
- Reducing barriers to information on the ability of shareholders (and potential investors) to assess corporate governance, both at member state level and at individual company level.

The allocation of a quota broken down by section is as in Table 2.

According to the above, a new way is being explored if there is a correlation between corporate governance, capital structure models and social enterprises in terms of the democratic and voluntary decision-making process that takes place (see also Tables 3 and 4).

4. Discussion and Concluding Remarks

The Greek capital market has changed greatly over the last 6 years. Corporate governance has been widely discussed between the business world and the relevant regulators. Voluntary and regulatory initiatives have been proposed or adopted in response to external and internal forces. Internally, in mid-1999, the Greek capital market faced an extended episode of overestimating the stock price. The crisis led to a significant fall in the stock price in the last quarter of 1999. The listed companies only were able to restore public confidence (Andersson, 1999). Reduced corporate accountability and inadequate disclosure of practices have sparked massive liquidation from investors. Externally, the upgrading of the Greek capital market to mature has had a significant impact. Institutional investors with an "emerging market" profile proceeded to substantially liquidate their portfolio (Becht, 1997). However, the Greek capital market has not been able to attract long-term, loyal institutional investors. The latter usually investigate extensively the governance structures (e.g. voting practices, composition of the Board of Directors and accounting standards) of the companies they intend to invest in, and decide on the basis of the available information. Without enough information of sufficient quality they will not invest. Self-regulation by individual companies on disclosure issues has proven to be inadequate (Galbraith, 1993). In this context, the main regulatory actions addressed issues such as corporate transparency, information and independent control. In this way, we hope that the Greek capital market will prove to be an attractive investment option, where investors' rights are adequately protected.

4.1 *New corporate governance frameworks for social enterprises*

It has been studied that the financial results of an enterprise are perfectly linked to corporate governance. Social enterprises have a different decision-making that does not follow the existing corporate governance frameworks.

The governance of a social enterprise, if incorporated well, helps to ensure the company's mission while allowing the management team to meet the requirements of various stakeholders such as investors, employees, customers and beneficiaries as well as compliance with public policies and regulations. However, few social enterprises use governance as a means of achieving their highest potential. Similarly, members of the board of social enterprises often feel they have more to offer than their social enterprise is currently employing. This is a strange missed opportunity. No governance mechanism suits all social enterprises. Governance, on the other hand, should be dynamic and adaptable to the changing needs of the management team, the operational and regulatory environment, and the larger goals and vision of the social enterprise in relation to its life span. According to Charkham and Simpson (1999), there are two basic principles for successful corporate governance:

- management is free to run the business with minimal interference and maximum incitement; and
- management must be accountable for the effective and efficient use of this freedom.

In order to be able to control the correct implementation of corporate governance in social enterprises, we need to look at their economic impact. This will be examined through the decisions of the members as a result of the capital structure of a business. The most prevalent capital structure theories are the trade-off theory, the representation cost theory, the Pecking order theory and market timing.

The above theories are quite important because with these social business executives they judge what financial tools they will use for social enterprises.

Financial instruments exclusively for social enterprises:

- **Unsecured debt:** A simple, stable or variable, non-secured loan.
- **Social bonds not listed on the stock market:** This is a collection of money from individuals or organizations that require a socially produced product as a guarantee.
- **Brokerage bonds:** This is an institution listed on a stock exchange specifically developed for charitable organizations, individuals and organizations.
- **Participation or semi-participation in equity investments:** A loan that delivers a risk-sharing between the investor and the business.
- **Third-party financing:** Two or more investors work together to provide different types of mixed finance with equity and loan, and where an investor is taking a higher risk.
- **Democratic funding:** This is the case where a social enterprise derives a grant, a loan, a share in the share capital.

Social enterprises offer the opportunity to study how governance systems facilitate an efficient performance reporting process. Of particular importance are the governance systems that promote transparency and efficiency. Therefore, these systems create accountability and sustainability, which are important if the social business sector is to continue to provide value to the social economy (Paton, 2003; Pearce, 2003).

The overall objective of this project is to optimize corporate governance monitoring mechanisms for decision-making and risk management in social enterprises. High quality disclosure about corporate governance status of social enterprises provides useful information for investors and facilitates their investment decisions. It also gives investors more confidence in the social businesses they invest in. Increasing transparency in the market can also bring benefits for business and legitimacy to the eyes of the players and society as a whole. Especially in the field of government subsidies, corporate governance does not provide a detailed regulatory framework for the governance of the objectives and their implementation. Then for the first time we will introduce capital structure models to measure the economic performance of the results of decisions made by members of social enterprises. The use of econometric models will clarify many factors and tell us about the risk management of members of social enterprises. In our research we are introducing for the first time the concept of the capital social enterprise that is closer to the regulatory and legal framework of corporate governance. However, a proposal is proposed that reconciles: (1) the capital principle based on the share of ownership on the capital held by the partner (2) the statutory commitment to promoting social goals (3) and the ownership and control structure ensuring equal rights for partners (one member — one vote).

It has been shown that there is a positive correlation between leverage and profitability, as socially profitable companies prefer borrowing to take advantage of the tax relief offered by interest-bearing interest. Since we are talking about social enterprises, existing corporate governance models should not be followed because profits are reinvested for social purposes.

Exploratory corporate governance models should provide information to stakeholders and should be useful at the practical level for boards of directors and managers of social enterprises (Dees, 1998; Low, 2006; Laville and Nyssens, 2001). From the point of view of the institutional economy there are many actors in the social enterprise that require careful consideration. The dominant model of stakeholders allows for governance that promotes diversity at board level and incorporates a variety of claims into strategic planning. However, management theory may be more appropriate to adapt the evolving characteristics of social enterprise (Dees, 1998; Dart, 2004; Low, 2006).

Business operation is a sine qua non for the social enterprise. The ability to make a profit is not an incidental activity: it must be continuous rather than occasional. The model of economic viability should be based on revenue from speculative activities. The generation of accounting profits may not necessarily be the case at any time with the business plan of the social enterprise, but it concerns distribution rather than its function, which is to offer services and products to the market in economically significant sources. Corporate governance has a framework for speculative business activities and you are against the concept of social enterprise.

Corporate governance rules determine how corporate goals are being achieved, how they set up corporate social risk monitoring and assessment systems. In social businesses, we often have ambiguities about the source of funding for the organization's permanence. Here, corporate governance cannot examine whether the agency's activities underlie speculation of a permanent type. For example, sports clubs are quite difficult to test or digital communities. Or even if they are active in the non-market sector and do not distribute profits and the participation of the members is not imposed by state law, and they follow corporate governance frameworks. Another key criterion for our study is the funding study criteria, there should be a separation of social enterprises into money and non-cash transactions. Finally, we should establish frameworks for the study of corporate governance's potential for the future planning of social enterprises because it is something they use enough and do not mention it in their minutes. Their ability to collect subscriptions and attract donations by reducing the financial burden on the Treasury. In the long run, however, the logic of cost compression is questioned as subscriptions and subsidies are reduced, voluntary work is replaced by tenant and government regulations are imposed.

The main challenge of this research is to integrate and exploit the extensive measurement of the social product with the growing sector of social business governance. Measuring performance is already a key aspect that affects internal and external responsibility (Paton, 2003; Somers, 2005). This research provides a critical remark on the rationale and effectiveness of performance measurement systems. In other areas, particularly in the private sector, performance measurement and governance are synthesized in scorecards (Strenger, 2004) and reference systems (Sherman, 2004). In the present thesis, the econometric model tries to measure the perceptual capacity of corporate governance as two factors: decision-making and risk management. Today's social enterprises have a high degree of autonomy, fed by state resources and private resources. And their sustainability depends on the efforts of members and employees to ensure sufficient resources and profits. Here we are trying to answer the question whether this democratic decision-making has enough knowledge to achieve enough social product either exportable or a profit percentage to invest in the local community.

4.2 *The adaptability of corporate governance to the specificities of social enterprises*

Corporate governance seeks to balance opposing forces and conflicting interests that are inherent in the nature of the business and the roles of those involved in it, which is not the case for the participatory and voluntary nature of the social enterprise. Under the existing corporate governance framework, there are no compliance directives for social enterprises regulating:

- Employee relations with each other, as many social enterprises lacking management;
- Danger management;
- Profit distribution;
- Assets and surpluses are used to generate community benefits;
- Grants from charitable and voluntary organizations where donors offer free of charge;
- Citizens' group initiative;
- Participatory character of employees and volunteers. Participation in projects and structures is open and voluntary.

A social enterprise needs special managerial skills in managing human resources, given the diversity of paid or voluntary staff. Human resources management is a central area where there are many issues, such as democracy, social and economic tensions, the need to meet the needs of the workers, and the maintenance of the people involved, etc. Permanent and effective management of social business staff is a challenge.

It is necessary to develop a corporate governance strategy to support the multiple objectives of social enterprises. Management must be able to analyze, understand and even anticipate the social needs expressed, in particular, by consumers, beneficiaries and the state. The current corporate governance framework is unable to determine the identity and scope of the social business, taking into account the organization's missions, goals and resources, as well as tensions between the social objective and the financial requirements. To do this, consistency, energy and a form of idealism are necessary behaviors. Through corporate governance, managers need to know how to communicate effectively in order to develop a dialogue tailored to different audiences. Innovation and adaptation capabilities are also assets to better manage change.

According to transnational criteria, the characteristics of social enterprises are:

- They do not belong to the state administrative authorities;
- Organized with structural business frameworks;
- The social culture and the ethos of social enterprise are based on volunteering, moral behavior;

- They help solve problems of unemployment and social reintegration of vulnerable groups;
- They seek to balance their Balance Sheets by drawing their revenue through their activation in the active market and through donations from their members, state and local government subsidies, donations, sponsorships and private business aid;
- The market for social products, which compete with other businesses, is carried out to achieve a social purpose rather than a private profit (Hart, 1995).

To classify a business as social, various social criteria and economic criteria have been formulated:

- Citizens' Action Group Initiative;
- Identifiable purpose and benefit to society;
- Incorporating all participants and volunteer groups into the process of achieving social actions and goals;
- Risk management models for capital remuneration;
- Democratic and participatory management model.

The economic criteria include:

- Economic viability through income generation from the sale of social goods and social services;
- Limited or no distribution of profits to participants;
- High degree of autonomy for all groups of social participation actions.

All the values and rules of social enterprises are based on the goal of achieving the maximum possible social benefit. The procedures for setting up a social enterprise are determined by a volunteering system based on self-commitment, which must be credibly documented and lead to efficiency. A legislative framework for corporate governance support should be developed in the field of social enterprises as well as in the instruments, resources and processes of their development.

In summary, the characteristics of social enterprises in terms of management issues that corporate governance should define, are:

- Increasing and participatory social participative decision-making;
- Democratic organization and operation of the action groups;

- Initiatives commensurate with the social character of businesses and local businesses;
- High degree of autonomy and local social and voluntary groups of actions;
- A decision system that does not favor participants' pay;
- Develop local cooperative models of actions, trust and mutual support between management and employees and between the social enterprise and the local community.

All of these demonstrate how corporate governance enhances the performance of social businesses and their effective and voluntary framework of action. Social enterprises can offer practical solutions to both public sector problems for the provision of social services (an area affected by the need for spending cuts) and a variety of social problems such as unemployment, insecurity, lack of social care for the elderly children and the general need to improve the standard of living of citizens.

The Commission of the European Union published an action program in May 2003 to reorganize corporate law and strengthen corporate governance. The European Commission's Corporate Action and Corporate Governance Action Plan helps to ensure sound and transparent corporate governance, for example since January 2005, all registered companies in the EU should apply the international accounting standards so that companies with common characteristics can be compared. New rules are in place to ensure that companies do not have a very close relationship with the auditors who control and validate the accounts. At the same time, it was approved as the basis for providing ongoing information on corporate governance practices of the companies involved, in the context of legislative regulation in the relevant sectors. In the same context, this Code was the cornerstone of the Compliance or Accountability Mechanism, even before it was adopted in EU law, by the provision of the Article 46a of the Directive 2006/46/EC. As highlighted in the 2011 Green Paper on the EU Corporate Governance Framework (hereinafter: "Green Paper"), these elements are crucial for both building citizens in the single market and at macroeconomic level to enhance the competitiveness of European businesses, in order to promote sustainable businesses that are working properly toward achieving the ambitious developmental strides set by the Europe 2020 strategy. With regard to the Greek legal order, the adoption of the legislation with the provisions of Law 3016/2002 "On Corporate Governance, Wage Matters and Other Provisions", Government Gazette 110A/17.5.2002, it was approved as a result of the Explanatory Report aiming to adapt the legislation on the operation and administration of public limited companies to the data arising from the listing of shares or other securities on a regulated market . It is noteworthy, however, that the acceptance of the decisive role and the advantages of the model of self-regulation, which is highlighted primarily in theory, is now crystallized by the incorporation into Greek law of the Directive 2006/46/EC of the European Parliament and of the Council of 14 June 2006, which, as will be presented below, is the cornerstone of the self-regulatory model through corporate governance codes. In particular, with the provisions of Law 3873/2010 (Government Gazette 150 A/6-9-2010): "Integration into Greek law of Directive 2006/46/EC of the European Parliament and of the Council on annual and consolidated accounts of certain types of companies and the Directive 2007/63/EC of the European Parliament and of the Council on the requirement to draw up a report by an independent expert in the event of a merger or division of public limited liability companies", and in particular Article 2 thereof, which made amendments to Article 43a of Codified Law 2190/1920. 2190/1920 on societies anonymous, the provision of Article 46a of the Directive 2006/46/EC was incorporated, resulting in the obligation of listed companies to include as a special part of the management report the Corporate Governance Statement, which obliges the mechanism "Compliance or justification", regarding the adoption of a certain Corporate Governance Code and the provision of explanations for any deviations from the recommendations of this Code.

4.3 *The EU directive/Communication on CG*

Corporate government (CG) as a voluntary commitment and as an obligation of business to society, which offers them profit and reason to exist in the market. The Code of Business Ethics and Ethics or Code of Corporate Government is the formulated and followed principles of behavior in which businesses/organizations support their goals, processes, and actions as to how they perceive Corporate Social Responsibility. In July 2002, the European Commission adopted the Communication on Corporate Government: A Business Contribution to Sustainable Development following the public debate launched by the Green Paper through particular proposals.

CG has been a subject of interest to the EU since 1999 when the European Parliament adopted a resolution calling on European businesses to adopt a "mandatory code of conduct" that respects both the environment and the rights of workers. Since then, many businesses have taken on board the various social and environmental aspects in their activities on a voluntary basis. The Council of the European Union, in 2000, and the European Commission in 2001 also advocated Corporate Government. And the European Parliament, bearing in mind that there is a growing image of confusion among citizens, as CG is essentially the will of every business, and it is natural for some of them to claim to be Corporate Government simply to improve their image, proposed the creation of common European rules, such as the multilateral forum at Community level, the Green Paper on the promotion of a European framework for CG. The Green Paper (2001) aims to launch a wider public debate on how the EU can promote CG at both European and international level, and in particular on how it can making the best use of existing experience, encouraging the development of innovative practices, introducing greater transparency and increasing the credibility of evaluation and validation. The Green Paper proposes an approach based on the deepening of partnerships in which all actors play an active role. (http://www.ab.gov.tr/files/ardb/evt/1_avrupa_birligi/1_6_raporlar/1_2_green_papers/com2001_green_paper_promoting_a_european_framework_for_corporate_social_responsibility.pdf) the document COM (2001) 366/F [18/08/2014) "GREEN PAPER: Promoting a European framework for Corporate Social Responsibility".

CG is also about managing change at management level in a socially responsible manner. CG is defined as business behavior that exceeds its legal obligations and is voluntarily adopted, and is closely linked to the concept of sustainable development as it incorporates the economic, social and environmental impact of its activities. In 2004, and following the publication of the EMSF report, the EU recognized that the social prosperity of the Eurozone can be ensured through growth and jobs. This was intended to achieve the revised Lisbon Strategy in February 2005, i.e. to focus on actions that promote growth and jobs in a way that is fully compatible with sustainable development. On 22 March 2006, the European Commission adopted the Communication "Implementing the Partnership for Growth and Jobs: Making Europe a Field of Excellence in Corporate Social Responsibility". (http://ec.europa.eu/) the document COM (2006) 136/F [22/09/2014], "Implementing the partnership for growth and jobs: making Europe a pole of excellence on corporate social responsibility".

In this context, the European Commission has launched a "direct" cooperation with European businesses, recognizing that they play a leading role in Corporate Social Responsibility. This cooperation took the form of a European Alliance for CG, with the aim of contributing, through concrete actions, to promoting Corporate Social Responsibility across Europe as a starting point for innovative corporate practices, to promote networking and to contribute to the creation of joint projects between businesses and stakeholders. The European Business Network for Corporate Social Responsibility (CG Europe) is Europe's business network for CG. The Enterprise 2020 program is a CG Europe initiative that supports the development of sustainable entrepreneurship, helps optimize synergies with stakeholders, and further enhances Europe's leading position on Corporate Social Responsibility. This will be feasible by developing, implementing and contributing business initiatives and synergies to key socioeconomic and environmental challenges. The most recent development at European Commission level in terms of Corporate Social Responsibility is the European Parliament's resolution of 8 June 2011 on the "external dimension of social policy, promoting labor and social standards and Corporate Social Responsibility" at a European level, which confirms the non-binding character of CG, and at the same time urges the EU to incorporate a "social clause", in line with other internationally agreed and recognized standards in all external EU trade agreements. (http://www.europarl.europa.eu/sides/getDoc.do?type=TA&reference=P7-TA-20110260&language=EL [23/08/201]).

5. Conclusions

The Hellenic Ministry of Development characterizes the institution of Private Capital Company (PCC) as successful, based on its penetration into the Greek business world. About 39% of the companies that are listed are PCC, and they even dominate the UK followed by 32%, EU follows with 15%, the EPE with 8% and SA with 6%. By analyzing the key features of the new form of company, we see the innovations it introduces and the benefits over other corporate forms. It is recommended through the one-stop service. Its statutes are generally drawn up by private agreement. No representation of a lawyer and attendance of a Notary is required, only published in GEMI. A notary agreement is required when it imposes a special provision of the law or when the company is transferred to property. The reimbursement cost is limited to the minimum because fees and publication fees are not paid to the Government Gazette SA and Ltd. The cost is limited to a €70 fee. The biggest innovation in this form of business is that a single person or multiple partners company can participate in the capital. The corporate form from the capital is disconnected while a minimum capital of €1 is required. The new corporate form responds to the separation of partner functions within the business. It is known that there are cash partners, assets, partners involved in daily activity (job offer), partners offering solvency, providing individual or tangible guarantees, partners with specific expertise and scientific capabilities. This new company type, facilitates cooperation and coexistence between these partners, making it suitable for family businesses as well as for businesses and partnerships of young entrepreneurs.

5.1 *The creation of a General Commercial Registry (GC)*

The need to set up a unified framework for the organization, updating and use of public administration registers has always been a fixed requirement for those dealing with public and wider public sector bodies. Particularly for the business community, data overlaps, nomenclature problems, different codings, fragmented data collection by operators, lack of business data, etc., were just a few of the problems they faced, resulting to problems in general business processes. It is widely accepted that the creation of a General Commercial Registry of all legal forms of business in Greece will assist in the follow-up of state-owned commercial enterprises and the better service of the enterprises themselves by the central administration and its competent bodies. In addition, many countries have implemented similar registers such as HOUSE OF COMPANIES (UK), PUBLIC REGISTER (America, Singapore) and others. For these countries, the e-business register is a factor of transparency, security of transactions (security and reliability) and acceleration of procedures and decision-making at both operational and state level. Thus, in Greece, the establishment of the General Commercial Registry, together with the "one-stop-shops", are decisive changes in the axis of simplification of the general business environment processes, both aiming to meet the needs and requirements of all kinds of stakeholders, as well as to the effective use and utilization of the information collected. The operation of a modern and up-to-date centralized business registry database will make it unlimited to reduce the bureaucratic processes of creating or changing a business, as well as issuing and submitting "corporate information" certificates for almost all of a company's transactions. At the same time, a general and unified business register creates wider conditions for information and exploitation of information for the entire public sector. Thanks to this, more effective statistical monitoring of company data, more accurate policy, legislative and/or audit power to businesses, and in relation to them, is possible. GC's work aims at radically reforming the operation of individual (fragmented) business registers of any legal form, the passage of today's manuscript — primarily — the way information is processed and current work management, into a single automated processing environment and high efficiency of a General Commercial Registry. The GC will be, amongst other things, a publicity tool, statistical analysis at national level and a third party protection instrument for both the GGE and the GC part of it and for the wider public sector when the project is completed. The simplification of the typical business activity framework expected to be achieved through the operation of GC aims to have as a result, among other things, the establishment of a regime of transparency in the exercise of commercial activity. AND to ensure the ability of businesses and citizens to be promptly served by "one-stop" procedures and the implementation of the requirements of Article 6 of Law 3242/2004. Finally, Greek innovation concerns the exercise of control and decision-making for each business, which can easily be achieved by the sector-specific public sector entities with the implementation and use of a single data bank, which will be used to exchange comprehensive information on relevant institutions and stakeholders.

Further Readings

Legal Bibliography

Law 1806/1986 on capital markets.

Law 2190/1920 on Anonymous Companies.

Law 3016/2002 on Corporate Governance.

Law 2076/1996 on banking activity.

Law 2396/1996 on institutions offering investment services.

Law 1969/1991 on institutional investors and the Securities and Exchange Commission.

Law 3823/2004 on mutual funds.

Law 2166/1993 on the Cyprus Securities and Exchange Commission.

Law 3152/2003 on the Cyprus Securities and Exchange Commission.

- Presidential Decree 258/1997 on the monitoring of banking institutions.
- Presidential Decree 350/1985 on listed companies on the Athens Stock Exchange.
- Presidential Decree 25/2003 on the Cyprus Securities and Exchange Commission.
- Bank of Greece instructions 2438/1998 on internal control of credit institutions.
- EU Directive 2001/107 on institutional investors with resumption of investment services in other EU countries.
- EU Directive 2001/108 on extending institutional investors to investment opportunities.
- Order of the Hellenic Capital Market Commission 195/2000 on public offering of quoted shares.
- Commission of the Hellenic Capital Market Commission 5/204/14/2000 on the behavior of listed companies.
- Annual Reports of the Capital Market Commission in 2000 and 2003.

Appendix

European Directives

COMMITTEE RECOMMENDATION

April 9, 2014
on the quality of corporate governance reports ("compliance or explanation")
(Text with EEA relevance)
(2014/208/EU)

THE EUROPEAN COMMISSION,

Having regard to the Treaty on the Functioning of the European Union and in particular the Article 292 thereof,

The following are considered:

(1) An effective corporate governance framework is crucial for society, as well as managed companies are likely to be more competitive and more sustainable in the long run. Good corporate governance is primarily the responsibility of this company, both at European and

national level, to be able to ensure that certain standards are met. These include legislation and compliant law, i.e. national codes of corporate governance.

(2) Corporate Governance Codes aim to establish principles for good corporate governance of listed companies in Europe based on transparency, accountability and a long-term perspective. They provide business models and best practices, enabling them to perform better and thus contribute to promoting growth, stability and long-term investment.

(3) Directive 2013/34/EU of the European Parliament and of the Council of 26 June 2013, the annual financial statements, consolidated financial statements and related reports of certain types of undertakings (1) require companies to include a corporate statement in their management report whether their securities are admitted to trading on a regulated market of any Member State within the meaning of Article 4(1) (14) of Directive 2004/39/EC of the European Parliament and of the Council of 21 April 2004 on markets in financial instruments (2).

(4) The corporate governance statement should provide the necessary information about the corporate governance arrangements of the company, such as information on the relevant corporate governance code(s) applied by that company, the internal control systems and risk management, the general meeting of shareholders and its responsibilities, the rights of shareholders, their administrative, management and supervisory bodies and their committees.

(5) High quality corporate disclosure of corporate governance provides useful information for investors and facilitates their investment decisions. It also gives investors more confidence in the companies they invest in. Increasing transparency in the market can also bring benefits for business and legitimacy to the eyes of the players and society as a whole.

References

Abor, J. (2007). Corporate governance and financing decisions of Ghanaian listed firms, and the cost of debt, *Journal of Accounting and Economics*, 37, 315–342.

Becht, M. (1997). Strong blockholders, weak owners and the need for European mandatory disclosure, European Corporate Governance Network, Executive Report, October.

Bedard, J. (2004). The effect of audit committee expertise, independence, and activity on aggressive earnings management, *Auditing*, 23, 23–36.

Berle, A.A. and Means, G. (1932). *The Modern Corporation and Private Property*. The Macmillan Company: New York.

Bloch, L. and Kremp, E. (1997). Ownership and Control in France, European Corporate Governance Network.

Brancato, C. (1997). *Institutional Investors and Corporate Governance: Best Practices for Increasing Corporate Value*. Irwin Professional Publishing: Chicago.

Breeden, D. and Viswanathan, S. (2006). Why Do Firms Hedge? An Asymmetric Information Model, Duke University Working Paper Capital Market Commission of Greece, 2002, Annual Report. Change: An Empirical Analysis of New Zealand listed Companies, *Journal of Business*.

Conference on: Convergence and Diversity in Corporate Governance Regimes and Capital Markets.

Eindhoven, The Netherlands, November 4–5. *Corporate Governance: International Journal of Business in Society*, 7.

Corporate Use of Interest Rate Derivatives, *Journal of Financial Research*, 27(2).

Dionne, G. and Garand, M. (2003). Risk management determinants affecting firm's values in economics, *Economics Letters*, 37(1), 39–65.

Fama, E.F. and French, K.R. (1993). Common risk factors in the returns on bonds and stocks, *Finance and Accounting*, 32(1), 255–295.

Fosberg, R.H. (2004). Agency Problems and Debt Financing: Leadership Structure Effects, *Corporate Governance: The International Journal of Business in Society*, 4, 31–38. https://doi.org/10.1108/14720700410521943

Galbraith, K.J. (1993). *A Short History of Financial Euphoria*. Whittle Books: Victoria.

Gietzmann, A. (2005). Derivatives usage, corporate governance, and legislative governance and compensation, *Journal of Finance*, 62(5), 2405–2443.

Hart, E. (1995). Diversification's effect on firm value, *Journal of Financial Economics*, 37, 39–95.

Hermalin, B. and Weisbach, M. (1988). The determinants of board composition, *Rand Journal of Economics*, 19, 589–606.

Maher, M. and Andersson, T. (1999). Corporate governance: Effects on firm performance and economic growth. Paper presented at the Tilburg University Mastering Risk.

Milton, H. and Raviv, A. (1998). Capital budgeting and delegation, *Journal of Financial Economics*, 50(3), 259–289.

Shamsul, N. A. (2004). Board composition, CEO duality and performance among Malaysian listed companies, *Corporate Governance: The International Journal of Business in Society*, 4(4), 47–61.

Shivadasani, A. and Zenner, M. (2004). Best practices in corporate governance: What two decades of research reveals, *Journal of Applied Corporate Finance*, 16, 29–41.

Stulz, R.M. (2000). Diminishing the threats to shareholder wealth, *Financial Times*, 25 April.

Vafeas, N. (1999). The nature of board nominating committees and their role in corporate governance, *Journal of Business Finance and Accounting*, 26, 199–225.

Wen, R., Mansi, S. and Reeb, D. (2002). Board characteristics, accounting report integrity.

Winter Report (2002). The High Level Group of Company Law Experts on a Modern Regulatory Framework for Company Law in Europe, Brussels, November.

https://doi.org/10.1142/9789811260506_0003

Chapter 3

New Corporate Governance Law in Greece: Key Elements and Analysis

Christos Lemonakis

Associate Professor Hellenic Mediterranean University, Department of Management Science and Technology, Ag. Nikolaos, Crete, Greece

lemonakis@hmu.gr

Abstract

The interest of this chapter focuses on corporate governance issues and current relevant developments in the international and Greek landscape. For this reason, the relevant issues are examined at both the theoretical and practical levels. The objective of this chapter is to examine and evaluate the new legal framework of corporate governance in Greece and to identify the main functions it integrates into corporate practice. The aim of this work is to study the practices that are applied in the application of the new law and differentiate them in relation to the Environment-Social-Governance (ESG) framework. Through this analysis, there is a scope to clarify the possible interventions of the law at the different levels of its interference in corporate practices. As part of the above, literature review on corporate governance issues and the main trends emerging in academic research is also carried out.

Keywords: Corporate governance, environment-social-governance (ESG), literature review

1. Introduction

The goal of corporate governance is to create an environment of trust, transparency and accountability. These are necessary conditions to promote long-term investment, financial stability and corporate integrity. This supports stronger growth of society as a whole (OECD, 2015). In general, corporate governance refers to all factors that determine the direction and control system of a company. Corporate governance is a concept rather than an isolated tool (The World Bank, 2005).

In the literature, corporate governance is defined in different ways, but most definitions fall into two categories. In the first category, definitions focus on corporate behavior, addressing issues of performance, profitability, growth, financial structure and treatment of shareholders and other stakeholders. In the second category, definitions refer to the regulatory framework within which companies should operate. The source of these rules can be laws, financial markets, labor markets, etc. (The World Bank, 2005).

According to the OECD, corporate governance "encompasses a set of relationships between a company's management, its board of directors, its shareholders, and other stakeholders. Corporate governance also provides the structure by which the company's objectives are defined, the means to achieve those objectives, and the monitoring of their performance" (OECD, 2015). This definition is also adopted by the International Financial Reporting Standards, which indicates that the strength of corporate governance is measured by aggregating variables related to the independence and functioning of the board of directors and the effectiveness of the audit committee (Sarieddine, 2018).

The modern form of corporate governance began in the United Kingdom with the establishment of the Cadbury Committee in 1991, the purpose of which was to regulate three interrelated areas. The first was growing concern about the use of "creative" accounting, which distorted the calculation of the value of shares. The second was concern about a series of corporate failures, mainly related to executives who were able to obfuscate financial data through the opacity of their control mechanisms. The third reason was growing public concern about rapid increases in executive pay, particularly in cases where these increases did not match corresponding corporate returns (Keasey *et al.*, 2005). The goal of the Cadbury Committee, as it stated at its inception, was "to help improve corporate governance standards and confidence in financial reporting and control by clearly defining what is considered and expected to be the responsibility of stakeholders" (Spedding, 2009).

At the global level, there are several initiatives aimed at convergence of corporate governance rules. One of the most important influences on corporate governance reform has been the introduction of international codes of corporate governance practice. The first comprehensive set of internationally recognized corporate governance standards was created by the Organization for Economic Cooperation and Development (OECD) (Solomon and Solomon, 2004). The OECD Corporate Governance Principles were originally introduced in May 1999 and revised in 2004. They provide concrete guidance for policymakers, regulators and market participants to improve the legal, institutional and regulatory framework that supports corporate governance, with a focus on listed companies. The OECD authorities also provide practical suggestions for stock exchanges, investors, companies and other stakeholders who play key role in developing good corporate governance. In 2010, the OECD published a series of action plans for improvements in priority areas such as compensation, risk management, board practices and the exercise of shareholder rights to address serious deficiencies in corporate governance exposed by the economic crisis. These recommendations also address how to improve the implementation of existing standards (Tophoff, 2013).

The structure of this chapter is as follows: Section 2 provides a literature review that presents empirical studies which examine the relationship between corporate performance and corporate governance. Next, in Section 3, the new legislation (whose validity started in July 2021) and the provisions of the Greek Corporate Governance Law are mentioned. Finally, in Section 4, this piece of work concludes by contrasting the main conclusions regarding the provisions of the new law on corporate governance in Greece.

2. Literature Review

This section presents empirical studies that examine the relationship between corporate performance and corporate governance. In particular, there is a look at studies that have examined how the quality of corporate governance at the outset and the ESG dimension then adopted by companies affect corporate stock returns and overall corporate value creation.

Value creation can be measured in a variety of ways, including financial indicators (e.g. returns on assets) or non-financial factors such as reputation and stakeholder trust in the company.

2.1 *Corporate performance and corporate governance*

Gaeremynck *et al.* (2010) examined the relationship between corporate governance ratings and corporate performance. The study was conducted in European countries (Austria, Belgium, Denmark, Finland, France, Germany, Greece, Ireland, Italy, the Netherlands, Portugal, Spain, Sweden and the United Kingdom) during 1999–2003, a period when corporate governance disclosure was voluntary. The results show that positive corporate governance ratings have a very significant and positive impact on firm's performance. Examining only endogenous factors (age of companies, growth rate of sales, level of capital debt and degree of ownership concentration), we found no relationship between corporate ratings and operating performance (return on equity and return on assets). However, with respect to the market measures (capitalization value and shareholder protection (anti-self-dealing index)), in contrast to the endogenous measures, it was found that there was a positive relationship with the stock market price-to-sales ratio and the stock market-to-book value ratio of equity. It was also found that companies in countries with strong shareholder protection laws or comprehensive corporate governance recommendations have higher corporate governance scores (above the average of 20.43 with a maximum score of 40 based on 300 OECD corporate governance principles) and lower performance effects than those in countries with weak shareholder protection laws. Finally, the relationship between corporate governance scores and returns was found to decrease over time, indicating that the more corporate governance is integrated into corporate practices, the less positively investors view it (Gaeremynck *et al.*, 2010).

In a survey conducted in 2015–2016, Blendinger and Michalski (2018) investigated how corporate competitiveness based on high quality corporate governance is related to the creation of long-term value (using the measures of economic value added (EVA) and return on capital employed (ROCE) in listed companies in Germany). The analysis first revealed that 80% of listed companies have high corporate governance standards, with no significant differences found between 2015 and 2016.

Of these companies, 38% have increased EVA and 54% have increased ROCE, indicating that the ROCE index is a better measure of value creation assessment.

Grant Thornton's (2020) questionnaire study on corporate governance and value creation in Greece (on a sample of more than 400 companies) found that strong governance has a positive impact on value creation. Specifically, companies with strong corporate governance are 43% more effective in developing and selling products and services and 29% more effective in generating profits. There are also positive effects on corporate solvency and liquidity, as companies are estimated to be 15% more solvent and 3.4 times more liquid. Good corporate governance also creates twice the returns for shareholders. Improving corporate governance of companies is associated with an average increase of 44% in operating cash flow, 46% in free cash flow and 10% in operating profit margin.

2.2 *Corporate performance and environmental social governance (ESG) framework performance*

The benefits of good corporate governance have been widely studied at the theoretical and empirical levels and are generally recognized as necessary to ensure healthy capital markets. Good corporate governance is also becoming an increasingly important factor in the investment decision-making process. Given the growing awareness of environmental and social issues, corporate governance is part of the evaluation of companies in terms of environmental, social and corporate governance issues. In the following, we present the empirical results of recent research that has examined the relationship between ESG ratings and stock returns and corporate value growth.

Ciciretti *et al.* (2019) examined the impact of ESG characteristics on stock returns in a global sample for the period 2004–2018 (in 2014, the sample included 1,349 companies and in 2017, 5,219 companies from countries (without mentioning the number of countries in the study) from North America, Europe, Japan, Asian countries in the Pacific excluding Japan, South America and Africa). The authors examined the contribution of ESG characteristics and their variability in explaining the expected excess returns of the stocks of companies in the cross-section. The results of the study show that ESG characteristics appear to explain expected excess stock returns to a much greater extent than ESG volatility.

Specifically, a one percentage point decrease in the standard deviation of the ESG score is associated with about a 13% increase in monthly expected returns. According to the researchers, investors are willing to hold the shares of companies with low ESG scores if they are compensated with higher returns, regardless of risk assessments. Although shareholder returns were highest for companies with low ESG scores in both long-term and short-term returns, the magnitude of returns changed by study period, as stock returns were lower during periods of increased scrutiny of ESG data.

Umar *et al.* (2020) examined the correlations between major global equity indices with the highest returns on ESG issues. Motivated by the rapid growth of socially responsible investments over the past two decades, they investigated whether investments in companies in countries that mandate strict ESG criteria are vulnerable to similar exogenous economic and financial shocks as the corresponding stock indices. The results of the study showed that there were correlations and dynamic patterns between stock indices and ESG criteria during three periods, namely the European sovereign debt crisis, Greece's systemic problems and the outbreak of the coronavirus pandemic. In particular, it was found that in countries where high ESG criteria are applied, changes in stock indices were similar and regressive during periods of economic crisis. Socially responsible investments (in companies with high ESG criteria) offer higher benefits during times of economic turmoil, such as higher stock returns and lower risk (price volatility). It was also noted that developed equity markets pass on shocks to Asian and other emerging markets. The survey results highlight the risk of transmission and the lower portfolio diversification benefits of these equity indexes in turbulent times.

A McKinsey (2020) survey conducted by Delevingne *et al.* examined how the ESG triptych affects short- and long-term value creation and corporate returns through the completion of questionnaires by investment professionals and managers. The survey was conducted online between July 16 and July 31, 2019 and collected responses from 558 respondents across a wide range of regions, sectors and company sizes (with no countries or number of respondents identified in the survey). Of these respondents, 439 were senior executives and 119 were investment professionals. The survey followed up on an earlier study conducted by the company in 2009 and sought to capture how perceptions of the issue have changed over the past decade. The 2009 survey was conducted among 84 executives and 154 investment professionals. The vast majority of respondents

(83%) believe that ESG plans will provide greater value to shareholders in 5 years and indicated that they are willing to pay a premium of about 10% to purchase the shares of companies that deliver high returns on ESG issues.

The majority of executives and investment professionals surveyed (57%) agreed that ESG programs create shareholder value, and 58% felt that developments in the policy environment during the 2009–2019 decade, i.e. growing government interest in ESG issues and institutionalization of new policies, have increased the importance of ESG programs to meet stakeholder expectations. Almost all respondents who believe that ESG programs add value also believe that the positive contribution is long-term in nature. Maintaining a good corporate reputation and attracting and retaining talent were cited more frequently as ways ESG programs improve corporate financial performance, as they were in 2009.

Kyere and Ausloos (2020) studied the impact of good corporate governance on corporate financial performance. The research was conducted on 252 companies listed on the London Stock Exchange in 2014. Specifically, five corporate governance mechanisms were examined in relation to two measures of financial performance, return on assets (ROA) and Tobin's Q index. Specifically, the independent variables in the survey were the degree of stock ownership by individuals within the company, the size of the board of directors, the degree of independence of the board of directors, the dual or unduplicated status of the individual in the position of chief executive officer and executive director, and the number of audit committee meetings. The results of the survey varied from company to company, as in some cases a positive correlation was found, in others a negative correlation, while in still other cases no effect of good corporate governance on the financial performance of the companies was found. The study of the results and causes showed that a company that chooses the right corporate governance mechanisms (participation of people involved in the management of the company with less than 10% of the share capital, a high percentage of independent members on the board of directors, the distinction between the position of chairman and managing director, and an increased number of meetings of the audit committee) can improve its financial performance.

Signori *et al.* (2021) studied the effect of ESG scoring on adding value to businesses using various value measures, such as gross profit, labor costs, tax amount, interest, dividends, the percentage of profit to the minority of shareholders and retained profits. The survey was conducted in 2018 on companies from Eurozone countries. Although the investigation found a positive relationship between ESG and EVA, this seemed to be more related to the size of the company than to its performance in ESG, as the results were the opposite when checking the size of the company. The analysis showed the absence of a direct link between social efficiency and ESG. Social efficiency was measured by the Method of Data Envelopment Analysis (DEA) with an incoming variable of retained equity and outgoing variables adding value to stakeholders and specifically employees, the state, investors and shareholders. This means that, despite a company's good performance from a social, environmental and intergovernmental point of view, ESG ratings are not able to capture or reflect the economic and social aspects of value creation and wealth distribution for stakeholders.

The research of the Tampakoudis *et al.* (2021) was to study the relationship between the environmental, social and governance performance of companies in shareholder wealth in the context of mergers and acquisitions before and during the pandemic (2018–2020). The sample of the survey was 889 completed acquisitions/mergers in the USA and the impact of ESG performance was studied in relation to the returns on the shares of the acquiring companies. The results of the survey showed a significant negative relationship between the effect of the ESG performance of the purchasing companies and the returns of the shareholders of the same companies. The negative effect was stronger with the onset of the pandemic crisis, possibly because during the economic turmoil the cost of long-term sustainability activities offsets capital gains, supporting the over-investment hypothesis. Based on this finding, it is suggested that the market considers sustainability activities costly during an economic crisis and rewards (with higher returns) companies with lower ESG performance. The main limitation of the survey is related to the availability of data on companies' ESG returns.

The Zumente and Bistrova survey (2021) examined whether ESG data can add long-term value to shareholders and in what ways. The survey was conducted in listed companies in eight Central and Eastern European countries (Croatia, Hungary, Czech Republic, Slovakia, Poland, Estonia, Lithuania and Latvia) in the period 2012–2021. The results of the analysis showed that companies with greater sustainability awareness ensure shareholder value creation through improved financial performance (profitability, returns on equity and equity returns), management quality (high degree of management accountability) as well as a reduced level of risk (volatility of stock returns and solvency risk). In addition, quality non-financial factors such as reputation, stakeholder trust and employee satisfaction provide an even more significant impact on long-term value than purely economic issues.

Huang's analysis (2021) of 21 empirical surveys found a positive and statistically significant relationship between ESG performance and corporate financial performance (CFP-Corporate Financial Performance) measured by operational, accounting and market variables, while from an economic point of view their relationship was moderate (possibly due to limited measures of economic governance performance that are unable to meet the concept of ESG). There was a stronger correlation between the ESG Performance (ESGP) measures and the operational CFP measures, while the correlation with market accounting and CFP measures was gradually smaller. This analysis showed that incentives to develop ESG activities can be mixed, motivated by both financial incentives and non-financial incentives such as the creation of a positive reputation and the development of functional skills that will help companies gain a competitive advantage, with the existence of theoretical and methodological issues for the determination of the ESG performance ratio and the PERFORMANCE CFP. Conflicting results may result from the heterogeneity that may exist in ESG measures.

3. New Corporate Governance Law in Greece — Key Elements and Assumptions

The key data of Greek Law 4706/2020, which regulates the functioning of corporate governance in Greece, are summarized below for each area of activity. The new Law 4706/2020 on Corporate Governance and Modernization of the Capital Market was published in Government Gazette No. 136A'/17.7.2020. The provisions of the law take into account the changes that have taken place so far in the regulatory framework, as well as the current trends in corporate governance (see also Table 1).

The new Law 4706/2020 does not make radical changes to the existing framework of corporate governance but introduces important regulations and safeguards for the activities of members of the Board of Directors and relations with shareholders. Regarding the Board of Directors, it better defines the responsibilities and duties of members, while establishing guidelines for the selection and evaluation of members. Law 4706/2020

Table 1: Greek Law 4706/2020: On corporate governance and capital market modernization — Main characteristics.

	Board of directors (BoD) Analysis
Role	Establish and monitor the corporate governance system, the internal control system, and ensure the independence of the corporate governance system, the internal control system and ensure the independence of the internal control system within a framework of clear, documented and enforceable responsibilities.
Composition of the BoD	Executive and non-executive members (and independent)
BoD Size	1/3 of the non-executive members of which at least 2 members are independent.
Tasks	— Executive: Implementing the strategy, evaluating it at regular intervals together with the non-executive members and informing the Board of Directors in emergency situations and in the event of risks. — Non-executive: Monitoring the implementation of corporate strategy, supervising the members of the Board of Management and reviewing the proposals submitted by the members of the Board of Management.
Capacity and duties of the President	Non-executive member.
Evaluation	Implementation of an appropriates policy for board members.
Internal audit	Monitoring, controlling, assessing and reporting risks on issues such as regulatory implementation, quality assurance, corporate governance and the use of funds raised from the regulated market. Reports and notifications are submitted to the Audit Committee on a quarterly basis.
Remunerations	The Compensation Committee is responsible for formulating a proposal to the Board of Directors on not only the compensation of the internal auditors and the Head of Internal Audit but also other senior executives.
Relations with shareholders	Informing shareholders, following the recommendation of the Nominating Committee for Directors, of their suitability both prior to their election and thereafter. Establishment of a Shareholder Services Department and a Corporate Communications Department.

also recommends new committees, the Nomination Committee and the Compensation Committee, while to better communicate with shareholders, the Corporate Communications and Shareholder Services Departments are also established.

Law 4706/2020 strengthens the role of the Board of Directors compared to the previous Law on Corporate Governance. Regarding the duties of the members of the Board of Directors, Law 4706/2020 describes the responsibilities for the executive and non-executive members separately, which was not the case in the previous legislation. In contrast, Law 4706/2020 did not contain provisions on the role of the Chairman, while a difference with the previous legislation is the clarification that the Chairman must be a non-executive member.

Regarding the evaluation of the members of the Board of Directors, Law 4706/2020 establishes the obligation to have a policy of suitability, regarding the principles for the selection and replacement of the members of the Board of Directors and the criteria for evaluating their suitability, as well as the provision of diversity criteria. The Audit Committee continues to be responsible for internal auditing under Law 4706/2020, but its role is also strengthened to safeguard the interests of third parties other than shareholders. Law 4706/2013 provides for the mandatory establishment of a Compensation Committee to operate on the basis of the Company's compensation policy (based on the provisions of Law 4811/2021). It also improves transparency toward and information of shareholders by introducing the obligation to establish a Shareholders' Service Department and a Corporate Communications Department, as well as the valid posting for the election and replacement of directors.

4. Conclusions

Corporate governance is a concept that encompasses several measures directly and indirectly related to all areas of a company's activities. It is of great significance and is becoming increasingly important because the adoption of best practices not only promotes the performance of the companies themselves but also contributes significantly to investment and the development of the economy. In the context of developing and improving corporate governance practices, a European directive was issued in 2017 to ensure the credibility of listed companies and facilitate the attraction of investors. This directive was incorporated into Greek legislation with the enactment of Law 4706/2020. This law establishes a stricter framework for the activities of the Board of Directors, the more precise definition of its responsibilities and the better protection of shareholders' interests.

Law 4706/2020 on Corporate Governance introduces regulations that better define the roles of board members and procedures that better monitor issues related to conflicts of interest and risks. An important provision of the law is the implementation of the Suitability Policy and the establishment of a Nomination Committee for the selection and evaluation of members of the Board of Directors. There are also provisions to strengthen the confidence of stakeholders, and in particular shareholders, by establishing rules for communication and disclosure of important information related to the members of the Board of Directors and internal audit.

In recent years, corporate governance has been integrated into a broader context that includes issues related to the environment and society. The triptych of environment, society and corporate governance is integral to the operations of many companies, especially those listed on the stock exchange, which aim not only at economic growth and prosperity but also at the sustainable development of the larger group in which they are integrated. Corresponding corporate actions, strategies and commitments have a significant impact on the financial performance of both their operations and their shares. Companies that advance the corporate interest in a context of defending the interests of investors and other stakeholders, as well as social and environmental concerns, receive greater recognition and gain value. This coordinated action is increasingly demanded by investors and society.

This is supported by empirical research showing that improving the quality of corporate governance and ESG criteria generally leads to higher stock returns and contributes to value creation by increasing companies' returns on capital while reducing the volatility of stock returns.

References

Blendinger, G. and Michalski, G. (2018). Long-term competitiveness based on value added measures as part of highly professionalized corporate governance management of German DAX30 corporations. *Journal of Competitiveness*, 10(1), 5–20.

Ciciretti, R., Dalò, A. and Dam, L. (2019). The contributions of Betas versus characteristics to the ESG premium. *CEIS Tor Vergata*, 15(7). Research Paper Series No. 413.

Delevingne, L., Gründler, A., Kane, S. and Koller, T. (2020). The ESG premium: New perspectives on value and performance. https://www.mckinsey.com/business-functions/sustainability/our-insights/the-esg-premium-new-perspectives-on-value-and-performance.McKinsey.

Gaeremynck, A., Sercu, P. and Renders, A. (2010). Corporate-governance ratings and company performance: A cross-European study, *Corporate Governance: An International Review*, 18(2), 87–106.

Grant Thornton (2020). Corporate Governance: How critical it is to business strategy and corporate value creation. Grant Thornton: Athina.

Huang, D.Z.X. (2021). Environmental, social and governance (ESG) activity and firm performance: A review and consolidation, *Accounting & Finance*, 61, 335–360.

Keasey, K., Thompson, S. and Wright, M. (2005). *Corporate Governance Accountability, Enterprise and International Comparisons*. John Wiley & Sons Ltd.: Chichester.

Kyere, M. and Ausloos, M. (2020). Corporate governance and firms financial performance in the United Kingdom. *International Journal of Finance & Economics*, 26, 1871–1885.

OECD (2015). *G20/OECD Principles of Corporate Governance*. OECD Publishing: Paris.

Sarieddine, M. (2018). *Role of IFRS in Enhancing Corporate Governance*. ACCA: London.

Signori, S., San-Jose, L., Retolaza, J.L. and Rusconi, G. (2021). Stakeholder value creation: Comparing ESG and value added in European companies. *Sustainability*, 13(3), 1–16.

Solomon, J. and Solomon, A. (2004). *Corporate Governance and Accountability*. John Wiley & Sons Ltd: Chichester.

Spedding, L.S. (2009). *The Due Diligence Handbook Corporate Governance, Risk Management and Business Planning*. Elsevier Ltd.: Burlington.

Tampakoudis, I., Noulas, A., Kiosses, N. and Drogalas, G. (2021). The effect of ESG on value creation from mergers and acquisitions. What changed during the COVID-19 pandemic? *Corporate Governance*, 21(6), DOI: 10.1108/CG-10-2020-0448.

The World Bank (2005). *Developing Corporate Governance Codes of the Best Practice Volume 1: Rationale*. The World Bank: Washington.

Tophoff, V. (2013). International Federation of Accountants. https://www.ifac.org/knowledge-gateway/contributing-global-economy/discussion/revision-oecd-corporate-governance-principles (Accessed 16 December 2021).

Umar, Z., Kenourgios, D. and Papathanasiou, S. (2020). The static and dynamic connectedness of environmental, social, and governance investments: International evidence. *Economic Modelling*, 93, 112–124.

Zumente, I. and Bistrova, J. (2021). ESG importance for long-term shareholder value creation: Literature vs. practice. *Journal of Open Innovation: Technology, Market, and Complexity*, 7(127), 1–13.

Legislation

Law 4706/2020, (Government Gazette A' 136/17-7-2020), Corporate governance of sociétés anonymes, modern capital market, incorporation into Greek law of Directive (EU) 2017/828 of the European Parliament and of the Council, measures for the implementation of Regulation (EU) 2017/1131 and other provisions.

https://doi.org/10.1142/9789811260506_0004

Chapter 4

Corporate Governance and Agency Problems

Menexiadis Marios

Hellenic Open University, Patras, Greece

mmenexiadis@hotmail.com

Abstract

In this chapter, the principal–agent problem is addressed. The agency problem is explained along with real cases used as examples that have been analytically described. The different types of the principal–agent problems are presented and analyzed, along with ways of mitigating the problem.

Key takeaways:

- The agency problem arises when incentives or motivations arise in the one party (agent) that does not act for the best interest of another (principal).
- Agency problems can be reduced through regulations or by incentivizing an agent to act in accordance with the principal's best interests.

Keywords: Corporate governance, principal–agent problems, agency costs

1. What is Agency Problem?

The agency problem is a conflict of interest. It is inherent and can be identified in any relationship where one party is expected to act not just for another, but for another's best interests. Consequently, the term best interests also needs to be explored and measured. Wearing the hat of the corporate finance professional, the agency problem usually refers to a conflict of interest between the company's management and the company's stockholders. The manager acts as the agent for the shareholders or principals and is supposed to make decisions that will maximize shareholder wealth even though it is in the manager's best interest to maximize his own wealth. Wearing the hat of the corporate governance professional, the question that should be addressed has to do with the meaning of buying shares in one company. It would mean placing confidence in the management of that company and its corporate governance system, whose decisions and proper management of corporate issues, would bring the wealth maximization. So, the agency problem in corporate governance is that large institutional shareholders who support management.

The agency problem can be better defined and easier understood as the conflict that takes place, when the agents who are entrusted with the responsibility of looking after the interests of the principals, chose to use the power or authority for their own personal benefits. In terms of corporate finance, it can be understood as a conflict of interest that takes place between the management of a company and its stockholders. Let us assume a theoretical example. Imagine that you have received a huge amount of money and you have hired a financial advisor to invest it for you. In this type of relationship, you are the principal, while the advisor acts as the agent. The advisor has the responsibility to act for the principal's best interest. However, incentives may exist for the advisor as well but in such a degree, that undermines the principal's interests and put the agent's needs first. Continuing with the theoretical example, suppose that the advisor, after learning the principal's financial targets, he/she knows that a growth stock mutual fund is the best option and solution for the money. But the advisor also knows that he/she can make a higher commission by placing the funds in an annuity, even though doing so, this compromises the principal's targets. This is a very classic theoretical example of the agency problem. The conflict of interest then, arises from the financial advisor who acts not in the best interest of the principal.

Conflicts may arise for the following reasons:

- **Remuneration:** Managers prefer greater levels of consumption and less intensive work. These are factors that do not decrease their remuneration and the value of the company's shares that they own.

- **Risk:** Managers prefer less risky investments and lower financial leverage. This is due to that fact, that in this way they may decrease the danger of bankruptcy and avoid losses on their managerial capital and portfolios.
- **Time horizon:** Managers prefer short term investment horizon.
- **Employment reduction:** Managers prefer to avoid problems that have to do with reductions in employment levels, which increase with the changes in control of a company.

It is quite usually argued that, managers tend to increase the size of companies even if it harms the interests of shareholders, as almost always their remuneration and personal prestige are positively correlated with company size. These inclinations cause conflicts of interest between managers who value expansion, and shareholders who are orientated toward the maximization of the value of their shares. If sufficient internal funds are available, managers may well be motivated to undertake investments of dubious profitability that would be rejected by the relevant monitoring authorities.

2. Understanding the Agency Problem

The agency problem is very common and it can be observed in almost every organization. The cause of agency problems arise from the relationship between the principal and the agent as already mentioned. Agents are commonly engaged by principals due to different skill levels, different employment positions as well as restrictions on time and access. The agency problem arises due to incentives and the presence of discretion in task completion. An agent may be motivated to act in a manner that is not favorable of the principal. However, the problem can be resolved, only if the organizations are willing to resolve it.

Agency problems are also common in fiduciary relationships, such as between trustees and beneficiaries, boards of directors' members and shareholders, lawyers and clients.

Some real world examples, would be helpful for the readers to understand the agency problem better.

- **Enron collapsed in 2001.** Accounting reports had been manipulated to make the company appear to have more money than what was actually

earned. The company's executives used fraudulent accounting methods to hide debt in Enron's subsidiaries and overstate revenue. These falsifications allowed the company's stock price to increase during a time when executives were selling portions of their stock holdings. In the 4 years leading up to Enron's bankruptcy filing, shareholders lost an estimated US$74 billion in value. Enron became the largest US bankruptcy at that time with its US$63 billion in assets. Although Enron's management had the responsibility to care for the shareholder's best interests, the agency problem resulted in management acting in their own best interest.
- **WorldCom case.** In 2001, the CEO took out US$400 million in loans at a rate of interest of 2.15%. The company did not report this in its annual report. The news of the accounting scandal came out later that year and the company took on debt to pay its executive.
- **Boeing Buyback case.** During 1998 to 2001, Boeing had about 130,000 shareholders, most of them were employees who bought stock through their retirement plans. Boeing was buying back the stock which drove prices lower. The executive actions damaged the employees' retirement account value.
- **Real Estate Bubble and Goldman Sachs case.** Goldman Sachs and other agencies created debt obligations and sold them short, with the thought that the mortgages would be foreclosed. In 2008, when the housing bubble occurred, the short sellers made millions and many people including homeowners lost money.

In all cases, all the scandals and failures at the end, were attributed in poor Corporate Governance practices and systems.

3. Types of Agency Problems

There are many reasons for agency problems. The root cause of these problems is the same in all cases, which is the mismatching of interests or even better the conflict of interests. When the agenda of the stockholder contradicts with the other groups, then the agency problem, is definitely going to arise.

Indicatively the following cases can be mentioned. In the case of employees, the reason would be the failure of stockholders to meet employees' expectations with respect to salary, incentives and bonuses, or working hours. In the case of customers, the cause would be the failure of stockholders to meet customers' expectations like the sale of poor quality goods, poor supply, high-pricing, low or none after sales service. In the case of management, the causes of agency problems could be the misalignment of goals, separation of ownership and management, stock options.

Every organization has its own set of long term and short-term goals and objectives that it wishes to achieve in a pre-determined period of time. Based on the above, it must also be noted that the goals of the management may not necessarily align with that of the stockholders as already described above. The management of an organization may have goals that are most likely derived with the motive of maximizing their personal benefits while on the other hand, the stockholders of an organization are most likely interested in their wealth maximization. This differentiation between the goals and objectives of the management and stockholders of an organization, may often become the basis for agency problems. There can be identified three types of agency problems:

- **Stockholders vs. Management:** Large organizations have a huge number of equity holders. It is always of high importance for an organization to separate the management from ownership since there is no actual reason for them to form a part of management. Segregating the ownership from management has numerous advantages as it does not have any implications upon the regular business operations and the company will hire professionals for managing the key operations. But hiring may become problematic for stakeholders. The hired managers may make unjust decisions and might even misuse the shareholders' money and this can be a reason for the conflict of interests between the two, so as to give space for agency problems.
- **Stockholders vs. Creditors:** The stockholders might pick up risky projects for making more profits, thus making high risks decisions. In case of project failure, the stockholders will have to participate in losses and this can result in agency problems with the stockholders and the creditors. Managers using debt agree to incur real agency costs and limit their freedom in making decisions. Conflicts between shareholders and debtholders manifest themselves in the choice of projects to make investment decisions and in determining how to finance these projects and how much to pay out as dividends. Increases in debt are directly related to increases in risk, especially bankruptcy risk. Debt not only reduces free cash flow, but also increases the probability of

bankruptcy. It should be noted that, from a legal point of view, bankruptcy is the process of scheduling the debt payments due to creditors when a company is in distress. From an economic point of view it is a mechanism for allocating resources. Managers cannot afford to waste the limited resources under their discretion in situations where the burden of debt is heavy. Therefore, increases in debt should increase the market value of a company, as long as bankruptcy costs are kept at a low level. Consequently, increasing financial leverage is therefore one of the possible ways of reducing the agency costs associated with equity. Managers that decide to increase debt limit their freedom to dispose of free cash flow and are subject to capital market discipline. Shareholders may use the increase in debt as a means of controlling managers. Managers have a very strong incentive to generate the financial resources needed to service the debt. Financial leverage is, therefore, used to restructure ownership claims and at the same time to change the aims and aspirations of managers to fully maximize the value of the company's assets at their disposal.

- **Stockholders vs. other Stakeholders:** The stakeholders of a company may have a conflict of interests with other stakeholders like customers, employees, society and communities.

4. Corporate Governance and Agency Problem

Corporate governance is in general the system with which companies are managed, controlled and directed. It is also a mechanism used to deal with agency problems. Managers are hired to operate the company. In order to prevent them from possible deviations that could leave space to agency problems, one solution is to monitor them by looking at their activities so that shareholders can stop any improper decisions before they become worse.

Governance is mostly exercised by the board of directors who control executives based on the company's rules and regulations. Usually board members are also firm executives. Debate exists as to whether executives can control themselves, then shareholders do not need to establish supervisory boards. Then outside directors, representatives of large shareholders, institutional shareholders, mutual funds and even the state are nominated for boards of directors with the expectation of increasing supervisory effectiveness.

To enhance the monitor role of the board of directors and to separate the power of executives and board members, independent non-executive directors' appointments become an inevitable trend. At first, outside directors execute their jobs to maintain their reputations in the field. Later on, to attract capable directors and to stimulate them, companies start offering stock-based incentive compensation.

However, there is also a question about whether these incentive compensations really encourage directors to work on behalf of shareholders' interests or to protect their incomes rather than their reputations. There are reasons for this skepticism. Agency problems appear in the same way as with executives' compensation packages. To protect their benefits, directors tend to depend on managers and to compromise in making financial reports. However, there exist arguments that boards which are less dependent on executives seem to perform worse than boards that are more dependent on company executives.

The question that arises is which agency problems will be solved effectively with the governance structure. Corporate governance is effective when agency risk is high and this happens when the company has surplus free cash flow. It is proved that direct monitoring is effective for small agency issues such as perquisite consumption. It is inferred that the direct intervention of directors will effectively impede managers from using cash resources in unproductive ways such as investing in projects or activities that do not generate value for shareholders but bring benefits for themselves. If the boards work effectively, cases like a generous donation, or an unnecessary overseas meeting, or purchasing a private airplane simply will not occur.

Some issues with corporate governance include high pay for chief executive officers, executives picking directors, as well as indirect resistance to regulations. The chief executive pay is not equal to their value to the company. Board members may get too comfortable in their positions. Financial matters are not transparent and directors are selected without a majority vote.

5. Corporate Governance and Agency Costs

Corporate governance mechanisms are used in various degrees in different countries, while corporate governance risk and agency costs are obvious in the non-finance sector. The agency costs do not have a positive impact on corporate governance in many countries. Agency costs are a type of internal cost that a principal may incur as a result of the agency problem. They include the costs of any inefficiencies that may arise from employing an agent to take on a task, along with the costs associated with managing the principal–agent relationship and resolving differing priorities.

There are three main types of agency costs:

(1) Costs occurring due to applying methods to monitor managers' actions such as fees for using independent auditors.
(2) Costs arising due to setting up the company's organization in order to limit the managers from diverging shareholders' interests.
(3) Opportunity costs that happen when shareholders take time to get a consensus before letting managers take action.

It can be concluded that agency costs are the sum of:

(1) the monitoring expenditures of the principal;
(2) the bonding expenditures by the agent;
(3) the residual loss.

By residual loss, it is meant the reduction in the value of the firm that arises when the entrepreneur dilutes his ownership. It is argued that this is the key cost, since the other two are incurred only to the extent that they yield cost-effective reductions in the residual loss. The shift out of profits into managerial discretion, induced by a dilution of ownership, is responsible for this loss. Monitoring expenditures and bonding expenditures can help to restore performance toward the pre-dilution levels. The irreducible agency cost is the minimum of the sum of these three factors.

6. Mitigating Agency Problems

The solution to the shareholders–managers agency problem is aligning the interests of managers with those of the shareholders, forcing them to work in a way that maximizes shareholders' wealth. The incentive compensation is used to encourage managers, for governance structure to monitor them, or for leverage to constrain them. To execute the solutions, costs occur, and they are called agency costs.

Next is the agency problem between equity holders and debt holders. The debtholders give loans to the firm and get returns from firm's cash flow in the form of interest payments. The interest rate applied for each loan is calculated based on the existing risk level of the firm at the time the loan is issued. After receiving the loan, the stockholders take action through their management in the company and change the risk level, such as selling some assets and investing in risky projects. The debt value decreases because more debt risk is borne. In case the risky project is successful, debtholders will not receive more returns because their income is fixed. However, if that project fails, debtholders have to share the risks. In this case, the interests of the two parties are not aligned. In order to protect their benefits, the debt holders will apply some mechanisms such as stricter covenants or rising interest rates. This causes the company difficulty in accessing the financial market and the debt costs increase. This obviously creates agency costs. To alleviate agency cost from debts, equity holders' and debt holders' benefits should be balanced.

Nowadays, with the evolution of the business world, many new agency problems occur. There are also other types of agency problems such as conflicts of interests between shareholders who are executing the company's control and shareholders who are not, or minority shareholders. This happens when controlling shareholders who usually own a substantial portion of a firm's ownership make decisions that are not beneficial for minority shareholders who do not have enough power to affect the decisions with voting rights. Overinvestment problems happen when there are surplus free cash flows and managers investing in projects that are not value added without facing financial constraints. Underinvestment problems arise when a company acquires too many debts, and the risk of default makes managers reluctant to invest and analyze thoroughly before deciding. Sometimes these managers ignore risky but high return projects and choose investments in safe projects without good returns.

Agency problems are also related to the structure of ownership. The problems occur when the owners do not totally operate their businesses by themselves and when the owners acquire debts to finance the business. In other words, the benefit sharing among parties make people think and act more for themselves and lead to conflicts of interests. The shareholders and the managers, the debtholders all invest in businesses, perhaps in different forms, and want their returns. However, with the participation of many parties, no one will be able to get all of the returns.

Each agency problem has its own core causes. Each mitigation mechanism also has its strengths and weaknesses. Thus, in order to deal effectively with a specific agency problem, the causes must be analyzed and select the most suitable approaches to deal with it.

While it is not possible to eliminate the agency problem, principals can take steps to minimize the risk, known as agency cost, associated with it. The relationship between the principal and the agent can be regulated through contracts, or laws in the case of fiduciary settings. Another method is to incentivize an agent to act in better accordance with the principal's best interests.

Regulations: Principal–agent relationships can be regulated, and often are, by contracts, or laws in the case of fiduciary settings. The fiduciary rule is an example of an attempt to regulate the arising agency problem in the relationship between financial advisors and their clients. The term fiduciary means that financial and retirement advisors are to act in the best interests of their clients. In other words, advisors are to put their clients' interests above their own. The goal is to protect investors from advisors who are concealing any potential conflict of interest.

For example, an advisor might have several investment funds that are available to offer a client, but instead only offers the ones that pay the advisor a commission for the sale. The conflict of interest is an agency problem whereby the financial incentive offered by the investment fund prevents the advisor from working on behalf of the client's best interest.

Incentives: The agency problem may also be reduced by incentivizing an agent to act in better accordance with the principal's best interests. For example, a manager can be motivated to act in the shareholders' best interests through incentives such as performance based compensation, direct influence by shareholders, the threat of firing or the threat of takeovers.

Principals who are shareholders can also tie the chief executive officer's compensation directly to stock price performance. If a chief executive officer was worried that a potential takeover would result in being fired, the chief executive officer might try to prevent the takeover, which would be an agency problem. However, if the chief executive officer was compensated based on stock price performance, the chief executive officer would be incentivized to complete the takeover. Stock prices of the target companies typically rise as a result of an acquisition. Through proper incentives, both the shareholders' and the chief executive officer's interests would be aligned and benefit from the rise in stock price.

Principals can also alter the structure of an agent's compensation. If, an agent is paid not on an hourly basis but by the completion of a project, there is less incentive to not act in the principal's best interest. In addition, performance feedback and independent evaluations hold the agent accountable for their decisions.

Compensation structure: The conflicts of interest between managers and shareholders cause agency costs. Shareholders put money into a company and they want their wealth maximized. Managers are hired to manage the company's day-to-day activities. They invest their human capital in the company and they want to maximize their investments as well. If the interests of the managers are attached to those of the shareholders', this divergence is solved. Based on this, companies offer incentive compensation to executives as a way of encouraging them to act in value-added ways to shareholders. Thus, in the executives' incomes, besides salaries and bonuses, there are some incentive payments tied to their company's performance in order to encourage executives to pay more attention to long term performances. There are two popular types of incentive compensation: stock ownership and stock option grant.

When the managers join the company, probably they are given a certain amount of stocks with preferred pricing or other ways to connect their interests with their company's interests. While stock ownership gives managers the feeling of keeping real wealth, the stock option grant, gives executives opportunities to purchase a certain amount of their company's stock at a predetermined price for a specific range of time in the future. Managers will own the stocks if they execute their rights, or their options will expire. The logic of these incentives is that managers will try their best to increase the company's stock price because they can get more returns. This behavior benefits shareholders as well.

It is easy to understand that even though managers' benefits are tied to those of the company, if the current stock price is higher than their predetermined price, it is a more attractive situation for managers. However, in the case of out of the money options, the current stock price is lower than the predetermined price. The reasoning for setting up the option price in this way is wise because it forces executives to do their best to push their company's performance, increasing stock price so that they gain when they exercise their options. However, the way the option price is set up may also have negative outcomes. In order to gain from their options, managers will do everything to enhance the stock price, including manipulating the performance data. This ruins the effect of the mechanism. Furthermore, the stock market responds negatively to such information about financial data restatement. As a result, this gives executives constraints, and these constraints are even stronger when they have stockownership.

The question that arises, is that of what types of agency problems that incentive compensation will mitigate. It is proved that the compensation mechanism works effectively with large agency problems such as choosing strategy and investment projects. Small agency problems such as perquisite consumption will be solved more effectively with direct monitoring. If increasing incentive compensation is used to alleviate the agency problem of equity, decreasing the compensation is applied to mitigate the conflicts of interests between shareholders and bondholders. When the incentive compensation works well, managers will act according to shareholders' benefits and choose investment policies that maximize shareholders' wealth at debtholders' expense. This hurts debtholders and it makes the conflicts more severe. In this case, reducing the compensation for managers could be a solution.

Capital structure: One of the roots of agency problems is the imperfect alignment of the principals and agents' interests. Managers do not only work for the company's benefit but also for themselves. These personal benefits include consuming excessive perquisites such as luxurious vacations, conferences abroad or investing in projects that are risky and do not enhance the value of the shareholders. It is mentioned that the existence of surplus cash flow is the condition that entitles managers to make unproductive investments. Thus, to impede the managers from acting in a way that is not value added, surplus free cash flow should be reduced. Therefore, the question arises of how to lessen the amount of cash available within a company and simultaneously encourage managers to work more value added. The answer is using leverage.

It is also mentioned that greater financial leverage can help reduce the agency costs by impacting managers including threat of liquidation, and the pressure of making money to pay for debt interests and principals. Leverage also helps reduce the conflicts between shareholders and managers in many ways, including choosing projects to invest and payout policy. However, the relationship between leverage and agency cost is not exactly negative. When the firm uses too much debt, the increase in cost of financial distress means that bankruptcy will be bigger than the decrease in the cost from the shareholders managers conflicts.

When the company uses debts, it has to pay for the interest and principal. The higher the debts, the greater the payment. To make more money to pay these debts puts stress on managers. If the company fails to make enough money to pay for its interest expenses and debt principal on the due dates, the company may come to default. If this happens, the managers may lose their jobs, their incomes, their perquisites and their reputations. Thus, to protect their benefits, managers will act in a way that keeps the company alive, healthy and prosperous. This is what the stockholders want.

One type of agency cost is the cost of overinvestment. It is stated that in a firm that is not levered and has excessive cash flow after investing in positive net present value projects, the surplus cash is usually overinvested in cash or real assets rather than delivered to shareholders. Furthermore, it is possible for managers to put money in projects that are not thoroughly analyzed or even risky because there are excess liquid funds; managers do not have constraints about financial funds. These investments may not create value for shareholders. When leverage is applied, debts such as long term loans are issued, and cash guaranteed for loan and interest payments consume significant parts of surplus cash, thereby reducing the free cash flow under the manager's discretion.

Other ways to reduce the available cash and reduce opportunities for managers to waste the company's resources is a payout policy share repurchase and dividend payout. When the company has excessive cash, the possibility of using it in unproductive ways by controlling managers is high. Cash extraction helps align interests between managers and shareholders, but payment is for creditors. There is no obligation for managers to distribute the surplus cash to shareholders; therefore, the question arises of how to make them do this. It is stated that if the company has surplus cash and investment opportunities are not plentiful, better managerial incentive alignment and closer monitoring by external shareholders are important factors stimulating such payout.

The use of leverage has two sides. It can reduce agency problems such as overinvestment due to surplus cash, but when too much debt is used the conflicts of interest between the equity holders and debt holders become serious and lead to the problem of underinvestment. Decreasing the incentive compensation will be the best choice to mitigate the conflicts of interests between shareholders and bondholders.

Mechanisms for dealing with agency problems are multifunctional. Each method mentioned above not only works effectively alone, but companies can substitute these mechanisms. It is posited that in order to alleviate the agency problems coming from surplus free cash flow, debt can be substituted for stock options. Debt and managerial equity ownership can also be used as alternative methods in controlling equity agency problems. Within debt use, convertible bonds have different effects in comparison with straight debts.

In dealing with agency problems between equity holders and debtholders, besides using the incentive compensation, convertible bonds are effective tools. With the overuse of ordinary debts, the risk of default is high. Therefore, equity holders through managers will try to gain value at debtholders' expenses. The introduction of convertible bonds into the existing structure of equity and straight debts gives the bondholders the right to convert debts into equity under some conditions. This conversion right reduces the conflict of interest between the two parties.

7. Recommendations

There are many approaches to mitigating the agency problems in which internal governance approaches such as compensation structure, direct monitoring, and capital structure can be applied by a company management decision. However, for external governance mechanisms such as government regulations or corporate takeover market mechanisms, the company cannot decide by itself. Which ones will be chosen: compensation, governance, capital structure or a mix? The answer is a mix because it is more feasible to use all available tools to solve the existing problems. Each mechanism has its own advantages and disadvantages, while in some cases, this tool can be a substitute or supplement for another. For instance, it is posited that, in order to alleviate the agency problems coming from surplus free cash flow, debt can be substituted for stock options. In addition, debt and managerial equity ownership can be used as alternative methods in controlling equity agency problems. Another option is issuing convertible bonds, which have different effects in comparison with straight debts. In any case, when choosing the use of a remedy, managers should consider the current status of the company, including country of origin, size, age, capital structure and type and level of existing agency problems.

Country of origin: Developed economies operate under market mechanisms. Businesses operating in emerging countries, especially in ones that do not fully operate under market mechanisms will have to analyze more conditions.

Company's size: If the firm is small or medium, the separation between ownership and management is smaller, so the agency problem is also smaller. In this case, a direct monitor mechanism is effective enough. When the company expands, the opportunity to waste resources becomes bigger. In addition to a direct monitor, the creditors' monitor and incentive compensation will be applied to mitigate agency problems.

Company's age: If the firm is young and has many investment opportunities, chances for conflicts of interests are not considered as important. In this case, direct monitors and compensation structures are effective. If the firm is mature and lacks investment opportunities, surplus cash flow is available and chances for wasting resources are also available. Debt should be introduced together with two other mechanisms. The use of a mix between straight debts and convertible debts should be considered because they work more effectively according to empirical studies.

Ownership structure: When the company has total equity, agency problems from debts do not exist. Thus, agency problems from equity will be analyzed. If the company's capital structure is a mix of equity and debts, both types of agency problems should be considered. With agency problems occurring between shareholders and managers, all three mechanisms including incentive compensation, governance and capital structure can be used with cost and benefit considerations to employ the remedy. When dealing with agency problems from debts, incentive compensation and convertibles seem more effective.

Type and level of agency conflicts: Agency problems from equity or debts as overinvestment or underinvestment, perquisite consumption or surplus free cash flow. The company usually looks for points where the benefit is bigger than the costs from agency problems.

Blockchain technology: It allows for the non-existence of internal and external monitoring that is necessary in corporate governance. The technology allows for guarantees to build trust to overcome agency problems. It's easier for a company to be efficient by lowering agency costs and relationship. Blockchain indeed offers solutions to agency problems by moving former supervisor tasks to a decentralized computer network that is not depended on human mistake or greed. It eliminates agency costs such as supervising agents by creating a trusting relationship between the agent and the principal. Its security system is immutable, which creates trust between the parties in their contractual relationship. Therefore, no party can bend the rules in the blockchain code. The principal has no reason to monitor agency costs since blockchain addresses the agency problems in corporate governance. Agency governance continues without intermediaries in the blockchain such as principal control, third party risk and intermediaries, as well as market performance and private investors.

The shareholders (investors) are the real owners of the company. They appoint directors to manage the affairs of the company on their behalf. The term managers mentioned herein refer to the highest level of management. In a small company, there is no difference between the shareholders and the board. As a company grows requiring more and more fund to finance expansion, the company has to approach the members of the public for financing. This is done through initial public offering (IPO). When public subscribe or invest in company's shares, real separation between ownership and management takes place. This is the only way out to manage the affairs of a big company. It is impossible for all shareholders to take part in the management of the company. The shareholders appoint persons to manage the company's affairs. They constitute boards. The board appoints one or two persons to manage the day to day affairs. The board as agents of the shareholders must optimally use the company's resources in the best interest of the investors and to truly represent the accounting numbers so that the investors can make decisions about their investment in the firm. Contrary to the above, if the board instead of utilizing the resources in the interest of the shareholders take a part of the resources for their own benefit, then the agency problem is created. This may happen in a number of ways. Supposing that the company is highly profitable and possesses high liquidity, this creates the agency problem of free cash flow. Ideally, there should be kept as much cash as it is required to finance expansion. The rest should be distributed as dividend. Another issue arises when management holding huge cash may go for costly acquisition by purchasing majority shares of other companies just to look big and mighty and such acquisitions may not be profitable in the long run. If too much cash is held for too long, the investors may sell the shares of the company in the fear of agency problem of high liquidity. Despite being profitable the share price may start going down. Agency problem results in cost and specifically in the form of loss of value. By the moment that there occurs separation of ownership and management, agency problem/possibility of agency problem occurs. Imagine a company where the board after an IPO may vanish overnight, taking away the investors' money. This is an extreme example of agency problem where management takes away all the resources put in by the investors. In fact, this is fraud. In order to minimize agency problem, in all market driven economies a series of mechanisms have developed. These are known as "corporate governance" mechanism. Corporate governance ensures that the interest of the shareholders are protected, the managers act in the best interest of the shareholders to prevent agency problem and so on. But the most of the corporate governance measures are market driven. The management knows if the governance mechanism is not put in place to prevent agency problem, the shareholders will sell the share of the company, value of the company will come down, promoters will suffer because of lower valuation and the company will become target of takeover by other companies.

Information asymmetry: This means that one party in a transaction knows more than the other party resulting in information asymmetry problem. The board in the case of our discussion, knows the working of a company and its future prospect much more than an individual shareholder. An individual investor tries to gather the information of a company from the managerial action as much as possible. It is the responsibility of the management to convey the worth and prospect of a company through appropriate managerial action like adequate and regular cash dividend distribution, issue of bonus shares, buy back of shares, share split, diversification, expansion, acquiring a firm, so that the investors can assess the worth of a firm. Lowering information asymmetry through appropriate managerial action has a significant role in minimizing agency problem between the corporate insiders and the investors.

Corporate governance is the system with which companies are managed, controlled and directed. Governance related to large businesses is called Corporate Governance. The corporate form of business raises large capital from public; therefore, there are millions of shareholders contributing small capital. Since contribution of shareholder is small, it is not practically possible for shareholders to run the day to day management of business. This management consists of professional managers who manage the company and make the important decisions. However, there is high chance that managers may pursue certain alternative objectives that are beneficial to themselves rather than owners. One solution to mitigate the agency problem is to appoint the honest and ethical managers. But the question is how to determine whether a manager is honest or ethical or not. Thus, there is need to do something beyond appointment of managers and this has to do with the audit. Auditors are expected to work on behalf of owners and examine the conduct of business run by managers and submit the report to owners. In addition to auditing, the corporate governance is used to resolve the agency conflict. Under corporate governance, the emphasis is on the board including the appointment of directors for the board, who are expected to be independent and expert in their fields. In addition, the board forms committees to have more close interaction with management.

References

Albrecht, W.S., Albrecht, C.C. and Albrecht, C.O. (2004). Fraud and corporate executives: Agency, stewardship and broken trust, *Journal of Forensic Accounting*, (5), 109–130.

Archer, M.S. (2003). *Structure, Agency and the Internal Conversation*. Cambridge University Press: Cambridge.

Arthurs, J.D., Hoskisson, R.E., Busenit, L.W. and Johnson, R.A. (2008). Managerial agents watching other agents: Multiple agency conflicts regarding underpricing in IPO firms, *The Academy of Management Journal*, 51(2), 277–294.

Barnes, S.B. (2000). *Understanding Agency: Social Theory and Responsible Action*. Sage Publications: London.

Bonazzi, L. and Islam, S.M.N. (2007). Agency theory and corporate governance: A study of the effectiveness of board in their monitoring of the CEO, *Journal of Modelling in Management*, 2(1), 7–23.

Damodaran, A. (1997). *Corporate Finance*. John Wiley: New York.

Davila, A. and Penalva, F. (2006). Governance structure and the weighting of performance measures in CEO compensation, *Review of Accounting Studies*, 11(4), 463–493.

Green, S. (1992). Managerial motivation and strategy in management buy-outs: A cultural analysis, *Journal of Management Studies*, 29(4), 513–535.

Hart, O. (1995). Corporate governance: Some theory and implications, *The Economic Journal*, 105(430), 678–689.

Jensen, M.C. (1986). The agency cost of free cash flow: Corporate finance and takeovers, *American Economic Review*, 76(2), 323–329.

Jensen, M.C. and Meckling, W.H. (1976). Theory of the firm: Managerial behavior, agency costs and ownership structure, *Journal of Financial Economics*, 3(4), 305–360.

Kaal, W.A. (2020). Blockchain solutions for agency problems in corporate governance, *Information for Efficient Decision Making*, 313–329.

Kim, K.A. and Nofsinger, J.R. (2004). *Corporate Governance*. Englewood Cliffs, Prentice Hall: London.

Klein, W.A., Ramsceyer, J.M. and Bainbridge, S.M. (2006). *Agency, Partnership, and Limited Liability Entities*. Unincorporated Business Association, 2nd edition. Foundation Press: Michigan.

Kolbjornsrud, V. (2017). Agency problems and governance mechanisms in collaborative communities, *Strategic Organization*, 15(2), 141–173.

Murphy, K.J. (1985). Corporate performance and managerial remuneration: An empirical analysis, *Journal of Accounting and Economics*, 30, 245–278.

Samuels, J.M., Wilkes, F.M. and Brayshaw, R.E. (1995). *Management of Company Finance*. Chapman & Hall: London.

Shapiro, A. (1999). *Modern Corporate Finance*. Englewood Cliffs, Prentice Hall: London.

Williamson, O.E. (1988). Corporate finance and corporate governance, *The Journal of Finance*, 43(3), 567–591.

https://doi.org/10.1142/9789811260506_0005

Chapter 5

Corporate Governance Gender Equality and Firm Financial Performance: The Case of Euronext 100 Index

Nektarios Gavrilakis[*,‡], **Christos Floros**[*,§], **and Emilios Galariotis**[†,¶]

[*]*Department of Accounting and Finance, Hellenic Mediterranean University, Greece*

[†]*Audencia Business School, Department of Finance, France*

[‡]*ngavrilakis@hmu.gr*

[§]*cfloros@hmu.gr*

[¶]*egalariotis@audencia.com*

Abstract

This chapter analyzes how financial performance indicators and gender equality of large cap stocks impact governance scores. In particular, we examine how the return on equity, reinvestment rate, price to book value, market capitalization and gender equality of large cap firms in Europe are related to their governance pillar scores. Based on the Euronext 100 index, we conduct a multiple regression analysis for the period, 2010–2020. As regards the above financial indicators, we find that return on equity and market cap have a significant positive impact on governance scores. In addition, we conclude that reinvestment rate and price to book value have a negative and significant effect on governance scores. Finally, the low percentage of female board membership is confirmed by the non-effect of gender inequality on governance scores. Our empirical investigation provides evidence in support of the moderate governance score in European companies. However, European companies should consider the benefits of good governance practices and apply sustainable strategies.

Keywords: Corporate governance, gender equality, return on equity, reinvestment rate, price to book value, market capitalization, Euronext 100

1. Introduction

Corporate governance is defined "as the procedures and processes according to which an organization is directed and controlled"; (OECD, 2004). The corporate governance structure specifies the distribution of rights and responsibilities among the board of directors, managers, shareholders and lays down the rules and procedures for decision-making (Bubbico *et al.*, 2012). According to Shleifer and Vishny (1997), corporate governance mechanisms are means to reduce the agency costs where they attempt to minimize two types of agency conflicts: the conflicts between shareholders and managers and the conflicts between controlling "majority" shareholders and minority shareholders. Capital market regulators and policy makers have been forced to concentrate their actions on corporate governance practices throughout Europe. A plethora of company owners and managers debate that the costs of adopting good corporate governance practices exceed the resulting benefits. In addition, costly governance strategies may not be esteemed or valued by investors. There has been a growing perception that, in order for companies across the world to become internationally competitive, they need to adopt commonly accepted standards of corporate governance. Board diversity is an essential element of corporate governance. Changes in the laws in several countries have increased the proportion of female presence on boards of directors by providing evidence that gender-diverse boards have beneficial effects on stock markets (Abad *et al.*, 2017).

In recent years, the role of good corporate governance has become crucial in financial markets, especially in Europe. The selection and construction of an investment portfolio that is based on companies with a high governance score might capture better long-term returns for investors and avail the society by influencing the social policy of companies. Consequently, it is interesting to investigate the effect of corporate governance, as investors are more frequently using it today for their investment decisions. The current study focuses on the question of how return on equity, reinvestment rate, price to book value, market capitalization and gender inequality of large cap firms in Europe are related to the governance pillar score. In numerous past studies, researchers investigate how governance affects firm performance or value. A major contribution of this study is that we explore how indicators of financial performance or value of a firm might lead to a higher governance score. There are few empirical studies that have analyzed how financial performance indicators are associated with governance pillar scores, thus the present study contributes to this debate by empirically investigating this issue. We applied a linear regression approach to analyze the performance of companies that constitute the Euronext 100 index.

Our empirical investigation provides evidence in support of the moderating role of some financial performance indicators on governance disclosure. More precisely, our results show that with regard to European companies, return on equities and market cap have a significant positive impact on governance scores. Furthermore, reinvestment rate and price to book value are negatively correlated with governance scores. Finally, our results indicate that there is no effect of gender inequality on the governance score, which is confirmed with the low percentage (38%) of women board membership.

The contribution of this study is crucial in the current literature by advancing investment decision making of investors and portfolio managers applying corporate governance strategies. Also, the financial performance of organizations is increasingly affected by governance factors; and thus, the current study has essential implications for companies that focus on sustainability. The remainder of the chapter is structured as follows. Section 2 reviews the related literature. Section 3 describes the data and methodology. The results are reported in Section 4, while Section 5 concludes the chapter.

2. Literature Review

Several studies have examined measures of corporate governance and their linkages to firms' financial performance. Karpoff *et al.* (1994) found a positive relationship between corporate governance structure and performance indicators, such as return on assets and market to book value. Gompers *et al.* (2003) analyzed the relationship between corporate governance, firm value and accounting measures for the U.S. market. They supported the hypothesis that well-governed companies outperform poorly governed firms. Bebchuk and Cohen (2005) used Investor Responsibility Research Center (IRRC) data to show that staggered boards impede firm value. In their study, Black *et al.* (2006) construct a corporate governance index for 515 Korean companies using a survey conducted by the Korean Stock Exchange and found a positive relation between the quality of corporate governance practices and market valuation (measured by market-to-book ratio). When examining the relation between the quality of corporate governance practices and firm valuation, Cheung *et al.* (2008) find no relation. Fisher-Vanden and Thorburn (2011) found that companies announcing membership in the Environmental Protection Agency (EPA), a center for corporate climate leadership, experience significantly negative abnormal stock returns. They conclude that the price decline is larger in firms with high market-to-book value. Moreover, Gupta *et al.* (2009) in their study concluded that the corporate governance rankings (high level of environmental performance) of companies operating in the Canadian capital market were not related to the firm value and firm financial performance. In their study, Fatemi *et al.* (2016) investigate the effect of environmental social and governance practices and their disclosure on firm value and found that strong corporate governance practices increase firm value and governance concerns decrease it. Contrary, Buallay *et al.* (2017) suggested that corporate governance did not have a significant impact on firm performance and concluded that the largest shareholder ownership has no impact on firm performance (ROE, ROA, Tobin's *Q*). Mishra and Kapil (2018) found that market-based measurements (Tobin's *Q*) were more affected by corporate governance than accounting-based measures (ROA). Mariana *et al.* (2020) examined the corporate governance perception index and profitability on firm value for the Indonesian Stock Exchange and found a partial and significant effect. In addition, Alsayegh *et al.* (2020) explored the impact of environmental, social and governance information disclosure on sustainability performance among Asian firms from 2005 to 2017. The results show that environmental performance and social performance are significantly positively related to economic sustainable performance. Those findings indicate that the corporate financial value and the value creation for society are interdependent. Recently, Borokova and Wu (2020) examined the resilience of more sustainable U.S. firms during the recent COVID-19 crisis. They report that losses of companies with low environmental social and governance scores were 50% higher than those of highly scoring companies. Eventually, it is not clear whether higher company valuation is in fact related to better governance, as the costs associated with the implementation of stronger governance mechanisms may outweigh the benefits (Gillan *et al.*, 2003; Chhaochharia and Grinstein, 2007; Bruno and Claessens, 2010).

A semantic aspect of corporate governance is the board gender diversity, which is defined as the presence of female directors on the boards of corporations (Carter *et al.*, 2003). There are some studies showing that the appointment of women directors has no influence on firm performance (Rose, 2007; Haslam *et al.*, 2010). According to Loukil *et al.* (2019), other studies provide evidence that diverse boards could suffer more conflicts of interests, slower decision-making and lower financial performance (Lau and Murnighan, 1998; Bohren and Strom, 2007). On the other hand, as Loukil *et al.* (2019) stated, it has been argued that board women members could have positive effects on financial and social performance (Boulouta, 2013; Alazzani *et al.*, 2017). In addition, the appointment of women as directors could be viewed as a positive signal by firms to stakeholders (Ismail and Manafe, 2016; Ahmed and Ali, 2017; Abad *et al.*, 2017). Recently, a study conducted by Puni and Anlesinya (2020) analyzed the relationship of corporate governance mechanisms with both market-based and accounting-based measurements and found a positive relationship between the board size, the frequency of board meetings, shareholder concentration and financial performance. Based on the above literature, we presume the presence of a positive or a non-effect of gender-diverse boards on governance pillar score.

Most of the previous studies focus on the relation between good governance practices and firm financial value. We further analyze whether performance, profitability, firm value, firm size and gender equality lead to higher governance pillar score, which is a key contribution of this study. High governance performance is a mechanism for improving the value of the company, protecting external investors and maximizing shareholder value (Beltratti, 2005). The literature review is summarized in the conceptual diagram (Fig. 1).

The conceptual framework shows that structure related indicators such as market capitalization and gender equality, as well as, performance-related indicators like return on equity, reinvestment rate and price to

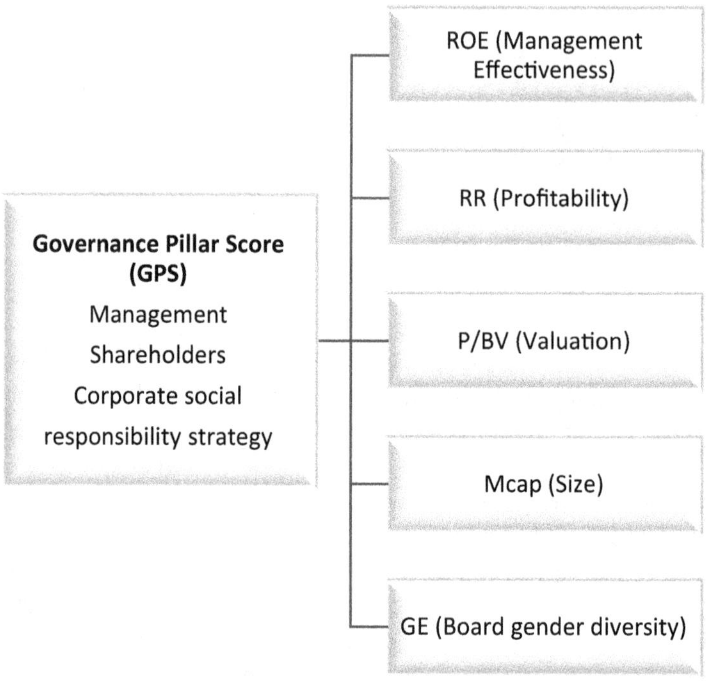

Fig. 1: Conceptual framework.

book value might affect the governance pillar score. According to Wallace *et al.* (1994), these variables are considered to be quite steady and constant over time. Based on the literature review, the current study examines the following hypotheses for European countries:

H1: The return on equity (ROE) has a positive effect on the Governance pillar score (GPS).

H2: The reinvestment rate (RR) has an effect on the GPS.

H3: The price to book value (P/BV) has an effect on the GPS.

H4: The market capitalization (Mcap) has a positive effect on the GPS.

H5: The gender equality (GE) has an effect on the GPS.

3. Methodology and Data Description

The governance pillar score was selected as the dependent variable, whereas independent variables consist of the return on equity, reinvestment rate, price to book value, market capitalization and gender equality. Datastream Refinitiv Eikon is chosen for retrieving yearly data since it offers one of the most comprehensive databases in the industry, covering over 80% of the global market cap across more than 47 metrics for governance pillar score (Breitz and Partapuoli, 2020). Table 1 presents the estimation formulas for the dependent and independent variables used in the analysis.

The current study determines the relationship of management effectiveness, profitability, value, size and gender equality for European companies on governance pillar score. We use the constituents of Euronext

Table 1: Methodology used for the construction of dependent and control variables.

Variables	Measurement
Dependent variable	
GPS (Governance pillar score)	The corporate governance pillar measures a company's systems and processes, which ensure that its board members and executives act in the best interests of its long-term shareholders (Refinitiv, 2020).
Independent variables	
ROE (Management effectiveness)	Return on equity is the net profit after tax/total equity.
RR (Profitability)	Reinvestment rate is the return an investor expects to make after reinvesting the cash flows earned from a previous investment.
P/BV (Valuation)	Price to Book Value is calculated by dividing the company's latest closing Price by its Book Value per share.
Mcap (Size)	Market cap (Market capitalization) is the total value of all a company's shares of stock. It is calculated by multiplying the price of a stock by its total number of outstanding shares.
Gender equality (Board gender diversity)	Gender equality is defined as the presence of female members on the board of directors.

Note: All data were retrieved from Refinitiv Eikon Database.

100 Index, which is the blue-chip index of the pan-European exchange, Euronext NV. The total period analyzed is from 01/01/2010 to 31/12/2020. We estimate multiple regression analysis to reveal which of the variables have the most and least influence on the stock returns of the selected indices. Our dependent variable is the governance pillar score (GPS*it)* of the stock *i* in year *t.* The panel data regression model is

$$\text{GPS}it = a + \beta_1(\text{ROE}) + \beta_2(\text{RR}) + \beta_3(\text{P/BV}) + \beta_4(\text{Mcap}) + \beta_5(\text{GE}t) + \varepsilon_{it} \tag{1}$$

where ROE is return on equity, RR is the reinvestment rate, P/BV is price to book value ratio, Mcap is the market capitalization and GE is the gender equality (percentage of women in firm's board meetings). These are the determinants or financial variables (for profitability, value and size) that investors and professionals mostly analyze before their investment decision. The terms α (constant) and β (regression coefficient) are parameters to be estimated and ε_{it} is the error term.

4. Empirical Results

To establish the relationship between the independent variables and the dependent variable, an inferential analysis using the SPSS software was conducted for descriptive statistics, correlation analysis, and a multiple regression analysis. As shown in Table 2, the mean of governance pillar score is **0.58** which means a grade of B^- according to the Refinitiv database (Refinitiv, 2020). Moreover, the mean of gender equality is **0.38** meaning that the percentage of female board membership is only 38%. The values of gender equality fluctuate between 0 and 0.5. The

Table 2: Descriptive statistics.

Euronext 100 index $N = 93$	Minimum	Maximum	Mean	Std. Dev.
Governance pillar score	0.151	0.943	**0.58**	0.203
Return on equity	−0.101	0.501	0.112	0.085
Reinvestment rate	−0.101	0.224	0.052	0.054
Price to book value	2.973	2.104	24.548	33.823
Market cap	0.424	11.59	2.56	2.045
Gender equality	0.171	0.637	**0.38**	0.091

Table 3: Correlations matrix.

$N = 93$		**GPS*t***	**ROE**	**RR**	**P/BV**	**Mcap**	**GE*t***
GPS*t*	Pearson Correlation	1					
	Sig. (2-tailed)						
ROE	Pearson Correlation	−0.111	1				
	Sig. (2-tailed)	0.288					
RR	Pearson Correlation	**−0.224***	**0.858****	1			
	Sig. (2-tailed)	0.031	0.000				
P/BV	Pearson Correlation	−0.194	**0.781****	**0.581****	1		
	Sig. (2-tailed)	0.062	0.000	0.000			
Mcap	Pearson Correlation	**0.280****	0.063	−0.019	0.026	1	
	Sig. (2-tailed)	0.007	0.550	0.859	0.804		
GE*t*	Pearson Correlation	−0.003	−0.143	−0.101	−0.182	0.071	1
	Sig. (2-tailed)	0.979	0.170	0.336	0.080	0.501	

Note: *Correlation is significant at the 0.05 level of certainty (2-tailed); **Correlation is significant at the 0.01 level of certainty (2-tailed).

diversity is maximized at the value of 0.5, where there is the same percentage of male and female board membership (Blau, 1977).

The correlation matrix is used to analyze the relationship between our variables. The statistics of Table 3 demonstrate a low negative (−0.224) significant correlation between reinvestment rate and the governance score, while market capitalization has a low positive (0.280) significant correlation with the governance score. In addition, return on equity has a high significant positive correlation not only with the reinvestment rate but also with the price to book value. The values of correlations are 0.858 and 0.781, respectively. Finally, the reinvestment rate has a positive (0.581) significant correlation with the price to book value.

The research hypotheses were tested by using regression analysis. The significance value is 0.002 (see Table 4), which shows that our research model is significant. The R^2 value measures the proportion of variation in the dependent variable (GSP) that is explained by the model, i.e. by variations in independent variables (ROE, RR, P/BV, Mcap, GE). Adjusted R^2 gives the value after adjusting the error term. The adjusted R^2 is 15%, which means that the independent variables contribute about 15% to the governance pillar score while other factors not studied in this research contribute 85%. The Durbin–Watson statistic is 1.806 and measures the

Table 4: Regression results for Euronext 100.

Model Summary					
Model	R	R^2	**Adjusted** R^2	**Std. Error**	**Durbin–Watson**
	0.443	0.196	**0.150**	0.187	1.806
ANOVA					
Model	**Sum of Sq.**	df	**Mean Sq.**	F	**Sig.**
Regression	0.745	5	0.149	4.251	**0.002**
Residual	3.049	87	0.035		
Total	3.794	92			
Coefficients					
	Unstandardized Coefficients				
Model	B	**Std. Error**	**Beta**	t	**Sig.**
Constant	**0.626**	0.094		6.647	**0.000*****$
ROE	**1.534**	0.611	0.645	2.509	**0.014****
RR	**−2.032**	0.729	−0.549	−2.786	**0.006*****
P/BV	**−0.039**	0.016	−0.396	−2.451	**0.016****
Mcap	**1.46**	0.000	0.243	2.484	**0.015****
GE*t*	−0.123	0.219	−0.055	−0.560	0.577

Note: Table 4 reports the estimated coefficients for the following model: $\text{GPS}it = a + \beta_1(\text{ROE}) + \beta_2(\text{RR}) + \beta_3(\text{P/BV}) + \beta_4(\text{Mcap}) + \beta_5(\text{GE}t) + \varepsilon_{it}$ GPS*it* is governance pillar score, *RR* is reinvestment rate, *P/BV* is price to book value ratio, *Mcap* is market capitalization, *GEt* is gender equality. ***Significant at 1% and **Significant at 5%.

Dependent Variable: GPSt/Predictors: ROE, RR, P/BV, Mcap, GE*t*/*N*=93.

autocorrelation between independent variables. Since the value lies between 1.5 and 2.5, there is no problem of serial correlation. A multiple regression analysis was conducted to identify which of the above indicators influence governance pillar score in Europe.

The regression equation (1) becomes

$$\text{GPS}it = 0.62 + 1.53(\text{ROE}) - 2.03(\text{RR}) - 0.039(\text{P/BV}) \\ +1.46(\text{Mcap}) - 0.123(\text{GE}t) + \varepsilon_{it}$$

Based on the regression equation, taking all the above variables constant at zero, the GPS would be 0.62. Table 4 shows some important statistics regarding the independent variables and their eligibility in impacting the dependent variable. According to the statistics, the beta value of ROE is 1.53, and it means that a 1 unit increase in ROE, keeping other things constant, impacts the governance pillar score with a 1.53 unit change. The significance value is 0.014 which means that the ROE indicator has a significant positive impact on the GPS. This finding is consistent with the results from the study of Fatemi *et al.* (2016) and Mariana *et al.* (2020), who found that firm profitability and the government perception index have a positive significant effect. Contrary, our results are not consistent with the study of Gupta *et al.* (2009) who indicate that companies with high corporate governance ranking in Canada were related neither to the firm financial performance nor to the firm value. The beta value of the second indicator (*RR*) is –2.03 which means that a 1 unit increase in reinvestment rate decreases the governance pillar score by 2.03, keeping other things constant. The reinvestment indicator has a significance value of 0.006, indicating that RR has a significant negative correlation with the governance score.

In fact, the P/BV indicator decreases governance score, as the corresponding regression coefficient (–0.039) is negative and significant. Furthermore, the coefficient of *M*cap is 1.46, which means that a 1 unit increase in *M*cap leads to a 1.46 unit change in governance score. This significant positive relationship between the market capitalization and governance suggests that European large cap companies possibly use good governance practices more than small cap firms do. Finally, there is no effect of gender inequality on the governance score for our sample. The above findings are consistent with the results of Karpoff *et al.* (1994) who found a relationship of market to book value with the corporate governance structure. In addition, we contradict the Black *et al.* (2006) study that found a positive relation between corporate governance and market value measured by the market to book ratio. Moreover, we support partly the results of Rose (2007) and Haslam *et al.* (2010) who found no influence of women directors on firm financial performance. Finally, we contradict the results of Boulouta (2013) and Alazzani *et al.* (2017) who concluded that women board members have a positive effect on financial and social performance. The summary of hypothesis testing is shown in Table 5.

Table 5: Summary of Hypothesis testing.

Hypothesis	Statement	Decision
H1	The return on equity (ROE) has a positive effect on GPS	Accepted
H2	The reinvestment rate (RR) has an effect on GPS	Accepted
H3	The price to book value (P/BV) has an effect on GPS	Accepted
H4	The market capitalization (Mcap) has a positive effect on GPS	Accepted
H5	The gender equality (GE) has an effect on GPS	Rejected

5. Conclusions

Previous studies report a positive relation of financial performance of a firm, measured both by accounting and market-based indicators and corporate governance. Other studies show a negative relation or no relation. In this study, this issue is examined by using recent data from Europe. We place the governance pillar score (Refinitiv, 2020) in a framework that aims to explain a firm's governance score as a function of profitability, valuation, size and board composition indicators. We focus on European countries by examining the constituents of the Euronext 100 index for a period of 11 years (2010 to 2020).

In particular, the current study examines whether return on equity, reinvestment rate, price to book value, market capitalization and gender equality lead governance pillar score. The findings show that return on equity and market cap have a positive and significant relationship with the governance score. In addition, the reinvestment rate and price to book value are significantly negatively correlated, which means that those two indicators reduce governance score. This valuable result possibly means that European investors are not sensitive to corporate governance issues. The same result is verified by the mean governance score which is B^- in European countries. Lastly, our results indicate that there is no effect of gender inequality on our selected European companies, as the percentage of women board membership is quite low (38%).

Overall, our findings are in line with empirical evidence documented in similar studies of the existing literature. This study offers insights into investors, finance professionals, and corporate owners helping them to understand how the financial performance of a firm, which is based on profitability and valuation indicators, may affect governance scores.

Finally, the results could improve the functioning of companies in order to follow vital governance practices.

Despite the valuable findings of this study, there are also possible extensions for further work. In particular, the study panel should be expanded to include more continents. In addition, more financial stock indicators, such as price to earnings (P/E) ratio, price to cash flow (P/CF) ratio, volatility, return on asset (ROA), should be taken into consideration. Furthermore, the examination of more pillars, such as environmental and social pillars, could be interesting.

Further Reading

Refinitiv (2020). Environmental, Social and Governance (ESG) Scores from Refinitiv. Available at: https://www.refinitiv.com/en.

References

Abad, D., Lucas-Perez, M.E., Minguez-Vera, A. and Yague, J. (2017). Does gender diversity on corporate boards reduce information asymmetry in equity markets? *BRQ Business Research Quarterly*, 20(30), 192–205.

Ahmed, A. and Ali, S. (2017). Boardroom gender diversity and stock liquidity: Evidence from Australia, *Journal of Contemporary Accounting & Economics*, 13(2), 148–165.

Alazzani, A., Hassanein, A. and Aljanadi, Y. (2017). Impact of gender diversity on social and environmental performance: Evidence from Malaysia, *Corporate Governance: The International Journal of Business in Society*, 17(2), 266–283.

Alsayegh, M.F., Rahman, R.A. and Homayoun, S. (2020). Corporate economic, environmental, and social sustainability performance transformation through ESG disclosure, *Sustainability*, 12(9), 1–20.

Bebchuk, L. and Cohen, A. (2005). The costs of entrenched boards, *Journal of Financial Economics*, 78, 409–433.

Beltratti, A. (2005). The complementarity between corporate governance and corporate social responsibility, *The Geneva Papers on Risk and Insurance-Issues and Practice*, 30(3), 373–386.

Black, B., Jang, H. and Kim, W. (2006). Does corporate governance predict firms' market values? Evidence from Korea, *Journal of Law, Economics, and Organization*, 22, 366–413.

Blau, P.M. (1977). *Inequality and Heterogeneity*. Free Press: New York, Glencoe, IL.

Bohren, O. and Strom, R.O. (2007). Aligned, informed, and decisive: Characteristics of value-creating boards. EFA 2007 Ljubljana Meetings Paper. Available at: http://ssrn.com/abstract=966407.

Borokova, S. and Wu, Y. (2020). ESG versus Financial Performance of Large Cap firms: The case of EU, U.S., Australia and South East Asia. Refinitiv, Boston, Massachusetts 02210, USA.

Boulouta, I. (2013). Hidden connections: The link between board gender diversity and corporate social performance, *Journal of Business Ethics*, 113(2), 185–197.

Breitz, C. and Partapuoli, P.J. (2020). How is ESG affecting stock returns? Lund University, School of Economics and Management.

Bruno, V. and Claessens, S. (2010). Corporate governance and regulation: Can there be too much of a good thing? *Journal of Financial Intermediation*, 19, 461–482.

Buallay, A., Hamdan, A. and Zureigat, Q. (2017). Corporate governance and firm performance: Evidence from Saudi Arabia, *Australasian Accounting, Business and Finance Journal*, 11(1), 78–98.

Bubbico, R., Giorgino, M. and Monda, B. (2012). The impact of corporate governance on the market value of financial institutions: Empirical evidences from Italy, *Banks and Bank Systems*, 7(2), 11–18.

Carter, A.D., Simkins, J.B. and Simpson G. (2003). Corporate governance, board diversity, and firm value, *The Financial Review*, 38, 33–53.

Chhaochharia, V. and Grinstein, Y. (2007). Corporate governance and firm value: The impact of the 2002 governance rules. Johnson School Research Paper Series No. 23-06, *AFA 2006 Boston Meetings Paper*.

Chhaochharia, V. and Laeven, L. (2009). Corporate governance norms and practices, *Journal of Financial Intermediation*, 18(3), 405–431.

Cheung, Y.L., Jiang, P., Limpaphayom, P. and Lu, T. (2008). Does corporate governance matter in China? *China Economic Review*, 19(3), 460–479.

Fatemi, A., Glaumb, M. and Kaiser S. (2016). ESG performance and firm value: The moderating role of disclosure, *Global Finance Journal*, 38, 45–64.

Fisher-Vanden, K. and Thorburn, K.S. (2011). Voluntary corporate environmental initiatives and shareholder wealth, *Journal of Environmental Economics and Management*, 62(3), 430–445.

Gillan, S., Hartzell, J. and Starks, L. (2003). Explaining corporate governance: Boards, bylaws, and charter provisions. Working Paper, University of Texas at Austin.

Gompers, P., Ishii, J. and Metrick, A. (2003). Corporate governance and equity prices, *Quarterly Journal of Economics*, 118, 107–155.

Gupta, P.P., Kennedy, B.D. and Weaver, C.S. (2009). Corporate governance and firm value: Evidence from Canadian capital markets, *Corporate Ownership & Control*, 6(3), 293–307.

Haslam, S.A., Ryan, M.K., Kulich, C., Trojanowski, G. and Atkins, C. (2010). Investing with prejudice: The relationship between women's presence on company boards and objective and subjective measures of company performance, *British Journal of Management*, 21, 484–497.

Ismail, K.N.K. and Manafe, K.B.A. (2016). Market reactions to the appointment of women to the boards of Malaysian firms, *Journal of Multinational Financial Management*, 36, 75–88.

Karpoff, M.J., Marr, M.W. and Danielson, G.M. (1994). *Corporate Governance and Firm Performance*. The Research Foundation of the Institute of Chartered Financial Analysts. Available at: https://www.cfainstitute.org/-/media/documents/book/rf-publication/1994/rf-v1994-n8-4449-pdf.ashx.

Loukil, N., Yousfi, O. and Yerbanga, R. (2019). Does gender diversity on boards influence stock market liquidity? Empirical evidence from the French market, *Corporate Governance*, 19(4), 669–670.

Mariana, Abdullah, S. and Mahmud, M. (2020). Corporate governance perception index, profitability and firm value in Indonesia, *Technology and Investment*, 11, 13–21.

Mishra, R. K. and Kapil, S. (2018). Board characteristics and firm value for Indian companies, *Journal of Indian Business Research*, 10(1), 2–32.

Puni, A. and Anlesinya, A. (2020). Corporate governance mechanisms and firm performance in a developing country, *International Journal of Law and Management*, 62(2), 147–169.

Rose, C. (2007). Does female board representation influence firm performance? The Danish evidence, *Corporate Governance: An International Review*, 15(2), 404–413.

Shleifer, A. and Vishny, R.W. (1997). A survey of corporate governance, *The Journal of Finance*, 3(2), 741–748.

Wallace, R.S.O., Naser, K. and Mora, A. (1994). The relationship between the comprehensiveness of corporate annual reports and firm characteristics in Spain, *Accounting and Business Research*, 25(97), 41–53.

Part II

CG and the Corporate Debt

https://doi.org/10.1142/9789811260506_0006

Chapter 6

A Bibliometric Overview of the State-of-the-Art in Bankruptcy Prediction Methods and Applications

Salwa Kessioui[*,§], Michalis Doumpos[†,¶], and Constantin Zopounidis[†,‡,||]

[*]*Department of Business, Economics, and Management, Mediterranean Agronomic Institute of Chania (CIHEAM-MAICh), Chania, Greece*

[†]*Technical University of Crete, School of Production Engineering and Management, Financial Engineering Laboratory, University Campus, Chania*

[‡]*Audencia Business School, Nantes, France*

[§]*salwakessioui@gmail.com*

[¶]*mdoumpos@tuc.gr*

[||]*kzopounidis@tuc.gr*

Abstract

This chapter aims to help future researchers and practitioners explore different statistical methods (discriminant analysis, logistic regression, probit analysis) and modern analytical methods (support vector machines, artificial intelligence, neural networks) to provide improved predictions. It is also intended to facilitate their research by providing a clear overview of their interests and finding relevant information for further research.

Over the past decades, the topic of bankruptcy prediction methods has developed significantly, becoming a relevant research area in many disciplines, including business economics, computer science, operations research, finance and accounting. Motivated by the severe impact that the 2007–2009 financial crisis and the recent COVID-19 global health crisis have had on companies of all sizes, and subsequently the need to develop new methodologies for predicting corporate failures, this chapter provides a systematic literature review, based on bibliometric analysis of 993 reviewed articles, and an in-depth review of 103 articles published on bankruptcy prediction methods over the period 1997–2019.

Keywords: Bankruptcy prediction, corporate failures, literature review

1. Introduction

Because of the dramatic increase in the number of bankruptcies in the world during the last few years, corporate bankruptcy has become a relatively common and complex issue that requires a thorough analysis. Since the beginning of the 20th century, one of the earliest studies on this subject was that of Fitzpatrick (1932). He analyzed data from 20 selected failed companies between 1920 and 1929 and compared their financial performance without using any statistical method to predict failure.

In 1966, the modern literature on bankruptcy prediction was initiated by Beaver. The most extensive univariate study was conducted on this topic at this time, as it provides a reference starting point for future research in terms of ratio analysis. He applied a univariate discriminant analysis to a sample of 79 bankrupt firms and 79 non-bankrupt US firms. Since then, the literature on the subject can be generally classified into three categories. First, the use of traditional models to predict business bankruptcy which are most commonly based on financial data. For example, Altman (1968) employed discriminant analysis and Ohlson (1980) used logistic regression. Second, the modern methods use hazard models (e.g. Shumway, 2001). In parallel, these models also include predictor variables based on stock market movements. Third, several studies carried out from the 1990s have used artificial intelligence systems such as neural networks, support vector machines or decision trees to predict bankruptcies (e.g. Lee *et al.* 1996; Charitou *et al.* 2004; Chen, 2011). However, all these bankruptcy prediction models are based on a statistical approach and a set of predictor variables.

Considering the importance of the subject, this chapter aims to provide an organized summary of existing research by identifying the first pioneers who initiated predictive bankruptcy methodologies in different fields as well as the new researchers who are currently involved in order to gain knowledge, understand and show the future direction of this research field. To this end, we used bibliometric analysis techniques that allow us to describe the main pillars and the evolution of the research field. Furthermore, we contribute to a specific way of showing the development of the main research aspects.

This chapter is organized as follows. In the next section, we highlight the motivation behind this literature review on bankruptcy prediction, and then we outline the data and all the steps followed to evaluate the bankruptcy prediction methods through different features based on a systematic bibliometric analysis using the latest version of VOSviewer. In the third section, we summarize the results obtained from our detailed research, discuss the limitations of the study, propose potential opportunities for future research, and provides a general conclusion on this important topic.

2. Methodology

According to Broadus (1987), a bibliometric review is a quantitative study of published articles. The assessment consists of data collection, analysis and synthesis. This means that to have a high-quality review, the scientific discipline required to complete those steps is crucial.

The increase in the number of scientific publications has stimulated a growth in the importance of bibliometrics. Because of the different characteristics of bibliometric data including titles, keywords, and references, authors, journals, direct citation networks and bibliometric linkage networks can be exploited for more in-depth and detailed analysis using these types of investigations (Najmi *et al.*, 2016); it is easy to recognize patterns in the literature, show the evolution of prominent topics, identify the impact of significant studies and analyze the relationship between articles and reference sources (Carvalho *et al.*, 2018).

Moreover, a bibliometric study related to bankruptcy prediction models was performed to provide a modern contemporary overview of the state-of-the-art of predicting business failure and evaluate the evolution of the research in this research area. The VOS viewer software was employed to analyze the academic literature in this area.

Following our research that identified the most relevant articles in top journals, the results that met the first selection were 993 international academic articles published from 1995 up to 2020. Figure 1 presents the evolution of the number of publications of models that concern bankruptcy prediction. Initially, the number of articles increased slightly in the first years until the global financial crisis in 2009. A significant increase was highlighted in the period 2008–2009, as the number of articles increased from 31 to 52. Starting from that period, the research area on bankruptcy prediction has increased, which is quite in line with the results obtained by Prado *et al.* (2016). Regarding the number of articles published, the most striking point was recorded during 2016 and 2020, reaching 102 articles and 92 for each year, respectively. This shows how intensely the academic research is debating the theme, possibly in response to the world economy's different events, such as the great financial crisis of 2008 and the global health crisis caused by the COVID-19 pandemic.

In the following section, the data and methods will be presented. First, we introduce the research design for data collection. Next, we exploit some mapping approaches to visualize the bibliometric analysis and the results of a systematic review to obtain a complete view of the research on bankruptcy prediction models.

2.1 *Research design*

As discussed in the previous section, this study aims to provide comprehensive research on predictive bankruptcy methodologies, investigate the

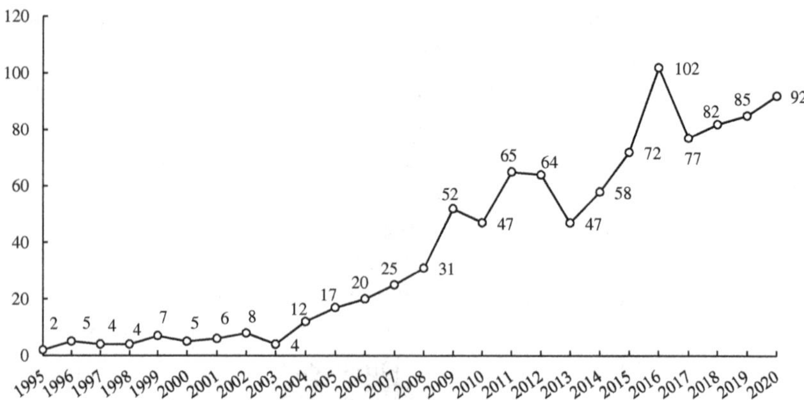

Fig. 1: The number of publications on prediction bankruptcy during the period 1995–2020.

field's evolution, propose a conceptual framework and provide a preview of upcoming trends and future perspectives. For this reason, a systematic review combining bibliometric analysis and content analysis, which helps to capture relevant information more accurately, was adopted in this analysis. Hence, this work can be classified as descriptive with the technique of bibliometrics to develop a conceptual framework that extends previous research and presents future research perspectives.

In this study, the research approach mainly encompasses a literature search, data collection and selection, a descriptive bibliometric analysis of articles, and a content analysis of recent highly cited papers. The study framework of this literature review is illustrated in Figure 2.

2.2 *Data collection*

The collection of data was completed through several procedures, consisting of keyword identification and query searching within the selected database. We began by identifying the keywords to be considered, seeking to identify the core topics on bankruptcy prediction. Researchers use different terms to refer to bankruptcy and prediction methods. This was a crucial step, as the involvement or elimination of a single keyword could lead to a larger or smaller initial set of contributions. We considered a series of keyword combinations used as search criteria to identify international academic articles related to the TITLE and TOPIC search. The following main terminologies were used in the search engine: "bankruptcy prediction", "corporate bankruptcy", "business failure" and "financial distress", which may be perceived as different concepts but have the common characteristic to predict the occurrence of failure over

Fig. 2: Research design of the systematic review study.

time using explanatory variables of the business and by applying various methods.

2.3 *Data selection*

Several bibliographic databases were used for the collection of the studies in this research, such as Google Scholar, Scopus and Web of Science. VOSviewer 1.6.16 supports several types of files, whether bibliographic database files like Web of Science, Scopus, Dimensions, and PubMed; or reference manager files, for example RIS, EndNote and RefWorks. Therefore, the software's technical characteristics led us to combine only those options mentioned above. We chose the Scopus and Web of Science (WOS) databases because they includes a wider range of journals, and many studies have compared major databases and concluded that WOS and Scopus are interchangeable and produce similar results for bibliometric analyses (Campbell, *et al.* 2009; Alakangas, *et al.* 2016).

A Boolean search was also used to identify the publications by running a search query for the titles of the papers. We searched simultaneously for "Bankruptcy prediction method*" OR "Financial failure*" OR "Financial distress*" AND "Insolvency*" OR "Default prediction*" OR "Failure Method*". We included the asterisk (*) because it implies that the search contained a variety of search variants. We limited our search to journal articles, thus excluding conference proceedings and other documents (Rodriguez, *et al.* 2004).

The first selection was carried out by combining a large selection of publications related to business failure prediction models, including different research areas such as "Business Economics", "Engineering", "Computer Science", "Mathematics" and "Social Sciences". In total, 993 documents met the first selection criteria.

After collecting the initial research results, a more in-depth examination was performed to eliminate some articles that do not present significant research for the prediction of business failures but were considered as a process of analysis. Hence, in-depth reading and review of 103 selected documents from Scopus and Web of Science were selected, published between 1997 and 2019, to describe precisely the methods adopted, to ensure the accuracy and reliability of the results, and provide a better understanding of the development and the state-of-the-art of bankruptcy prediction methodologies.

The final articles are gathered from over 35 scientific journals, which are related to information systems, operation research, econometrics, finance, accounting, economics, innovation and entrepreneurship, and general management fields. Table 1 highlights the list of the top 10 journal sources in our selection. As the table shows, most of the papers are from the *Review of Quantitative Finance and Accounting, the Journal of Banking and Finance* and *the Journal of Business Finance & Accounting.* All the publications come from journals belonging to business, finance and accounting studies (*Journal of Business Research, Decision Support Systems, Journal of Operational Research Society, Omega, Computers & Operations Research, Journal of Risk & Insurance, The British Accounting Review*).

3. Results and Findings: Bibliometric and Network Analysis

3.1 *Keyword analysis*

The keyword network map was created to find the major research themes. A co-occurrence was selected as the type of analysis to obtain this map, all keywords as the unit of study and fractional counting as the calculation method. The total number of keywords was 2,143, which was excessive to be included on a map. Therefore, a threshold of five occurrences was

Table 1: Top 10 journals selected.

Journals	**Number of Articles**
Journal of Banking and Finance	10
Review of Quantitative Finance and Accounting	10
Journal of Business Finance & Accounting	8
Journal of Business Research	7
Decision Support Systems	7
Journal of Operational Research Society	6
Omega	6
Computers & Operations Research	5
Journal of Risk & Insurance	3
The British Accounting Review	2

set, which 230 keywords met. The normalization method was fractionalization, and the visualization weight was occurrences.

Due to the different ways in which authors describe a term as plural or singular, the same expressed and written text may be counted separately. Numerous publications have appeared in the literature during the last few decades, the most frequent keywords: “bankruptcy prediction”, “financial ratios”, “discriminant analysis”, and “neural networks” had the highest occurrence, total link strength and largest size. The biggest node, which represents the bankruptcy prediction, displays thick lines (i.e. strong connections) which rely on other terms.

Figure 3 shows the main keywords that were used in the literature reviews. The closeness of two terms and the thickness of the lines connecting them show the frequency of their co-occurrence as keywords. The frequency of its occurrence determines the size of a node as a keyword. Other keywords with high occurrence were “support vector machine”, “macroeconomic” and “SMEs.” To avoid repeating tags, VOSviewer does not display items close to a big title in the static image of the map, which prevents specific phrases from being displayed. Therefore, these recurring keywords that traverse the entire field without adding additional information were removed from the visualization to simplify it and reveal the structure of the area in the space.

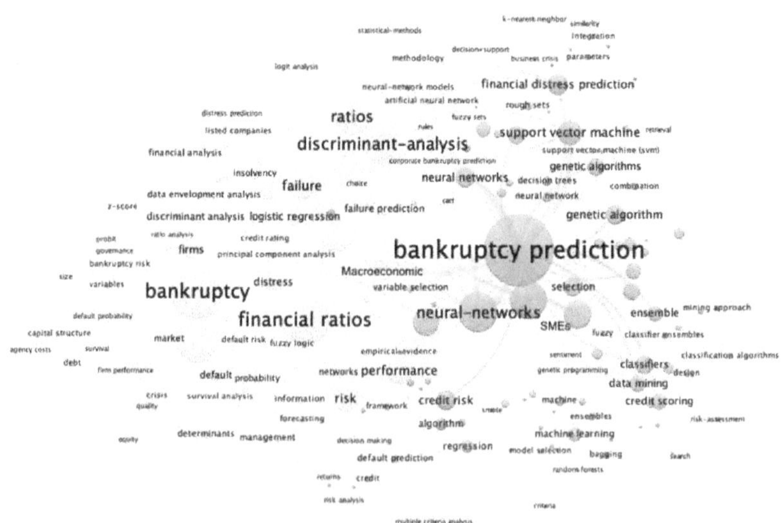

Fig. 3: Keyword co-occurrence map.

3.2 *Co-authorship/Co-citation analysis*

In this subsection, we explore the ability to cooperate and connect researchers' work using different methods in the field of bankruptcy prediction. The VOSViewer software was used to build a network of individual co-authors. For illustration shown in Figure 4 covers author with at least five publications (35 authors out of 220), with the thickness of the connections indicating the strength of the relations between the authors. The colors represent the number of citation indexes; the yellow color means that the author has an average of more than 40 citation indexes. In other words, for each of the 35 authors, the total strength of the bibliographic linkage with other authors will be calculated, and the authors with the highest total linkage strength are selected. The distance between two nodes shows the strength of the relationship, i.e. when two nodes are closer to each other, they tend to have a strong relationship. Bigger nodes represent authors who have a higher importance in terms of citations and publications.

According to Figure 4, four colors differentiate each author according to the average number of citations. The most important nodes are represented by the yellow and green colors, which have the highest citation weight and total link strength, varying between 30 and 40. The other authors have a significantly weaker citation and publication weight and fewer collaborative links. We also notice the high concentration in the network of co-authors connected with Li and Sun and a considerable difference in terms of total link strength compared to the rest of the authors.

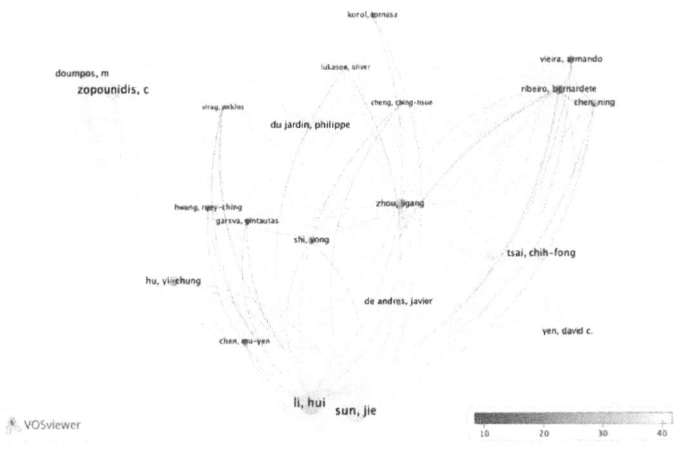

Fig. 4: Illustration of co-authorship map.

3.3 *Country citation analysis*

In this study, a citation analysis by country was conducted as it reflects the collaboration between nations and the most influential countries in a particular research area (Zeng, *et al.*, 2018). Figure 5 shows an overlay visualization map of the citation network by country. The map covers 41 countries with at least five papers. The colors in this visualization represent that average publication year for all papers from a given country, with yellow colors indicating more recent years.

As illustrated in Fig. 5, the size of a node depends on the number of publications. In this map, several large nodes indicate the countries with the largest number of publications and the largest number of total links in this bankruptcy prediction domain: China and the US. However, South Korea is not shown as the largest node on the map even though it has the highest total linkage capacity for maximum connection and collaboration with various countries and regions in different continents.

In terms of an average year of publication, shown in Fig. 5, the yellow color indicates that the Czech Republic, Slovakia, Scotland, Vietnam, and Sweden, have a high volume of publications after 2016, evidence that researchers from these countries have shown increasing interest in this research topic in recent years. Greece and Canada in blue color show a peak of publications before the year 2012, revealing their significant historical contribution and importance in this field. The increase in the number of publications during this year is mainly explained by what happened after the financial crisis of 2008.

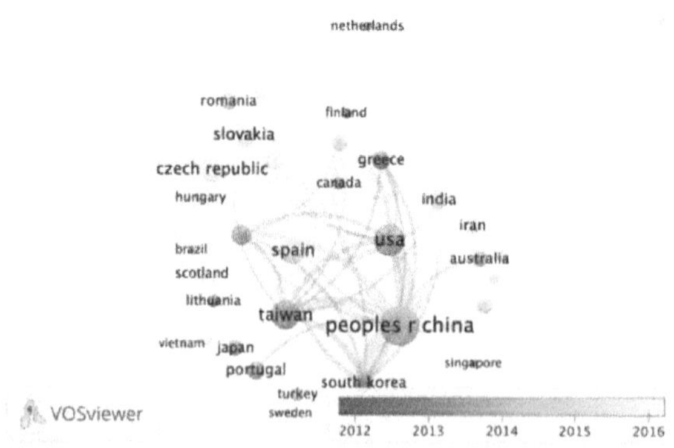

Fig. 5: Country map based on publications.

3.4 *Research area analysis*

After reviewing many studies published between 1997 and 2019, several statistical and intelligent models were applied to overcome bankruptcy prediction challenges in different sectors, including manufacturing and industrial companies, banks, etc. According to full set of all 993 articles published from 1997 to 2019, the authors elaborated several models dealing with different research areas: business economics, engineering, computer science, etc. (see Table 2).

Table 2: Overview of the research area in different articles.

Research Areas	Record Count	% of Full Sample
Business Economics	480	48.34
Computer Science	400	40.28
Operations research management science	202	20.34
Engineering	198	19.94
Mathematics	63	6.34
Mathematical Methods in social sciences	31	3.12
Science, technology other topics	26	2.62
Social sciences, other topics	23	2.32
Telecommunications	14	1.41
Automation control systems	13	1.31
Environmental sciences ecology	12	1.21
Educational research	8	0.81
Government law	8	0.81
Public administration	8	0.81
Construction building technology	7	0.71
Information science library science	7	0.71
Physics	6	0.60
Agriculture	4	0.40
Development studies	3	0.30
Neurosciences/Neurology	3	0.30
Robotics	3	0.30
Urban studies	3	0.30
Chemistry	2	0.20

In the following section, we present the results, analysis, and discussion of the systematic review in the summaries of all the articles examined. The results are used to evaluate each model according to specific criteria. The criteria were assessed and discussed in the context of bankruptcy prediction models as variables (e.g. quantitative and qualitative innovative variables).

4. Content Analysis: Discussion and Research Findings of the Systematic Review

4.1 *Description of quantitative methods for bankruptcy prediction*

Different models for predicting bankruptcy have been applied previously (Appendix A). First, the univariate model developed into the multiple discriminant analysis. Then the Logit/Probit regression analysis succeeded it, followed by methods such as the recursive partitioning algorithm and neural networks.

Various researchers have used different parameters to examine and develop models for predicting bankruptcy. However, based on a detailed and comprehensive review of existing and recent studies in this area, nine elements have been identified as the most common and essential for our analysis: country of the sample, year of the sample, industry of firms, the main method adopted, list of variables, test sample, number of firms used in a sample and the accuracy related to the classification of failed firms and non-failed firms.

Many papers on bankruptcy prediction models have used test data accuracy to measure the effectiveness of the models, considering that holdout testing ensures the independence of both training data and testing data. For example, McKee and Greenstein (2000) adopted the recursive partitioning method (RSP) using five groups of training data sets that created decision trees for predicting financial distress and obtained 97% predictive accuracy (Doumpos and Zopounidis, 2002). However, McKee and Greenstein (2000) demonstrated that models could not recognize failed firms correctly in their tests of three bankruptcy prediction methods: Logistic regression, Neural Network and the ID3 algorithm. They showed that the performance of corporate failure prediction models is a function of the balance between each class in the data. In other words, the results of the study showed that the developed model had a higher percentage accuracy than the logit model and the neural network model.

The variable that has been proven significant for bankruptcy in all companies is “net income & ratio of total assets”. These variables were employed by McKee and Greenstein (2000) in their decision tree models to predict bankruptcy.

After the global financial crisis of 2007–2009, which was characterized by a severe restriction of financial market regulation, the use of multiple criteria decision support (MCDM) techniques, which deal with sorting issues in investment analysis, has notably increased (Doumpos and Zopounidis, 2002). For example, in a recent study, Doumpos *et al.* (2017) used an MCDM approach to predict business failures in the energy sector using a large sample from 18 countries. They combined traditional financial characteristics with non-financial qualitative characteristics related to the macroeconomic and business environment to predict financial distress, obtaining significant results.

Other studies have relied on banks’ financial ratios and credit agency ratings (Doumpos, *et al.*, 2020). They have proposed the development of early warning systems to predict bank failures.

Li and Miu (2010a) reported that logistic regression is a superior compared to discriminant analysis, while other studies conclude the opposite. For example, Bardos (1998) obtained better results from discriminant analysis than from the logit model.

In his paper, Shumway (2001) provided three major criticisms of Altman’s (1968) work. The first concerns the time horizon; he argues that single-period models are invalid because a firm’s risk of bankruptcy changes over time and because its health is related to the age and the final financial data. The second criticism concerns the financial condition of the failing firm. Shumway (2001) states that as firms get closer to bankruptcy, their financial situation deteriorates. The final criticism involves the financial ratios used in the analysis. Shumway (2001) argues that several bankruptcy models do not take into consideration several market-related variables, such as market size, stock returns and idiosyncratic risk, which are strongly related to the probability of bankruptcy. In addition, he argues that most of the financial ratios used in previous models have proven to be poor predictors.

In the same context that concerns the last criticism, Du Jardin and Severin (2011) criticize models with very short prediction horizons, noting that prediction rates are often good one year before failure but weak when the horizon is expanded to three years or more.

In recent work, Ciampi *et al.* (2018) highlight the necessity for SMEs to use prediction models based on quantitative predictors other than financial ratios and macroeconomic variables. Using Kohonen map-based trajectories, they notice that the use of variables related to the firm's prior payment behavior improves prediction accuracy, especially for small firms and for a horizon longer than one year.

Some authors, such as Laitinen (1998) and Hensher (2004) have analyzed the use of financial ratios combined with "statistical" variables (mean, standard deviation, variance, logarithm, estimated from financial data). These computations have often been used to standardize data to increase their reliability, mainly when these data characterize companies whose size is not homogeneous and when this size can affect the informational content of traditional ratios.

McGurr and Devaney (1998) applied failure prediction models developed on mixed samples of industries and reported that a failure prediction model developed using firms from one set of industries may not be very accurate in predicting the failure of firms from other industries. Thus, they demonstrated that there is an industry impact in the prediction of failure. Grice and Ingram (2001) also supported the notion that failure prediction studies should use industry-specific samples. The authors concluded that the model developed using only manufacturing samples had significantly higher overall accuracy than the model developed using both manufacturing and non-manufacturing samples.

Similarly, Pendharkar (2005) selected five financial indicators from the *Z*-Score model. Because the bankruptcy prediction performance of neural network (NN) models has often been compared to discriminant analysis and logistic regression, Pendharkar (2002) demonstrated that the performance of NNs was superior to that of statistical methods.

Pendharkar and Nanda (2009) also looked at bankruptcy prediction models by integrating cost-sensitive learning with a genetic algorithm to minimize the total cost of misclassification, which allowed the model to improve the performance of the models with unbalanced samples.

Later, Premachandra (2011) used data envelopment analysis (DEA) as a method for corporate failure prediction. In a similar context, Avkiram and Cai (2014) applied a slacks-based DEA model (SBM). Many studies have estimated DEA efficiency scores of firms using financial accounting variables, e.g. total assets, total liabilities, total sales, employees and cash flows. In contrast, the study of Avkiran and Cai estimated efficiency indicating the ability to improve the efficiency of firms using inputs and outputs defined through market-based variables, e.g. market capitalization, annual stock return, liquid assets, etc.

In addition, Agarwal and Taffler (2008) compared two approaches — the Z-score model and market-based models — and found that each method provides different information about business failures, but neither method replaces the other.

Serrano-Cinca and Guttierrez-Nieto (2013) employed partial least squares discriminant analysis (PLS-DA) to predict the 2008–2011 US banking crisis. They found that the results were similar to those of discriminant analysis and support vector machines. They further noted that PLS-DA has the advantage of not being affected by multicollinearity.

Another paper that applied linear programming was developed by Kwak *et al.* (2012). The authors proposed a multi-criteria linear programming (MCLP) method to predict bankruptcy for Korean firms, using the accounting variables that Altman (1968) and Ohlson (1980). The results of the MCLP approach showed that it performs at the same level as traditional multiple discriminant analysis or logit analysis using only financial data. Furthermore, the overall prediction accuracy of this model is comparable to that of decision trees and support vector machines.

Hensher and Jones (2007) presented a theoretical and econometric basis of advanced models for predicting business failures, like the mixed logit model, the nested logit model, and the error component logit model. These models are considered potentially efficient models due to their statistical and explanatory performance, providing significantly better results than the standard logit models.

Tsenga (2005) proposed a quadratic programming approach that combines the advantages of logit models and an interval regression model. The objective is to improve the accuracy of early identification and incorporate binary response variables into logistic regression. They also reported that it allows the logit model to have better discrimination performance.

4.2 *The use of qualitative information for bankruptcy prediction models*

Several studies have considered the use of non-financial factors in combination with financial data for business failure prediction. For instance,

Lussier and Pfeifer (2001) studied the role of organizational variables for small enterprises and the characteristics of owners; they showed that SEs considerably increase their degree of success when they combine adequate capitalization, control and planning systems, and adequate levels of owner education with skilled and competent entrepreneurs.

Similar variables have also been used in other studies, such as those of Lennox (1999), Beynon and Peel (2001), Becchetti and Sierra (2003), Lee (2004) and Lussier and Halabi (2010). Among others, such studies have considered management efficiency and the characteristics of the managers, the strategy, the market share, the concentration of the clientele, the sector of activity, and the age of the firm. Moreover, macroeconomic data have been used including interest rates, inflation, economic trends, access to financing, and the profitability of the market.

In the endeavor to integrate accounting-based models, Andrikopoulos and Khorasgani (2018) eventually came up with a hybrid default prediction model, combining traditional financial ratios of listed and unlisted SMEs with market information. Likewise, Lee and Yeh (2004) considered the combination of accounting information and corporate governance variables. Using data from Taiwan, they found that ownership concentration may be a relevant factor in reducing the risk of bankruptcy.

From these points discussed below, it can be inferred that a weak corporate governance situation leads to the expropriation of minority shareholders' wealth by major shareholders to gain individual profit and, subsequently, to lower firm valuations and increase the risk of financial distress.

Fich and Slezak (2008) state that higher ownership concentration has an important role in reducing the probability of firm failure and should have a smaller effect on the risk or probability of bankruptcy in countries with stronger organizational performance. On the other hand, Cheng *et al.* (2010) find that good corporate governance has a positive effect on stock returns. Wilson (2013) found that stock market information is an important determinant of bank failure because it incorporates information about future cash flows, increases the timeline, and allows us to measure volatility.

4.3 *Exploring the potential of audit variables for bankruptcy prediction failures*

Several studies have examined the usefulness of audit reports and variables for the prediction of bankruptcies. For instance, Lennox (1999) analyzed the accuracy and informational value of audit reports when identifying failing firms in the UK, and found that audit reports are reliable predictors of bankruptcy.

For Jeffrey *et al.* (2000), auditors have the responsibility to assess the continuity of each company as part of the audit, and they must decide whether the company is able to continue its operation. Hence, they consider the audit report an early warning indicators of failure risk. In their work, they conclude that although auditors are not able to justify the legal proceedings, they could detect the worst possible scenarios, giving qualified opinions to companies that are in default and whose prospects are uncertain.

4.4 *The role of banking data in bankruptcy prediction analysis*

Some previous studies have used bank-specific determinants of financial distress of financial institutions and firms. Among these studies, Bongini *et al.* (2000) consider variables such as loan loss reserves to capital, loan growth, net interest income, and loans to borrowings are essential indicators for predicting banking distress. They compared different sets of indicators and regulatory measures. Their findings suggest that there is no unique approach and that a variety of financial indicator sets can be used simultaneously, depending on the availability of appropriate and reliable data. Wong (2010) focused on the predictive power of bank-level indicators based on the asset side of the bank balance sheet, such as capital adequacy, liquidity, inflation, the growth rate of gross domestic product and default risk.

Bongini *et al.* (2002) used stock market data to measure bank fragility. They showed how government intervention, encouraged by political connections, helps to save troubled banks, and concluded that during the 1997 East Asian crisis, traditional CAMELS-type[1] indicators predicted the eventual distress and closure of financial institutions.

The results of Agarwal and Taffler's (2007) suggest that in terms of predictive accuracy, there is a relatively small difference between market-based and accounting models. They state that bankruptcy refers to the re-creation of a new type of capital that may include the devaluation of

[1]Capital adequacy, assets' quality, management efficiency, earning capacity, liquidity.

some loans and converting some bonds into equity. It also refers to the government's intervention or when creditors/suppliers decide to disrupt the business operations and transactions of the firms. All these elements can serve as indicators that a company will fail, which leads to corrective or alternative measures for the companies.

In the United States, Morrison (2007) found that the presence of secured creditors has an impact on the outcome of the bankruptcy insofar as the greater the number of secured creditors, the lower the likelihood of reorganizing the debtor, particularly in bankruptcy systems where reorganization requires the approval of creditors.

4.5 *The potential of intelligent models*

During the decades following the work of Altman (1968) on the use of discriminant analysis for bankruptcy prediction, this field has been dominated by statistical approaches. More recently, the computational and algorithmic advances, together with the widespread availability of big data, have motivated the use of artificial intelligence approaches, mainly based on the framework of machine learning. In this context, methods like neural networks (NNs), decision tree algorithms, support vector machines (SVMs) and ensembles have become popular tools for building powerful models for predicting corporate failures.

The studies of West *et al.* (2005) and Alfaro *et al.* (2008) used NNs with ensemble algorithms such as bagging and boosting and found that the ensemble NNs models had higher generalization capability than the single model. Boosting and bagging are the two most common ensemble methods that apply a single learning algorithm to different versions of a given data set.

Sun *et al.* (2014a) proposed an ensemble for imbalanced credit evaluation combining SMOTE with the bagging algorithm using a SVM classifier. They proved that it outperforms the SMOTE-SVM ensemble method and the dataset partition-based ensemble.

Furthermore, Barboza *et al.* (2017) tested models to predict bankruptcy and compared their performance with the results of linear and nonlinear SVMs, as well as discriminant analysis, logistic regression, NNs and ensembles, using data from 1985 to 2013 on North American firms. Comparing the best models, the ensemble with the random forest algorithm provided the best results, reaching an accuracy rate of 87%, whereas logistic regression and discriminant analysis had the worst performance.

Olson *et al.* (2012) used logistic regression, NNs, SVMs, and decision trees to predict bankruptcies. They noted that analysts face a trade-off between model accuracy, model transparency and transportability. For instance, to increase the model's transportability or apply it to new data sets and observations, the level of accuracy will decrease. NNs have also been considered in studies such as those of Brockett *et al.* (1997) and Youn and Gu (2010a).

To obtain linear functions without statistical constraints and the appropriate discriminant criteria, Varetto (1998) applied a genetic algorithm (GA). However, its performance in predicting financial distress was not as efficient as that of discriminant analysis.

Despite the success of machine learning models, a common issue of criticism is that complex models cannot identify and explain the determinants of a firm's performance and its risk of failure. Recently, the main goal of scholars and practitioners in this area has been to address this weakness and make machine learning models more transparent and comprehensible.

5. Conclusion

Predicting bankruptcy is one of the most critical problems in business decision-making. The importance of predicting the economic failure of a company leads researchers to find a model that can act as early warning systems for the identification of weaknesses and risks that can lead to corporate failure. Starting from the traditional bankruptcy prediction models (e.g. discriminant analysis, logistic regression), new models are constantly appearing that are likely to be the most appropriate to predict the bankruptcy of companies evolving in a specific economic and financial environment.

The framework presented in this study provides a basis for understanding the status and the emerging trends in this area. More specifically, the bibliographic analysis enables the investigation of the theoretical underpinnings, network structure and thematic evolution in this research area. Moreover, the analysis revealed the theoretical foundations of the field through scientific maps and showed the development of key themes in the research area across countries.

Of course, a bibliometric analysis, such as the one presented in this paper is its limitations too. For example, such an analysis does not reflect the content and the way authors refer to other studies, so the bibliometric analysis cannot capture the full description of the source structure in detail. Nevertheless, despite focusing on the major points of the results in each article, the presented analysis cover several models and could serve as a reference for future research on the subject.

As the area of corporate failure continues to evolve, many opportunities exist to develop improved analytical models based on new various new predictive factors. The incorporation of new information in bankruptcy prediction models is particularly important considering the rapidly evolving economic situation related to the global health crisis caused by COVID-19 and the turmoil caused due to the recent crises in the global supply chain and the energy sector.

Appendix A: In the following appendix we included all the papers considered and reviewed in-depth in the present study.

Authors	Year of Publication	Country Sample	Main Method
Agarwal and Taffler	2007	UK	Logistic regression
Agarwal and Taffler	2008	UK	Logistic regression
Alexeev and Kim	2012	Korea, US	—
Alfaro *et al.*	2008	Spain	Adaboost
Andrikopoulos and Khorasgani	2018	UK	Merton model
Astebro and Winter	2012	USA	Multinomial model
Avishur and Tsoref	2001	Israel	—
Baidoun *et al.*	2018	Palestine	Logistic regression
Balcaen and Ooghe	2006	—	Statistical methods
Barbozaa *et al.*	2017	North America	Various machine learning models
Bardos	1998	France	Discriminant analysis
Barniv and Mcdonald	1999	—	Logit, Probit models
Barniv *et al.*	2002	USA	Logistic regression
Barniv *et al.*	2000	—	
Beaver and McNichols	2010		
Becchetti and Sierra	2003	Italy	Logit model, stochastic frontier approach
Beynon and Peel	2001	UK	Rough sets
Bhimani *et al.*	2010	Portugal	Logistic regression
Bongini *et al.*	2002	East Asian countries	Logistic regression
Brockett *et al.*	1997	USA	Neural network
Brockett *et al.*	2006	USA	ANN method
Bruneau *et al.*	2012	France	Vector autoregression
Casterella *et al.*	2000	USA	Logistic regression
Cecchini *et al.*	2010	USA	SVM
Charalambous *et al.*	2000	USA	Neural network

(*Continued*)

Appendix A: (*Continued*)

Authors	Year of Publication	Country Sample	Main Method
Charitou *et al.*	2013	USA	Black–Scholes–Merton model
Chen	2014	Taiwan	Particle swarm optimization, SVM
Chen *et al.*	2011a	Poland	Nearest neighbor, particle swarm optimization
Cheng *et al.*	2010	USA	Hazard model
Ciampi *et al.*	2018	Italy	Logistic regression, hazard models, Kohonen maps
Cipollini and Fiordelisi	2012	EU	Probit model
Cole and Gunther	1998	USA	Probit model
Cole and Gunther	2013	USA	Partial least square discriminant analysis
Cummins *et al.*	1999	USA	Logistic regression
Demyanyk and Hasan	2009	USA	Neural network
Dewaelheyns and Van Hulle	2006	Belgium	Logistic regression
Dierkes *et al.*	2013	Germany	—
Dionne and Laajimi	2009	Canada	Merton model
Doumpos *et al.*	2017	18 EU Countries	MCDA
Du Jardin	2010	France	Neural network
Fich and Slezak	2008	—	Hazard model
Fiordelisi and Marec	2013	Italy	Discrete-time survival model
Foste *et al.*	1998	USA	Logistic regression
Gadenne and Iselin	2000	—	Statistical models
Grice and Dugan	2001	—	Logistic regression

Appendix A: (*Continued*)

Authors	**Year of Publication**	**Country Sample**	**Main Method**
Grice and Ingram	2001	—	Discriminant analysis
Gupta *et al.*	2014	UK	Hazard model
Gyimah *et al.*	2019	Ghana	Logistic regression
Hensher and Jones	2007	—	Mixed logit model
Hernandez Tinoco and Wilson	2013	UK	Logistic regression
Hwang	2012	—	Hazard model
Hwang and Chu	2013	—	Hazard model
Jardin and Severin	2011	France	Kohonen map
Jones and Hensher	2004	—	Multinomial logit analysis
Kahya and Theodossiou	1999	—	Discriminant analysis
Kemal Avkiran and Cai	2014	—	Data envelopment analysis
Kim and Kwok	2009	—	Logistic regression
Kim and Nabar	2007	—	—
Kolari *et al.*	2018	EU	Adaboost
Kwak *et al.*	2012	Korea	Multiple-criteria linear programming
Laitinen and Laitinen	1998	Finland	Logistic regression
Lee and Urrutia	1996	USA	Hybrid system
Lee and Yeh	2004	Taiwan	Logistic regression
Lee *et al.*	1996	Korea	Neural network
Lennox	1999	UK	Probit analysis
Li and Miu	2010	—	Binary quantile regression
Li and Sun	2011	China	Discriminant analysis
Li *et al.*	2011	China	MCDA
Lin *et al.*	2012	UK	Binary logistic model

(*Continued*)

Appendix A: (*Continued*)

Authors	Year of Publication	Country Sample	Main Method
Loffler and Maurer	2011	US	Hazard Model
Lussier and Halabi	2010	Chile	Logistic regression
Lussier and Pfeifer	2001	Croatia	Logistic regression
Lyandres and Zhdanov	2013	USA	Discriminant analysis
McGurr and DeVaney	1998	—	Mix of five models
Mckee and Greenstein	2000	—	Various machine learning models
Morrison	2007	USA	Hazard model
Nasir *et al.*	2000	UK	Neural network
Neophytou and Molinero	2004	UK	Multidimensional scaling methodology
Olson *et al.*	2012	USA	Various machine learning models
Peat	2007	—	Hazard model
Pendharkar	2002	—	Data envelopment analysis
Pendharkar	2005	—	Neural network
Pendharkar and Nanda	2009	—	Neural network
Powell and Yawson	2007	UK	Logistic regression
Premachandra *et al.*	2011	USA	Data envelopment analysis
Qi *et al.*	2014	—	—
Reynolds *et al.*	2002	Thailand	Probit, logit models
Richardson *et al.*	1998	—	Statistical models
Salcedo-Sanza *et al.*	2005	—	Genetic programming
Sharma and Stevenson	1997	Australia	—
Shumway	2001	US	Logistic regression
Sun	2006	—	Hazard model

Appendix A: (*Continued*)

Authors	**Year of Publication**	**Country Sample**	**Main Method**
Sun and Li	2009	China	Case-based reasoning
Sun and Shenoy	2007	USA	Bayesian network
Sun *et al.*	2014	—	SVM
Tseng and Lin	2005	UK	Quadratic interval logit model
Varetto	1998	—	Genetic algorithm, discriminant analysis
West *et al.*	2005	Australia, Germany	Neural network
Wilson and Altanlar	2014	UK	Hazard models
Yang *et al.*	1999	USA	Neural network
Youn and Gu	2010	—	Logistic regression, neural network
Zopounidis and Doumpos	1999	Greece	Rough sets

References

Agarwal, V. and Taffler, R.J. (2007). Twenty-five years of the Taffler z-score model: Does it really have predictive ability? *Accounting and Business Research*, 37(4), 285–300.

Agarwal, V. and Taffler, R. (2008). Comparing the performance of market-based and accounting-based bankruptcy prediction models, *Journal of Banking and Finance*, 32(8), 1541–1551.

Alakangas, S. and Harzing, A.W. (2016). Google scholar, scopus and the web of science: A longitudinal and cross-disciplinary comparison, *Scientometrics*, 106, 787–804.

Alfaro, E., GarcIa, N., Gamez, M. and Elizondo, D. (2008). Bankruptcy forecasting: An empirical comparison of AdaBoost and neural networks, *Decision Support Systems*, 45(1), 110–122.

Altman, E. (1968). Financial ratios, discriminant analysis and the prediction of corporate bankruptcy, *Journal of Finance*, 589–609.

Andrikopoulos, P. and Khorasgani, A. (2018). Predicting unlisted SMEs' default: Incorporating market information on accounting-based models for improved accuracy, *British Accounting Review*, 559–573.

Åstebro, T. and Winter, J.K. (2012). More than a dummy: The probability of failure, survival and acquisition of firms in financial distress, *European Management Review*, 9(1), 1–17.

Avkiran, N.K. and Cai, L. (2014). Identifying distress among banks prior to a major crisis using non-oriented super-SBM, *Annals of Operations Research*, 217(1), 31–53.

Balcaen, S. and Ooghe, H. (2006). 35 years of studies on business failure: An overview of the classic statistical methodologies and their related problems, *British Accounting Review*, 38(1), 63–93.

Barboza, F., Kimura, H. and Altman, E. (2017). Machine learning models and bankruptcy prediction, *Expert Systems with Applications*, 83, 405–417.

Bardos, M. (1998). Detecting the risk of company failure at the Banque de France, *Journal of Banking and Finance*, 22(10–11), 1405–1419.

Barniv, R. and Mcdonald, J.B. (1999). Review of categorical models for classification issues in accounting and finance, *Review of Quantitative Finance and Accounting*, 13(1), 39–62.

Barniv, R., Agarwal, A. and Leach, R. (2002). Predicting bankruptcy resolution, *Journal of Business Finance and Accounting*, 29(3–4), 497–520.

Barniv, R., Mehrez, A. and Douglas, K. (2000). Confidence intervals for controlling the probability of bankruptcy, *Omega*, 28(5), 555–565.

Beaver, W.H. (1966). Financial ratios as predictors of failure, *Journal of Accounting Research*, 4, 71–111.

Becchetti, L. and Sierra, J. (2003). Bankruptcy risk and productive efficiency in manufacturing firms, *Journal of Banking and Finance*, 27(11), 2099–2120.

Beynon, M.J. and Peel, M.J. (2001). Variable precision rough set theory and data discretisation: An application to corporate failure prediction, *Omega*, 29(6), 561–576.

Bhimani, A., Gulamhussen, M.A. and Lopes, S.D.R. (2010). Accounting and non-accounting determinants of default: An analysis of privately-held firms, *Journal of Accounting and Public Policy*, 29(6), 517–532.

Bongini, P., Ferri, G. and Kang, T.S. (2000). *Financial Intermediary Distress in the Republic of Korea: Small is Beautiful?* World Bank Publications: Washington, D.C.

Bongini, P., Laeven, L. and Majnoni, G. (2002). How good is the market at assessing bank fragility? A horse race between different indicators, *Journal of Banking and Finance*, 26(5), 1011–1028.

Broadus, R.N. (1987). Early approaches to bibliometrics, *Journal of the American Society for Information Science*, 38, 127–129.

Brockett, P.L., Cooper, W.W., Golden, L.L. and Xia, X. (1997). A case study in applying neural networks to predicting insolvency for property and casualty insurers, *Journal of the Operational Research Society*, 48(12), 1153–1162.

Bruneau, C., de Bandt, O. and El Amri, W. (2012). Macroeconomic fluctuations and corporate financial fragility, *Journal of Financial Stability*, 8(4), 219–235.

Campbell, A. and Lindsay, D. (1996). A chaos approach to bankruptcy prediction, *Journal of Applied Business Research*, 12(4), 1–9.

Cecchini, M., Aytug, H., Koehler, G.J. and Pathak, P. (2010). Making words work: Using financial text as a predictor of financial events, *Decision Support Systems*, 50(1), 164–175.

Charalambous, C., Charitou, A. and Kaourou, F. (2000). Comparative analysis of artificial neural network models: Application in bankruptcy prediction, *Annals of Operations Research*, 99, 403–425.

Charitou, A., Neophytou, E. and Charalambous, C. (2004). Predicting corporate failure: Empirical evidence for the UK, *European Accounting Review*, 13, 465–497.

Chen, Yang, Wang, Liu, Xu, Wang and Liu, Da-You (2011). A novel bankruptcy prediction model based on an adaptive fuzzy k-nearest neighbor method, *Knowledge-based Systems*, 24(8), 1348–1359.

Cheng, K.F., Chu, C.K. and Hwang, R.-C. (2010). Predicting bankruptcy using the discrete-time semiparametric hazard model, *Quantitative Finance*, 10(9), 1055–1066.

Ciampi, F., Cillo, V. and Fiano, F. (2018). Combining Kohonen maps and prior payment behavior for small enterprise default prediction, *Small Business Economics*, 54(4), 1007–1039.

Costa, D.F. (2018). Behavioral economics and behavioral finance: A bibliometric analysis of the scientific fields, *Journal of Economic Surveys*, 33(1), 3–24.

Cummins, J.D., Grace, M.F. and Phillips, R.D. (1999). Regulatory solvency prediction in property-liability insurance: Risk-based capital, audit ratios, and cash flow simulation, *Journal of Risk and Insurance*, 66(3), 417–458.

Hensher, David A. and Jones, Stewart (2007). Forecasting corporate bankruptcy: Optimizing the performance of the mixed logit model, *Abacus*, 43(3), 241–264.

Demyanyk, Y. and Hasan, I. (2010). Financial crises and bank failures: A review of prediction methods, *Omega*, 38(5), 315–324.

Dionne, G. and Laajimi, S. (2012). On the determinants of the implied default barrier, *Journal of Empirical Finance*, 19(3), 395–408.

Doumpos, M.A. (2017). Corporate failure prediction in the European energy sector: A multicriteria approach and the effect of country characteristics, *European Journal of Operational Research*, 347–360.

Doumpos, M. and Zopounidis, C. (2002). *Multicriteria Decision Aid Classification Methods.* Springer: New York Inc.

Du Jardin, P. and Severin, E. (2011). Predicting corporate bankruptcy using a self-organizing map: An empirical study to improve the forecasting horizon of a financial failure model, *Decision Support Systems*, 51(3), 701–711.

Elango, B. (2019). A bibliometric analysis of franchising research (1988–2017), *Journal of Entrepreneurship*, 223–249.

Fich, E.M. and Slezak, S.L. (2008). Can corporate governance save distressed firms from bankruptcy? An empirical analysis, *Review of Quantitative Finance and Accounting*, 30(2), 225–251.

Fitzpatrick, P.J. (1932). A comparison of the ratios of successful industrial enterprises with those of failed companies, *Certified Public Accountant*, 12, 656–662.

Manthoulis, G., Doumpos, M., Zopounidis, C. and Galariotis, E. (2020). An ordinal classification framework for bank failure prediction: Methodology and empirical evidence for US banks, *European Journal of Operational Research*, 282, 786–801.

Grice, J.S. and Ingram, R.W. (2001). Tests of the generalizability of Altman's bankruptcy prediction model, *Journal of Business Research*, 54(1), 53–61.

Gupta, J., Gregoriou, A. and Healy, J. (2014). Forecasting bankruptcy for SMEs using hazard function: To what extent does size matter? *Review of Quantitative Finance and Accounting*, 45(4), 845–869.

Gyimah, P., Appiah, K.O. and Lussier, R.N. (2019). Success versus failure prediction model for small businesses in Ghana, *Journal of African Business*, 21(2), 215–234.

Hosaka, T. (2019). Bankruptcy prediction using imaged financial ratios and convolutional neural networks, *Expert Systems with Applications*, 117, 287–299.

Hwang, R.-C. (2012). A varying-coefficient default model, *International Journal of Forecasting*, 28(3), 675–688.

Jeffrey, R., Casterella, J.R., Lewis, B.L. and Walker, P.L. (2000). Modeling the audit opinions issued to bankrupt companies: A two-stage empirical analysis, *Decision Sciences*, 31(2), 507–530.

Jones, S. and Hensher, D.A. (2007). Modelling corporate failure: A multinomial nested logit analysis for unordered outcomes, *British Accounting Review*, 39(1), 89–107.

Kahya, E. and Theodossiou, P. (1999). Predicting corporate financial distress: A time-series CUSUM methodology, *Review of Quantitative Finance and Accounting*, 13(4), 323–345.

Kim, Y. and Nabar, S. (2007). Bankruptcy probability changes and the differential informativeness of bond upgrades and downgrades, *Journal of Banking and Finance*, 31(12), 3843–3861.

Kwak, W., Shi, Y. and Kou, G. (2012). Bankruptcy prediction for Korean firms after the 1997 financial crisis: Using a multiple criteria linear programming data mining approach, *Review of Quantitative Finance and Accounting*, 38(4), 441–453.

Laitinen, E.K. and Laitinen, T. (1998). Cash management behavior and failure prediction, *Journal of Business Finance and Accounting*, 25(7–8), 893–919.

Lee, K.C., Han, I. and Kwon, Y. (1996). Hybrid neural network models for bankruptcy predictions, *Decision Support Systems*, 18(1), 63–72.

Lee, T.-S. and Yeh, Y.-H. (2004). Corporate governance and financial distress: Evidence from Taiwan, *Corporate Governance*, 12(3), 378–388.

Lennox, C.S. (1999). The accuracy and incremental information content of audit reports in predicting bankruptcy, *Journal of Business, Finance and Accounting*, 26, 757–778.

Li, H., Adeli, H., Sun, J. and Han, J.-G. (2011b). Hybridizing principles of TOPSIS with case-based reasoning for business failure prediction, *Computers and Operations Research*, 38(2), 409–419.

Li, M.Y.L. and Miu, P. (2010a). A hybrid bankruptcy prediction model with dynamic loadings on accounting-ratio-based and market-based information: A binary quantile regression approach, *Journal of Empirical Finance*, 17(4), 818–833.

Lin, S.-M., Ansell, J. and Andreeva, G. (2012). Predicting default of a small business using different definitions of financial distress, *Journal of the Operational Research Society*, 63(4), 539–548.

Loffler, G. and Maurer, A. (2011). Incorporating the dynamics of leverage into default prediction, *Journal of Banking and Finance*, 35(12), 3351–3361.

Lussier, R.N. and Halabi, C.E. (2010). A three-country comparison of the business success versus failure prediction model, *Journal of Small Business Management*, 48(3), 360–377.

Lussier, R.N. and Pfeifer, S. (2001). A crossnational prediction model for business success, *Journal of Small Business Management*, 39(3), 228–239.

McGurr, P.T. and Devaney, S.A. (1998). Predicting business failure of retail firms: An analysis using mixed industry models, *Journal of Business Research*, 43(3), 169–176.

McKee, T.E. and Greenstein, M. (2000). Predicting bankruptcy using recursive partitioning and a realistically proportioned data set, *Journal of Forecasting*, 19(3), 201–217.

Morrison, E.R. (2007). Bankruptcy decision making: An empirical study of continuation bias in small-business Bankruptcies, *Journal of Law and Economics*, 50(2), 381–419.

Najmi, A., Rashidi, T.H., Abbasi, A. and Travis Waller, S. (2016). Reviewing the transport domain: An evolutionary bibliometrics and network analysis, *Scientometrics*, 843–865.

Noga, T.J. and Schnader, A.L. (2013). Book-tax differences as an indicator of financial distress, *Accounting Horizons*, 27(3), 469–489.

Ohlson, J.A. (1980). Financial ratios and the probabilistic prediction of bankruptcy, *Journal of Accounting Research*, 18(1), 109–131.

Olson, D.L., Delen, D. and Meng, Y. (2012). Comparative analysis of data mining methods for bankruptcy prediction, *Decision Support Systems*, 52(2), 464–473.

Peat, M. (2007). Factors affecting the probability of bankruptcy: A managerial decision based approach, *Abacus*, 43(3), 303–324.

Pendharkar, P.C. (2002). A potential use of data envelopment analysis for the inverse classification problem, *Omega*, 30(3), 243–248.

Pendharkar, P.C. (2005). A threshold-varying artificial neural network approach for classification and its application to bankruptcy prediction problem, *Computers and Operations Research*, 32(10), 2561–2582.

Pendharkar, P.C. and Nanda, S. (2006). A misclassification cost-minimizing evolutionary-neural classification approach, *Naval Research Logistics*, 53(5), 432–447.

Powell, R. and Yawson, A. (2007). Are corporate restructuring events driven by common factors? Implications for takeover prediction, *Journal of Business Finance and Accounting*, 34(7–8), 1169–1192.

Prado, J.W., Castro Alcântara, V., Melo Carvalho, F., Vieira, K.C., Machado, L.K. and Tonelli, D.F. (2016). Multivariate analysis of credit risk and bankruptcy research data: A bibliometric study involving different knowledge fields (1968–2014), *Scientometrics*, 106(3), 1007–1029.

Premachandra, I.M., Chen, Y. and Watson, J. (2011). DEA as a tool for predicting corporate failure and success: A case of bankruptcy assessment, *Omega*, 39(6), 620–626.

Qi, M., Zhang, X. and Zhao, X. (2014). Unobserved systematic risk factor and default prediction, *Journal of Banking and Finance*, 49, 216–227.

Richardson, F.M., Kane, G.D. and Lobingier, P. (1998). The impact of recession on the prediction of corporate failure, *Journal of Business Finance and Accounting*, 25(1–2), 167–186.

Serrano-Cinca, C. and Gutierrez-Nieto, B. (2013). Partial least square discriminant analysis for bankruptcy prediction, *Decision Support Systems*, 54(3), 1245–1255.

Shumway, T. (2001). Forecasting bankruptcy more accurately: A simple hazard model, *Journal of Business*, 74(1), 101–124.

Sun, J., Shang, Z. and Li, H. (2014a). Imbalance-oriented SVM methods for financial distress prediction: A comparative study among the new SB-SVM-ensemble method and traditional methods, *Journal of the Operational Research Society*, 65(12), 1905–1919.

Tsenga, Fang-M. and Lin, L. (2005). A quadratic interval logit model for forecasting bankruptcy, *Omega*, 33(1), 85–91.

Tyler, S. (2001). Bankruptcy more accurately: A simple Hazard Model, *The Journal of Business*, 101–124.

Varetto, F. (1998). Genetic algorithms applications in the analysis of insolvency risk, *Journal of Banking and Finance*, 22(10–11), 1421–1439.

Webster, J.A. (2002). Analyzing the past to prepare for the future: Writing a literature review, *MIS Quarterly*, 26(2), 13–23.

West, D., Dellana, S. and Qian, J. (2005). Neural network ensemble strategies for financial decision applications, *Computers and Operations Research*, 32(10), 2543–2559.

Whittaker, J. (1989). Creativity and conformity in science: Titles, keywords and co-word analysis, *Social Studies Science*, 473–496.

Wilson, N. and Altanlar, A. (2014). Company failure prediction with limited information: Newly incorporated companies, *Journal of the Operational Research Society*, 65(2), 252–264.

Wilson, N. and Tinoco, H.M. (2013). Financial distress and bankruptcy prediction among listed companies using accounting, market and macroeconomic variables, *International Review of Financial Analysis*, 30, 394–419.

Wong, B., Partington, G., Stevenson, M. and Torbey, V. (2007). Surviving chapter 11 bankruptcies: Duration and payoff? *Abacus*, 43(3), 363–387.

Wong, J., Wong, T. and Leung, P. (2010). Predicting banking distress in the EMEAP economies, *Journal of Financial Stability*, 6(3), 169–179.

Yang, Z.R., Platt, M.B. and Platt, H.D. (1999). Probabilistic neural networks in bankruptcy prediction, *Journal of Business Research*, 44(2), 67–74.

Youn, H. and Gu, Z. (2010a). Predicting Korean lodging firm failures: An artificial neural network model along with a logistic regression model, *International Journal of Hospitality Management*, 29(1), 120–127.

Zeng, S. and Ni, X. (2018). A bibliometric analysis of blockchain research. *Intelligent Vehicles Symposium (IV)*. IEEE, Changshu, pp. 102–107.

Zopounidis, C. and Doumpos, M. (1999). Business failure prediction using the utadis multicriteria analysis method, *Journal of the Operational Research Society*, 50(11), 1138–1148.

https://doi.org/10.1142/9789811260506_0007

Chapter 7

CG and Viable Corporate Debt

Ioannis Passas[*,¶], Konstantina Ragazou[†,], Panagiotis Giannopoulos[‡,††], and Paschalis Kagias[§,‡‡]**

[*]*Hellenic Mediterranean University, Department of Business Administration and Tourism, Heraklion, Greece*

[†]*University of Thessaly, Department of Planning and Regional Development, Volos, Greece*

[‡]*Department of Public Administration, Panteion University of Political and Social Sciences, Athens, Greece*

[§]*University of Western Macedonia, Department of Accounting and Finance, Kozani, Greece*

[¶]*ipassas@hmu.gr*

[**]*kragazou@gmail.com*

[††]*Pannos@gmail.com*

[‡‡]*paschaliskagias@hotmail.com*

Abstract

This chapter presents a basic level explanation about corporate debt and its viability. Also, it presents basic corporate governance types and their relationship with corporate debt and its manifestations worldwide.

It is an indisputable fact that corporate governance is increasingly appearing on the world stage. How listed companies are controlled and managed has begun to concern the firm environment in its totality, such as the Board of Directors, senior executives, shareholders, employees and those who present a relative interest in that company. After the pressure of the collapse of many large companies, the supervisory authorities of almost all economies began to look for systems to deal with and solve the problems of protecting shareholders and creditors of stock exchange-listed companies. The main objective of corporate governance systems is the fully transparent and effective management of a company, which will maximize its financial value and protect shareholders and creditors. A large part of corporate governance concerns the financial viability of businesses, and that is where loans and corporate debts, in general, come in. Corporate debts in the modern economy have skyrocketed and are now determining the economic scene worldwide.

Keywords: Corporate debt, corporate governance, management responsibility, accounting

1. Introduction

Firstly, (Berle and Means, 1933) set the terms of the modern corporate governance debate by observing the separation of ownership and control in the modern American company. Triantis and Daniels said that the divergence in interest between owners (the shareholders) and those who control the decisions of the firm (the managers) is now well understood through managerial agency theory. Corporate governance is the cornerstone for the organization of effective internal control systems by modern organizations (Triantis and Daniels, 1995).

The System of National Accounts (SNA) defines debt "as a specific subset of liabilities identified according to the types of financial instruments included or excluded. Generally, debt is defined as all liabilities that require payment or payments of interest or principal by the debtor to the creditor at a date or dates in the future" (Paragraph 22.104) (Bwanakare, 2019). Essentially, debt is the money borrowed by one part from the other to serve a financial need that otherwise cannot be covered. Many organizations use debt to procure goods and services that they cannot afford to pay in cash. Increasing corporate debt levels from the Great Depression of 2009 becomes more and more a speech point among many analysts.

The debt of global non-financial companies amounted to US$81 trillion in the third quarter of 2020 and exceeded the value of global GDP for the first time. Companies in emerging markets made about 31% of this debt — a number that has grown steadily over the last decade increases from 9% in 2008. China is by far the largest publisher of corporate debt. The quality of Chinese debt has fallen in previous years. That did not happen in the case of Japan, France and Germany, where the share of "profit" debt issued by non-domestic companies decreased over time. In the United States, 35.68% of the debt of the company's non-intensive company was considered at risk in 2019, which was the highest value among other developed economies.[1]

2. Corporate Governance and Its Importance

The term "Corporate Governance System" means the framework of statutory or non-statutory rules under which an organization's governance is exercised. More simplistically is the system or how organizations are guided and managed. An integral element of corporate governance is how the organization is governed by the competent bodies and its impact on its results. An essential reason for implementing effective corporate governance practices is the necessity of subordinating the special interests that characterize individual stakeholder groups (e.g. managers, shareholders, Board of Directors, etc.) to the general interest of the organization and its shareholders. Corporate governance is mainly exerted by the Board of Directors of Organizations, whose operations are limited by direct or indirect interest. It is essential to separate those interests in the process of the body within it, and they are respective except. The second category concerns stakeholders. Specifically, the stakeholders are responsible within the organization, which is responsible for the corporate governance process and its effectiveness, shareholders associated with administration, among other ways and through the financial statements, while outside the organization are the Workers, customers, creditors, banks, public bodies, etc. The day-to-day management of the Agency is in the hands of the administration and the directors it has designated and to whom it has delegated responsibilities. The results are submitted for

[1] Global corporate debt — Statistics & Facts | Statista. https://www.statista.com/topics/5724/global-corporate-debt/.

approval to shareholders at the General Meeting. It is crucial to undergo structures and operating procedures to ensure that the agencies concerned are not subject to the operators' actions or omissions of the latter. As the administration manages corporate issues, it also attributes the burden of applying correct corporate governance rules. It is vital to manage the Agency in the best possible way for shareholders, workers and other third parties (Bank, 2005).

3. The Evolution of Corporate Governance Over Time

In 1970, Friedman in *New York Times* (Gheraia *et al*., 2019) defined corporate governance (CG) as the firm managements' effort to meet owners or shareholders' expectations, considering basic social rules, legal requirements and native customs. Elkington (1998) through its theory of "Triple Bottom Line", highlights three key concepts at the heart of the activities, which the firms should develop to ensure their viability. These are the profits in the financial benefits that the company creates for society, the people by meaning the human resources and the society where the business operates, and finally, the planet (known as the 3Ps). The company has to grow its activity by taking into account environmental protection at the same time. Also, firms should maintain sustainability and operate in a social responsibility context. As Hemingway and Maclagan (2004) argued even if firms do not work toward this direction, eventually, market demands will lead them to adopt practices to improve their social and environmental efficiency while at the same time being financially efficient (Maravelaki *et al*., 2021).

Bibliography had suggested five elements of CG that unable firms to confront financial hazards:

(1) Firm's culture, meaning the values, beliefs, concepts and ways to act that an organization's members adopt and use in routine procedures. Each organization is a smaller group of people who interact with each other. Being such, it develops a cultural framework that represents itself. A firm that criticizes unethical behavior phenomena, or illicit internal competition, promotes feelings of security and trust among its internal environment and sets boundaries. All these principles shape the firm's image also the external environment.

(2) Leadership, referring to the management. Management defines the requirements of the team member's ethical behavior and promotes education on matters of corporate ethics. Managers on higher levels may acknowledge and reward the employees who support the firm's values and operate in that framework. On the other hand, top management sets the example and represents the organizational culture.
(3) Cooperation among firm subgroups. Risk management, internal and external control, and guidelines compliance could be proven extremely difficult if not regulated by a system that organizes and sets goal priorities on the various departments to avoid conflicts of interest. Managers are necessary to pay attention to the internal cooperation and orientation of responsibilities.
(4) Operational Systems developed to address organizational needs. They need to be designed to support the firm's operations and be evaluated regularly to support decision-making and strategic planning. The appliance of operational systems ensures information credibility when combined with control procedures providing constant data feed.
(5) Organizational structure is the fundamental element for effective CG. When significant changes in internal and external environments occur, the firm's structure should be revised and redesigned to ensure that firm does not divert from its objectives. Organizational change mainly refers to human resources, operations, and technological issues. Top management needs to make vast decisions in such cases to adjust to the competition (Maravelaki *et al.*, 2021).

CG shareholders try to ensure that managers achieve satisfying returns on their invested capital supported by (Foerster and Huen, 2004). Corporate governance confronts the agency problem, which refers to the shareholders' need for assurance for their investment (Shleifer and Vishny, 1997). The agents–managers are the third parties assigned to act in the best interests of the owners' (Jensen and Meckling, 1979). There are conflicts of interests between principals-owners and agents; the phenomenon of information asymmetry occurs. CG guidelines have been promoted, among other tools, in order for the firms to provide essential and reliable information to the external parts of interest. The most common of them involve financial reposting. Most companies have adopted and customized these guidelines to suit their needs. It is commonly believed that firms in compliance with existing CG rules are positively evaluated by the markets and investors (La Porta *et al.*, 2000).

4. Business Scandals and their Economy Impact

Over the years, a multitude of speculative incidents and business scandals have been recorded worldwide. Starting from 1720, when the financial scandal of the South Sea company erupted in Britain, continuing with the panic created on the New York Stock Exchange in 1873, the great crash of 1929, the collapse of Wall Street in 1987 until the recent accounting scandals and the wave of bankruptcies of influential giants such as Enron, WorldCom, Guinness, Blue Arrow, Polly Peck, BCCI, Maxwell Group, Barings Bank and others. The negative impact on the economies they operated on was significant and had negative consequences for those directly or indirectly linked to them. Shareholders, suppliers, customers, creditors, workers, and the countries' governments in which the organizations mentioned above were active have been negatively affected. The failure of these organizations is mainly due to the inadequacy of their administrative boards and the lack of organized and effective control mechanisms by administrations (Menexiadis, 2021).

Any regulated capital market must enhance transparency, the valid and timely information of shareholders, continuous, independent, and effective audits, strengthening the supervisory role of the Board of Directors, and preparing reliable accounting statements. All these elements promote the adequate protection of shareholders' rights and prevent mistreatment and business dysfunction. Almost always, major economic crises signal new and more effective measures. After the crash of 1929,[2] the US authorities drew up a series of new measures, creating the Securities and Transactions Commission, controlling compulsory treasury rates, and creating a pyramid scheme. In the United Kingdom, we have the Cadbury Commission's recommendation in December 1992 following the scandals of companies such as Maxwell and BCCI. The Cadbury Committee designed a voluntary code for corporate governance. Following the recent financial scandals of large companies, the US Congress was also led, in July 2002, to create a new law on corporate governance. Subsequently, the New York Stock Exchange defined new criteria for listing companies on the stock exchange, such as the majority of the Board of Directors being composed of independent members, the audit committee is composed only of independent members, of which at least one

[2] https://money-zine.com/investing/stocks/stock-market-crash-of-1929/.

member possesses financial knowledge and, finally, a limitation on the services provided by external auditors to their clients (Winter *et al.*, 2002).

On the 21 May 2003, the European Commission sealed the modernization of company law and corporate governance at the community level by adopting a new action plan. With this program, he defined the existence of collective responsibility of the members of the Board of Directors, the reinforcement of the information that will come from the companies and the establishment of a detailed statement referring to the implementation of the Corporate Governance Code. The action plan combines the new legislative regulations developed within the European Union and emphasizes corporate governance initiatives to increase confidence in the capital markets. The main objectives of the action plan are:

- To strengthen the rights of shareholders/investors and the protection of creditors, employees and other stakeholders with whom the companies carry out transactions, and the simultaneous adaptation of the rules of company law and corporate governance to the different types of enterprises.
- To strengthen the competitiveness and efficiency of businesses, paying particular attention to specific cross-border issues.

The action program stresses the need to modernize company law and corporate governance based on the increasing drive of European companies to operate cross-border in the internal market, the continuous development of information and communication technologies, changes in capital markets, and the adverse effects of the various economic scandals. The European Parliament aims to strengthen public confidence in the financial statements and annual reports of European companies. Directive 2006/45/EC of the European Parliament and the Council amending Council Directive 78/660/EC was thus adopted on 14 June 2006, concerning the annual accounts of companies of specific types and Council Directive 83/349/EC on consolidated accounts (European Commission, 2013).

The European Commission has defined the following:

- The obligation to draw up and publish an annual corporate governance statement. This declaration should contain all the main elements of implementing the Corporate Governance Code, such as presenting internal control systems, compliance with the Code, the composition and functioning of the Governing Council and its committees.

- To create a legislative framework to support the different rights of shareholders. Rights such as abstention and participation in general meetings by electronic means. These facilities will be provided to all shareholders in the European Union to resolve all problems relating to cross-border voting.
- Recommendation 2005/162/EC on date 15 February 2005, concerning the promotion of (independent) non-executive or supervisory directors. Member States should lay down provisions concerning the role of non-executive and supervisory directors and the committees of the administrative or supervisory board.
- Recommendation 2004/913/EC on date 14 December 2004, concerning the promotion of an appropriate remuneration regime for the directors of the listed companies. This Recommendation calls on the Member States to establish a regulatory system that will offer shareholders greater transparency and influence and provide complete and detailed information on individual remuneration.
- The European Forum for Corporate Governance, with a view to the coordination and convergence of national corporate governance codes and how they are implemented and controlled.

In addition to all the above, the action program also deals with better information on the role of institutional investors in corporate governance, the promotion of the principle of proportionality between control and capital; to give the listed companies a choice between multi-level and single-level administrative structures and to strengthen the responsibilities of the management concerning the various financial statements. Understandably, corporate governance concerns both the European and the global economies. Good corporate governance is a key condition for the existence of integrity and credibility in a company. The purpose of corporate governance is to build investor confidence and promote companies' long-term success and development.[3]

5. Alternative Corporate Governance Systems

In developed economies, we identify two systems of corporate governance. The Anglo-Saxon system, also known as the market-based system

[3]http://data.europa.eu/eli/dir/2013/34/oj.

and the continental Europe and Japan system, is called relationship-oriented or group-based (Carati and Rad, 2000; Kaplan, 1997). Essential elements of the Anglo-Saxon corporate governance system (followed, among other things, by the USA and the United Kingdom) are the existence of extensive capital markets with high liquidity, the large dispersion in company equity and the existence of aggressive takeovers. The problem of the mandator arises between the weak shareholders and the strong executive. The capital market is the essential mechanism of executive discipline; the shareholders are characterized by their inability to exercise effective control over the functions of the executive board. Therefore, where the executive board does not protect shareholders' rights and interests, the shareholders follow the path of exit from the company's shareholding, by, of course, immediately lowering the price of the share and by mobilizing the executive to change its policies and to move toward effective safeguarding of the interests of shareholders. Companies are also exposed to the threat of aggressive takeovers. Thus, when there is an active corporate control market, shareholders can better control the executive.

A typical example is the United Kingdom, where 200 acquisitions and mergers have taken place per year in the last decade. All the evidence showed that in the 90% of aggressive takeovers, we had replaced the Board of Directors of the acquired company and in the so-called "friendly" we have had some changes to the board members. So we understand that aggressive takeovers are a key mechanism for changing the governing boards in the UK. That is not the case in continental Europe, where things are entirely different. A typical example is Germany, where 50 acquisitions and mergers took place per year (Brancato, 1997; Goergen and Renneboog, 2001). Based on the market, we note that the large spread of shares leads to short-term behavior for both the executive and the shareholders. Intense competition among investors motivates them to seek short-term returns from the companies they invested in without showing any disposition to obtain long-term benefits. According to several CEOs, such investors create instability and pressure them to turn to strategies that bring them recent capital gains (Daily *et al.*, 1996, Coffee, 1991). In recent years, both in the United Kingdom and the United States, there has been an ever-increasing trend toward the concentration of shares by institutional investors. (Brancato, 1997; CEPS, 1995).

On the other hand, we have the partnership governance system such as "long-term relations-oriented" or "group-based" (which takes place in

Japan, France, Germany, etc.). There is also a high concentration of voting rights or ownership of shares, and the problem of the mandate. In Germany, 90% of the 200 largest companies, have one shareholder with a share of 25% of the total number of companies in total issued units (Franks and Mayer, 2001). Significant shareholders of a company other than the investment they make can communicate with each other and make joint decisions on how to control the executive power. Current corporate governance system aggressive takeovers are minimal. Most of the shares are distributed to company owners, banks and (non) financial institutions which have long-term relations with the executive and are, of course, in line with its policies. Germany, where a majority of 75% is required at the general meeting to approve the replacement of the shareholders' representatives of the Supervisory Board (Maher and Andersson, 2000).

6. Corporate Debt in Accounting Terms

The account of "Participations in Companies" contains shares of subsidiaries or related firms. Thus, firms that aim to manipulate their results may show these shares in their acquisition value and not trading on the Stock Exchange (for the listed ones) or the actual value at the end of the fiscal year. Therefore, Income Statement does not include gains or losses by the over or under evaluation of subsidiaries and participations' shares. In addition to that, firms may transfer their holdings of debt instruments that belong to the current assets to improve their liquidity ratios. However, the ROI index is also affected, the securities do not correspond to sales and are not included in the Operating Assets as the participants do. Thus, the denominator of ROI is reduced, and the company will show increased profitability. Of course, that is a big problem (Maravelaki *et al.*, 2021).

7. Corporate Debt and Its Viability

According to OECD, "by the end of 2019, the outstanding global stock of non-financial corporate bonds reached an all-time high of USD 13.5 trillion in real terms. This record amount is the result of an unprecedented build-up in corporate bond debt since 2008 and a further USD 2.1 trillion

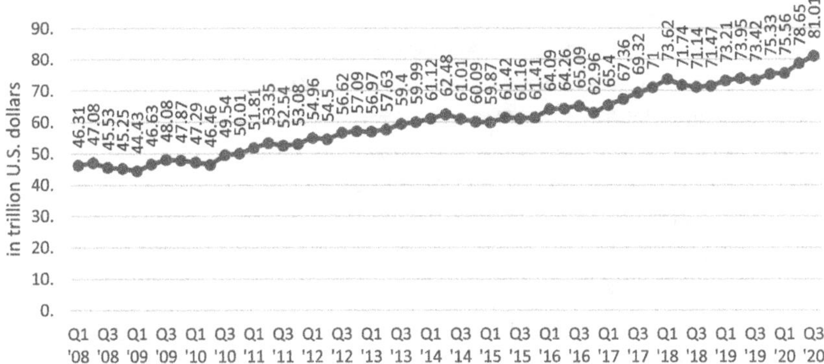

Fig. 1: Debt of non-financial corporations worldwide quarterly 2008–2020.

Source: Bank of International Settlement (2021). Total credit to non-financial corporations (core debt) in billions of USD. https://stats.bis.org/statx/srs/table/f4.2.

in borrowing by non-financial companies during 2019, in the wake of a return to more expansionary monetary policies early in the year"[4] (Çelik *et al*., 2020).

Furthermore, as mentioned above, the debt of global non-financial companies amounted to US$81 trillion in the third quarter of 2020 and exceeded the value of global GDP for the first time (see Figure 1). In addition, policy makers need to believe that the quality and dynamics of the excellent stock of corporate bonds have changed to its growing size. Compared to previous credit cycles, the current stock of outstanding corporate bonds has lower overall credit quality, higher repayment requirements, more significant maturities and insufficient deal protection. These characteristics can reinforce the negative impact that an economic downturn would have on the non-financial corporate sector and the overall economy. As a result, today's corporate bond markets' size, quality, and dynamics have become a factor to consider in the various scenarios that underpin monetary policy (Çelik *et al*., 2020).

As for the companies worldwide with the largest long-term debt, the first for 2020 is AT&T, a telecommunications company (see Figure 2). It

[4]https://insights.londonfs.com/the-role-of-default-dependency-in-a-world-of-rising-debt.

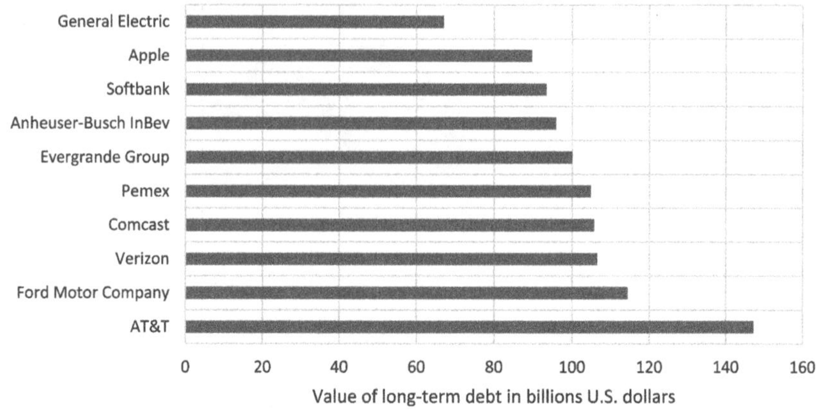

Fig. 2: Companies with largest long-term-debt globally 2020.

Source: Global Economic Data (2020). Corporate Debt Kings: The World's Most Indebted Companies 2020. https://www.gfmag.com/global-data/economic-data/companies-largest-debt-world-2020.

is followed by Ford Motor Company, Verizon, Comcast and Pemex, ending with General Electric. We notice that most of the companies on this list are based in the United States of America (Menexiadis, 2021).

7.1 *Is China the biggest debtor of corporate debt?*

China is by far the biggest debtor of corporate debt. The quality of Chinese debt has declined in previous years. That was not the case for Japan, France and Germany, where the share of "speculative" debt issued by non-financial corporations has decreased over time. In the United States, 35.68% of non-financial corporations' debt was considered at risk in 2019, the highest value among other developed economies (Figure 3).

The "Chinese giant" has dramatically increased its corporate debt. The debt share increased from 35.73% in 2009 to 49.74% in 2019. In contrast, despite the above figures, over the same 10-year period, the United States saw only a slight increase, from 43.17% to 47.98%. Speculative debt is debt that has not been deemed to be of investment grade quality by a credit rating agency. In general, speculative debt provides investors with higher returns, but at the cost of higher risk.

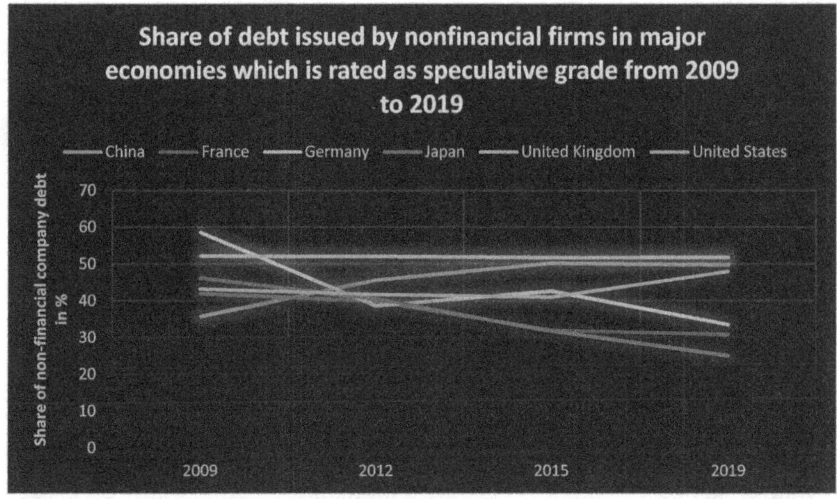

Fig. 3: Share of speculative grade corporate debt in major economies 2009–2019.

Sources: IMF. https://www.imf.org/en/Publications/GFSR/Issues/2019/10/01/global-financial-stability-report-october-2019.

8. Conclusion

In a modern business world, it is imperative for companies to be at the level of corporate governance, as the business environment faces unprecedented challenges (Hussain *et al.*, 2018). One of the key elements of the structure of companies is the full implementation of a framework of rules, regulations and procedures governed by the relevant legislation (Lehn, 2021). At the same time, the role and exercise of corporate social responsibility is also considered catalytic, as it not only promotes the company's offer and sensitivity to society but also creates a competitive advantage, causing respect and commitment of customers (Puni and Anlesinya, 2020).

Based on the literature, a distinction is made between corporate governance models: the Anglo-Saxon, and the continental Europe and Japan system (Ciampi, 2015). The Anglo-Saxon model (typical examples are the US and the UK) is characterized by large size and liquidity capital market, large dispersion in the share capital of companies, increasing concentration of shareholder power in institutional investors and the acquisition of control through acquisitions (Siepel and Nightingale, 2014). Shareholders basically seek short-term benefits from their participation in companies. The second model is also called as a "relationship-oriented" or "group-based system". This model reflects the strong government intervention in this for the formulation of a national plan and sectoral policies. It is characterized by less liquid markets and a concentration of shareholder power in banks, households and governments (Forcadell *et al.*, 2020).

However, whichever corporate governance system is adopted, it is important to highlight the role of the corporate governance on the corporate debt and its viability (Lipton, 2019). Regionally speaking, Chinese corporate debt is the "biggest threat" to the global economy (Ding *et al.*, 2021). This comes from the fact that many companies in China are struggling to deal with a slowdown in growth stemming from the trade war and other factors. Debt has been a problem in the world's second largest economy, but China has already made a lot of efforts to reduce its reliance on it by tightening regulations to speed up deleveraging — or the process of reducing debt (Pessarossi and Weill, 2013).

References

Bank, T.H.E.W. (2005). External debt statistics: Guide for compilers and users. In *External Debt Statistics: Guide for Compilers and Users*. https://doi.org/10.5089/9781589063013.069.

Berle, A. and Means, G. (1933). *The Modern Corporation and Private Property*. Macmillan Company: London.

Brancato, C. Kay. (1997). *Institutional Investors and Corporate Governance: Best Practices for Increasing Corporate Value*. Irwin Professional Pub: Burr Ridge.

Bwanakare, S. (2019). The System of National Accounts. In *Non-Extensive Entropy Econometrics for Low Frequency Series*. https://doi.org/10.1515/9783110605914-007.

Carati, G. and Rad, A.T. (2000). Convergence of corporate governance systems, *Managerial Finance*, 26(10), 66–83. https://doi.org/10.1108/03074350010766945.

Çelik, S., Demirtaş, G., and Isaksson, M. (2020). Corporate Bond Market Trends , Emerging Risks and Monetary Policy, *OECD Capital Market Series*, 1–58.

CEPS (1995). *Corporate Governance in Europe, Report of a CEPS Working Party* (Issue 12).

Ciampi, F. (2015). Corporate governance characteristics and default prediction modeling for small enterprises. An empirical analysis of Italian firms, *Journal of Business Research*, 68(5), 1012–1025. https://doi.org/10.1016/J.JBUSRES.2014.10.003.

Ding, Y., Xiong, W. and Zhang, J. (2021). Issuance overpricing of China's corporate debt securities, *Journal of Financial Economics*, 144(1), 328–346. https://doi.org/10.1016/j.jfineco.2021.06.010.

Elkington, J. (1998). Accounting for the triple bottom line, *Measuring Business Excellence*, 2(3), 18–22. https://doi.org/10.1108/eb025539.

European Commission (2013). Proposal for a directive of the European Parliament and of the Council on the Annual Financial Statements, Consolidated Financial Statements and Related Reports of Certain Types of Undertakings, *Official Journal of the European Union*, 1–87. https://eur-lex.europa.eu/legal-content/EN/TXT/PDF/?uri=CELEX:32013L0034&from=EN.

Foerster, S. and Huen, B. (2004). Does Corporate Governance Matter to Canadian Investors? Canadian Investment Review, 17, 19–25.

Forcadell, F.J., Sanchez-Riofrio, A., Guerras-Martín, L.Á. and Romero-Jordán, D. (2020). Is the restructuring-performance relationship moderated by the economic cycle and the institutional environment for corporate governance? *Journal of Business Research*, 110, 397–407. https://doi.org/10.1016/J.JBUSRES.2020.01.055.

Franks, J. and Mayer, C. (2001). Ownership and control of German corporations, *The Review of Financial Studies*, 14(4), 943–977. https://doi.org/10.1093/RFS/14.4.943.

Gheraia, Z., Saadaoui, S. and Abdelli, H.A. (2019). Business ethics and corporate social responsibility: Bridging the concepts, *Open Journal of Business and Management*, 7(4), 2020–2029. https://doi.org/10.4236/OJBM.2019.74139.

Goergen, M. and Renneboog, L. (2001). Investment policy, internal financing and ownership concentration in the UK, *Journal of Corporate Finance*, 7(3), 257–284.

Hemingway, C.A. and Maclagan, P.W. (2004). Managers' personal values as drivers of corporate social responsibility, *Journal of Business Ethics*, 2004, 50(1), 33–44. https://doi.org/10.1023/B:BUSI.0000020964.80208.C9.

Hussain, N., Rigoni, U. and Orij, R. P. (2018). Corporate governance and sustainability performance: Analysis of triple bottom line performance, *Journal of Business Ethics*, 149(2), 411–432. https://doi.org/10.1007/S10551-016-3099-5.

Jensen, M.C. and Meckling, W.H. (1979). Theory of the Firm: Managerial Behavior, Agency Costs, and Ownership Structure. In: Brunner, K. (eds) Economics Social Institutions. Rochester Studies in Economics and Policy Issues, Springer, Dordrecht, 1, 163–231. https://doi.org/10.1007/978-94-009-9257-3_8.

Kaplan, S. (1997). The words of risk analysis, *Risk Analysis*, 17(4), 407–417. https://doi.org/10.1111/J.1539-6924.1997.TB00881.X.

La Porta, R., Lopez-de-Silanes, F., Shleifer, A., and Vishny, R. (2000). Investor protection and corporate governance, *Journal of Financial Economics*, 58(1–2), 3–27.

Lehn, K. (2021). Corporate governance and corporate agility, *Journal of Corporate Finance*, 66. https://doi.org/10.1016/J.JCORPFIN.2021.101929.

Lipton, D.A. (2019). Rebalancing China: International lessons in corporate debt — Remarks at the Chinese Economists Society Conference on Sustainable Development in China and the World, *China Economic Review*, 57. https://doi.org/10.1016/J.CHIECO.2017.09.011.

Maher, M. and Andersson, T. (2000). Corporate governance: Effects on Firm Performance and Economic Growth, *SSRN Electronic Journal*. https://doi.org/10.2139/SSRN.218490.

Maravelaki, A., Zopounidis, C., Lemonakis, C. and Passas, I. (2021). *Corporate Governance as a Tool for Fraud Mitigation*, 1998, 1–15. https://doi.org/10.4018/978-1-7998-4805-9.ch001.

Menexiadis, M.E. (2021). Corporate governance: Introduction, roles, codes of corporate governance. In *Applications for Accounting Disclosure and Fraud*. https://doi.org/10.4018/978-1-7998-4805-9.ch003.

Pessarossi, P. and Weill, L. (2013). Choice of corporate debt in China: The role of state ownership, *China Economic Review*, 26(1), 1–16. https://doi.org/10.1016/J.CHIECO.2013.03.005.

Puni, A. and Anlesinya, A. (2020). Corporate governance mechanisms and firm performance in a developing country, *International Journal of Law and Management*, 62(2), 147–169. https://doi.org/10.1108/IJLMA-03-2019-0076/FULL/HTML.

Shleifer, A. and Vishny, R. W. (1997). A survey of corporate governance, *The Journal of Finance*, 52(2), 737–783. https://doi.org/10.1111/J.1540-6261.1997.TB04820.X.

Siepel, J. and Nightingale, P. (2014). Anglo-Saxon governance: Similarities, difference and outcomes in a financialised world, *Critical Perspectives on Accounting*, 25(1), 27–35. https://doi.org/10.1016/J.CPA.2012.10.004.

Triantis, G.G. and Daniels, R.J. (1995). The role of debt in interactive corporate governance. *California Law Review*, 83(4), 1073. https://doi.org/10.2307/3480898.

Winter, J., Garrido Garcia, J.M., Hopt, K.J., Rickford, J., Rossi, G., Schans Christensen, J., Simn, Joelle, Thienpont, D. and Van Hulle, K. (2002). *Report of the High Level Group of Company Law Experts on a Modern Regulatory Framework for Company Law in Europe*, November, 132.

https://doi.org/10.1142/9789811260506_0008

Chapter 8

Corporate Governance and Financial Fraud Detection

Maria Tragouda[*,‡], **Michalis Doumpos**[*,§], **and Constantin Zopounidis**[*,†,¶]

[*]*Technical University of Crete*
School of Production Engineering and Management
Financial Engineering Laboratory
University Campus, Chania

[†]*Audencia Business School*
Nantes, France

[‡]*tragouda_maths@outlook.com*

[§]*mdoumpos@tuc.gr*

[¶]*kzopounidis@tuc.gr*

Abstract

In this chapter, we approach fraud detection using the fraud diamond theory, which utilizes the concepts of motivation, opportunity, pressure, and a fraudster's ability to perform fraudulent acts. The dataset used includes information of Greek companies obtained from the Athens Stock Exchange from 2014 to 2019. We employ a machine learning approach (ML) to develop a model for identifying fake financial reports. The results are quite satisfactory in terms of accuracy and open the possibility of providing a basis for the study of other variables that affect elements of corporate governance. The development of a financial statement fraud identification and risk assessment (FFS) model could act as an early warning system and mitigate losses for investors, auditors, and all other internal and external stakeholders.

Keywords: Corporate governance, financial fraud detection

1. Introduction

Corporate governance (CG) includes the principles, such as rules, processes or laws, by which a company should operate or to be controlled. CG affects the stakeholders' interests, including shareholders, customers, vendors and management. Within a firm, the principles of good CG involve all top-level management committees, including the board, the audit committee and the CG committee.

Although the principles of CG are now well-established and widely accepted, the number of cases of corporate fraud is growing, raising the need to investigate thoroughly factors that can be used as early-warning signals. Among the various types of corporate fraud, financial frauds are among the most important ones. The auditors' weakness to detect financial scandals renders the usage of specific audit methods and tools necessary (Lin *et al.*, 2003). An ample number of academic researchers (Dechow *et al.*, 2011; Price *et al.*, 2011) have proposed various methods to detect financial fraud, often based on information derived from financial statements (Ngai, 2011). Nowadays, even if the audits are intensive, the fraudsters can override them, and auditors cannot detect the scams on time. Thus, it is imperative to approach the detection of frauds studying the motivation, the opportunity, the pressure and the ability of a fraudster to conduct fraudulent actions.

These four elements constitute the fraud diamond theory, which this chapter adopts for the application of a machine learning approach. The results show a high accuracy (overall accuracy over 83%), thus setting a basis to investigate more variables which are from fraud diamond theory and more generally, are corporate governance elements.

The structure of this chapter is as follows: In Section 2, there is a general approach of financial fraud with several definitions and some popular examples. In Section 3, there is an empirical analysis of financial fraud detection of Greek companies listed in the Athens Stock Exchange. Finally, Section 4 concludes this chapter, and discusses some issues for future research.

2. Financial Fraud

The fierce competition in the financial environment and the decline in business performance, combined with the great pressure on business executives to achieve higher and higher goals, are some of the reasons that have led to widespread falsification of accounting statements, and the so frequent use of misleading accounting practices to meet unrealistic market expectations (Jennings, 2004). However, in recent decades, the cases of falsified financial statements that have come to light have become alarmingly serious, with the global business community having been severely shaken by numerous financial scandals (Humpherys *et al.*, 2011; Kamarudin *et al.*, 2012; Kirkos *et al.*, 2007; Yeh *et al.*, 2010).

Many of the world's most prominent companies and organizations have been hit by large-scale financial fraud of the companies involved (Zerban, 2018). Examples of financial statement fraud that have had a tremendous impact in different international environments are Enron, Parmalat, WorldCom, Freddie Mac, Tyco, Xerox, Lehman Brothers, Satyam, HIH Insurance (Basilico *et al.*, 2012), proving that fraud is a phenomenon mostly emerging from strong economies (Carnegie and Napier, 2010). International financial scandals have had multiple adverse effects on the global economy, while leading companies, employees, creditors and investors themselves into huge financial losses (Abdulahi and Mansor, 2015; Rezaee, 2002). Although these scandals have occurred in recent decades, wide-range operational turmoil, conflicting interests and the collapse of governance standards have been the catalyst for the shake-up of stakeholder confidence in the functioning of the financial markets and the weakening of its credibility (Abdulahi and Mansor, 2015; Albeksh, 2016; Bierstaker *et al.*, 2006; Peterson and Buckhoff, 2004; Rezaee *et al.*, 2004).

Focusing furthermore on the thematic of the present study, "financial fraud" relates the activities of misusing financial or payment systems for obtaining financial gain. In addition to the purely financial costs for companies and organizations, financial crime also has significant negative effects on employee morale, corporate reputation and business relationships.

2.1 *The cost of financial fraud*

The global study by the Association of Certified Fraud Examiners-ACFE (2018) analyzed data from 125 countries and estimated that about 5% of annual corporate revenues are lost due to fraud. The largest part of this cost is attributed to financial statements fraud, which, although not as frequent as other types of financial fraud, it has a much higher cost. The same study estimated that the damage from investigative fraud cases exceed $7 billion. In the case of fraud, the average loss was found to be US$130,000, whereas the average loss due to corruption an average was US$250,000. The sectors with the highest incidence of corruption were energy (53%), industry (51%) and government/public administration (50%). According to the study, the most common methods of committing fraud include the creation of forged physical and electronic documents, the falsification of physical/electronic documents, the destruction of physical documents, as well as the creation of fraudulent transactions and alternations in accounting transactions.

Research and the experience of professional investigators have shown that the longer a fraud lasts until it is exposed, the more it grows and affects its victims. Specifically, the ACFE study notes that fraud cases that last more than 5 years, cost 20 times more than those revealed within 6 months. On the other hand, the perpetrators tend to start with small-scale scams and rapidly increase their acts in less than 3 years. Therefore, it is imperative that companies use fraud prevention and timely repression mechanisms to minimize the damage caused. Moreover, according to ACFE, the predominant methods for detecting fraud are the complaint (in 40% of cases), the internal audit (15% of the cases) and the management review (13% of the cases). Complaints come at a rate of 53% from within the firm (employees) and less frequently from outside agents (customers, suppliers, competitors).

In an earlier study, Karpoff *et al.* (2008) mentioned that when news of a company's misbehavior is exposed, it loses 38% of its market value, indicating that the market is responding to a more accurate portrayal of a firm's financial situation. This is the adjustment to the "true" corporate value if the company's books had not been tampered with.

2.2 *Ways to convict fraud*

Examples of criminal acts that are included conceptually to the above-mentioned definition of fraud, are the following (Reiner, 2017):

- Over and under-invoicing of goods and services. This type involves activities of misrepresentations of price of the good or service to conduct illegal transferring of additional value between the importer and exporter.

- Multiple invoicing of goods and services. This kind of fraud involves a more complicated series of transactions whereby the same good or service is invoiced more than once, often using several different financial institutions to make the payments.
- Recording revenue before it is earned.
- Creating fictitious revenue.
- Boosting profits with non-recurring transactions.
- Shifting current expenses to a later period.
- Failing to record or disclose liabilities.
- Shifting current income to a later period.
- Shifting future expenses to an earlier period.
- Land grabbing/Real estate frauds.
- Corruption and bribery of public servants.
- Illegal foreign trade.

These tricks aim at boosting current year earnings or current-year earnings to the future to create an illusion of steady income over years. Together with merge and acquisition and advanced financial products, such as holding derivatives or other off-balance activities, financial accounting became more and more complex, making the detection of financial fraud more difficult than ever. In an overall perspective, financial fraud is expressed through numerous criminal acts, each one affecting different economic activities.

2.3 *Fraud triangle*

An ample number of researchers in the previous years, dealt with financial fraud detection in companies using only financial variables. Nowadays, it is crucial for enhancing the results of detection of financial fraud to examine more qualitative factors in combination with the financial ones.

In 1953, Donald Cressey published his survey — among many others — on organized crime, called *Other People's Money: A Study in the Social Psychology of Embezzlement.* Due to his academic studies on sociology and criminology and having an honest interest on why fraudsters get tempted to commit fraud, he conducted extended research that included the interviewing of 200 fraudsters convicted for embezzlement. It was after identifying three basic elements that were common to all fraudsters, in relation to their motivation for committing fraud, that Cressey developed his theory on Fraud Triangle.

According to Cressey's theory (1953), there are three conditions that accompany fraud: opportunity, pressure/motivation and rationalization. These three conditions create the concept of the "triangle of fraud", which refers to a set of conditions that must exist for a criminal activity or act of fraud to take place. The three components of the fraud triangle are defined as follows:

(1) The *opportunity*, which must be sufficient enough to commit fraud. Therefore, situations or the environment must allow criminal activity to take place. Generally, opportunity includes weakening of restrictive measures that allow a person to move easily toward the thought of committing fraud and eventually implementing it.
(2) The *rationalization* of the individual, which is the most important element, as this includes the mentality of an individual that leads him or her to commit crime or act unlawfully. By giving oneself excuses for the righteousness or the unharmful of the act, the potential fraudster attempts to justify the act of fraud.
(3) The *pressure* that the person receives or the motivations that influence him to commit fraud. No person commits a crime or fraudulent activity without motive. Motivation is most frequently created by feelings of revenge or distress, or when money is scarce or in great need or when the potential fraudster is being blackmailed.

These three factors that create opportunities for fraud, can be examined through an alternative/opposite scope, referring to the environment of opportunity (Brink *et al.*, 2013; Dorminey *et al.*, 2012):

(1) *Lack of internal control*: Lack of segregation of duties, lack of proper organization in a company, lack of physical controls and ineffective supervision are characteristics of an inadequate internal control system that nurtures criminal activities.
(2) *Ineffective board*: When the board of directors is inadequate and weak or lacks independence, senior management is being given an opportunity to commit fraud as they believe that there is no strong control mechanism to monitor its conduct and practices.
(3) *Practices of impunity*: When there are no penalties for offenders in a company, employees are encouraged to commit fraud, as they believe that revealing it will not lead to dismissal or any severe reprimand.

(4) *Lack of ethical guidance and leadership*: There is a need for the competent people, who are usually the management and the senior executives of the departments of a company, to take the responsibility to properly inform and guide those involved in all departments of an organization, most importantly in the accounting team. In addition to providing ethical guidance, management must also act as a model of ethical behavior.

Furthermore, rationalization represents a code of moral values or behavior that allows individuals to commit a fraud voluntarily and intentionally, justifying the act. People do not commit fraud if they cannot justify it according to their own beliefs. For example, to justify an act of fraud, executives invoke opinions such as that everything should be sacrificed for the good of the business or that competitors apply similar practices. On the other hand, employees can justify an act by claiming that they feel that they are underpaid, that everyone does the same, that one must do anything in order to move up the hierarchy (Gabbioneta *et al.*, 2013).

The motives and reasons that lead a company to financial fraud in the form of publishing falsified financial statements, come from both the internal (employees, management) and the external environment (industry, state, competition). The growth rate of companies in recent decades and the competition of companies for higher profits, have led executives and employees to commit fraud either for the benefit or to the detriment of the company. The expectations and motivations that are created are the reasons for cultivating to the individual the desire to commit fraud. The most important motivations/pressures that push individuals, executives and non-executives, can be located in (Mayhew and Murphy, 2014):

(1) The intense competition.
(2) The pressure to meet the expectations of investors and the capital markets.
(3) Financial incentives from the company itself. For example, executives may be better paid or get a raise when the organization's financial results are satisfactory or present a raising tendency. These goals can easily lead to adopting practices that lead to distorted financial statements or equivalent acts of fraud.
(4) The composition of the board of directors.
(5) The managing director holding the position of chairman of the board. It is possible that in such a case there is no proper separation of responsibilities between the two roles.

(6) The growing growth rate and size of a business.
(7) The specialization and high training of the external auditor.

2.4 *Fraud diamond*

Completing and evolving the fraud triangle theory, Wolfe and Hermanson (2004) proposed a new improved theory that introduced a new parameter to the fraud triangle conditions, namely the capability of the fraudster to commit fraud. The fraud diamond theory, as it was named, is more oriented to the human factor that plays an important role in committing fraud. Opportunity paves the way for fraud, while motivation and rationalization allow the individual to go forward with it. However, it is considered as a prerequisite that the individual must have the ability to recognize the opportunity and seize it, not just once, but repeatedly.

2.4.1 *Ability*

Ability is defined as a state where the individual has the necessary characteristics or skills and abilities to commit fraud. These characteristics play an important role in whether there is a real possibility of fraud. A potential fraudster must be able to recognize the specific opportunity for scam and possess the ability to turn it into reality. As Wolfe and Hermanson (2004) state in their research, important characteristics for committing fraudulent actions are the position, intelligence, ego, coercion, deception and stress that a fraudster may feel. According to Bressler and Bressler (2007), as reported by Mackevicius and Giriunas (2013), having incentives, opportunities and justification of one's behavior, does not necessarily mean that a person is able to commit fraud, due to lack of the ability to do so or hide it. Albrecht *et al.* (1995) propose that this aspect is particularly important when extensive or prolonged fraud is committed. In addition, the authors believe that only the person with extremely high capacity will be able to understand the existing internal control techniques and procedures, identify its weaknesses and use them in planning and implementing fraud.

2.4.2 *Position/Operation*

Wolfe and Hermanson (2004) state that the position or function of the individual within the organization may provide the opportunity to create or seize an opportunity for fraud that is not available to others. In addition, when individuals perform a particular task repeatedly, such as banking agreements or creating new vendor accounts, their ability to commit fraud increases as their knowledge of the procedures and control mechanisms increases over time.

2.4.3 *Intelligence/Creativity and ego*

The potential fraudster is someone who can grasp and is able to exploit the weaknesses of internal control procedures and use his/her position, function or some authorized access to his/her advantage. Smart, experienced, creative people with a consistent understanding of the controls and vulnerabilities of the systems they handle are usually the ones committing most of the biggest scams today. The Association of Certified Fraud Examiners (2003) revealed that 51% of scammers had at least a college degree and 49% were over 40 years old. In addition, directors or executives committed 46% of the frauds based on a study of the Association.

Additionally, fraudsters are characterized by a strong ego and great confidence in the fact that their act will not be detected or share the belief that they can easily be acquitted if by chance, they get caught. This self-confidence, reaching to the point of arrogance, can affect a person's evaluation of the pros and cons regarding their involvement in fraud. Furthermore, as personality traits are concerned, a need for admiration and a lack of empathy for others are the most frequently observed. People with this behavior believe they are superior or remarkable and they believe that achieve a better performance at all fields than they really do.

2.4.4 *Coercion, deceit and stress*

A successful scammer can force others to commit or conceal fraud (Rudewicz, 2011). A person with a very persuasive personality may be able to persuade others to commit fraud or simply conceal the fact. According to Wolfe and Hermanson (2004) and Rudewicz, (2011), an effective scammer must also lie successfully and continuously. To avoid detection, the scammer must present to auditors, investors and others a realistic, yet untrue, version of facts and convince them of an unrealistic situation. Thus, fraudsters must also keep track with their lies so that the overall story remains consistent. Another common characteristic of fraudsters is their ability to handle stressful situations (Manurung and Hadian, 2013). Fraud also requires fraud management over a long period of time, a situation that can clearly be stressful. As the risk of detection has not been eliminated, along with the personal consequences an arrest may induce, there is a constant need to hide the fraud daily. The individual must be able to control his/her anxiety, as committing and concealing an unlawful act can be an extremely stressful process (Rudewicz, 2011).

3. Empirical Analysis

The theoretical framework of the fraud triangle/diamond is adopted for the implementation of an empirical study on the identification of falsification in financial statements (FFS) for Greek listed firms, through a machine learning approach, namely using a neural network model.

3.1 *The sample*

The initial dataset includes information from 135 Greek companies obtained from the Athens Stock Exchange from 2014 to 2019. The composition of the sample by the sector of the companies is shown in Table 1.

Following earlier studies (Spathis *et al.*, 2002; Kotsiantis *et al.*, 2006), the classification of a financial statement as falsified or not, was based on evidence which were derived from the opinion of auditors published in the

Table 1: Number of companies by sector.

Sectors	**Number of Companies**
Health services	5
Industrial materials & services	25
Manufacturing	12
Media	9
Raw materials	16
Technology	10
Trade	58
Total	135

Table 2: Number of falsified and non-falsified statements per year.

Year	Non-FFS	FFS	Total
2014	97	34	131
2015	94	37	131
2016	93	38	131
2017	92	35	127
2018	94	25	119
2019	90	23	113
Total	560	192	752

financial statement of each company. Having examined the official notes of auditors into the financial statements, the following opinions were employed for the classification of the financial statements as falsified or not:

(1) Serious doubts on the accuracy of the accounts,
(2) equity capital less that the half of share capital or negative,
(3) existence of court proceedings or some other evidence which can alter the financial situation of the company,
(4) re-financing uncertainty,
(5) total short-term liabilities more than total current assets,
(6) lack of necessary documents (e.g. invoices, vouchers, supporting documents, etc.),
(7) erroneous categorization of financial accounts (e.g. reporting long-term liabilities as short-term debt).

Table 2 shows falsified and non-falsified cases per year. It is clear, that in the first years 2014–2017, the percentage of FFS cases is approximately 35–40%, whereas in the following years the percentage is lower than 30%. Overall, the total FFS occasions to the total companies from 2014 to 2019 is 34%.

3.2 *Variables*

The variables employed in the analysis were selected following the existing literature on falsified statements as well as through various statistical

Table 3: Selected variables.

Variable	Description	Category
FAMILY	1 if there are family members in the board of directors, otherwise 0	Capability
CHANGE OF DIR.	1 if there the chairman of the board of directors changed in year t, otherwise 0	Capability
IND. BOARD	The number of independent members in the board of directors to the total members	Capability
SHARE&BOARD	1 if the members of board of directors are also shareholders, otherwise 0	Capability
BIG4	1 if the audit company is one of the Big 4, otherwise 0	Opportunity
LN(SUBSD)	Natural logarithm of the number of subsidiaries	Opportunity
LN(EMPL)	Natural logarithm of the number of employees	Opportunity
COSTSOLD/INV	Cost of sales/Inventories	Pressure
AMORT./FIXEDASSETS	Amortization/Fixed assets	Pressure
(CASH+CASHEQUIV)/CURRLIAB	(Cash+cash equivalents)/Current liabilities	Pressure
CURRASSETS/CURRLIAB	Current assets/Current liabilities	Pressure
EBIT/T.ASSETS	Earnings before interest & taxes/Total assets	Pressure
LN(T.ASSETS)	Natural logarithm of total assets	Pressure
T.LIAB/T.ASSETS	Total liabilities/Total assets	Pressure
P/BV	Price per book value	Pressure
AUDSWI	1 if the audit company changed in year *t*, otherwise 0	Rationalization

tests (e.g. *t*-test, Mann-Whitney, χ^2 test, correlation analysis), which helped examine the statistical significance of the variables in describing the falsified and non-falsified statements in the sample. The final list of variables is presented in Table 3, classified according to the fraud diamond categories (pressure, opportunity, capability and rationalization). The variables and their categorization are discussed in more detail below.

3.2.1 *Pressure*

According to SAS No. 99, managers feel pressure to proceed in fraudulent actions on the financial statements when financial stability and/or profitability is threatened by the economic conjuncture, sector or operating conditions (Skousen *et al.*, 2008). Due to pressure caused by current conditions, fraud may occur to meet the high earnings expectations by investors and shareholders. Furthermore, executives may use fraudulent financial reporting to meet the requirements of the debt contracts. This shows that the probability of fraudulent reports at high debt levels has increased (Indarto and Ghozali, 2016).

Financial target pressure is the risk of excessive pressure on the management to achieve targets by the management, including targets for acquisition and profit promotion (Supri *et al.*, 2018). Variables, such as COSTSOLD/INV, (CASH+CASHEQUIV)/CURRLIAB, CURRASSETS/CURRLIAB, EBIT/T.ASSETS, T.LIAB/T.ASSETS and P/BV are used in the present study to identify anomalies in the financial position of the firms that could be FFS signals.

Moreover, companies try to increase the value of their assets, either through real value increases in asset items such as asset acquisition, development of existing assets, or by active growth through valuation of existing assets. Often, the acquisition of new assets and the improvement of existing assets, are reported at values different from the real ones (Ozcelik, 2020). A variable, such as LN(T.ASSETS) or AMORT/FIXEDASSETS can be used for the identification of falsification in asset valuations.

3.2.2 *Opportunity*

Effective monitoring (e.g. by an independent audit committee) can minimize the risk of fraudulent behavior (Sunardi and Amin, 2018). Evidence from the literature indicate that audit quality is improved when the audit company belongs in top audit firms (Behn *et al.*, 2008; Verriest, 2013). This is explained because large audit firms seek to main their reputation, while employing more experienced auditors. Nowadays, the four major auditing companies are known as "BIG4" (Deloitte, Ernst and Young, KPMG, PricewaterhouseCoopers).

One of the first ways to commit accounting fraud is to fall into the category of improperly accounting for subsidiary with overstatement of income-revenues or understating expenses. Moreover, foreign subsidiaries play an important role by "permanently reinvesting" foreign earnings to avoid reporting the earnings and paying taxes locally (Troy *et al.*, 2009). Schilit (2002) provided evidence of earnings management relating to acquisitions activity involving subsidiaries. To control for these issues, we use the number of subsidiaries (in logarithmic form).

Moreover, Dechow *et al.* (2011) revealed that during misstatement years the number of employees is declining. They found that if assets are overstated, then the difference between the change in the number of employees, which is not likely overstated, and the change in assets, which is overstated, might be useful evidence of the real economic situation of the company. To check this possibility, we use the number of employees (in logarithmic form).

3.2.3 *Capability*

The category of indicators that refers to "capability" involves the type of management of the companies. First, the existence of family members in the boards of directors has been found to increase the likelihood of fraud due to insufficient board oversight (Lin *et al.*, 2015). Moreover, Sunardi and Amin (2018) found that the change of the director was a fraud risk factor. The composition of the board of director is also important. In this study, we consider the existence of independent members on the board, which has been found to increase the effectiveness of the internal audit protocols (Indarto and Ghozali, 2016). Finally, we also examine whether board members are also stockholders, in which case fraudulent behavior is more likely.

3.2.4 *Rationalization*

According to Chow and Rice (1982), Craswell (1988) and Krishnan and Krishnan (1996), qualified opinions are associated with subsequent auditor switching. Lou and Wang (2009) found that the more the auditor changes, the higher is the frequency of fraudulent reporting. To account for this factor, a dummy indicator is employed regarding change in the auditors (AUDSWI).

3.3 ***Results***

Given the classification of the companies in the sample as FFS and non-FFS, and the variables described above, a machine learning (ML) approach is implemented to develop a model for the identification of falsified financial reporting. The development of an FFS identification and risk assessment model could act as an early-warning system, mitigating the losses for investors, auditors, and all other internal and external stakeholders.

ML approaches have recently become popular tools in the auditing domain and are widely used for fraud detection purposes (Baesens *et al.*, 2015). In the present study, we compare various popular ML methods, namely a multi-layer perceptron (MLP), decision trees, support vector machines with linear kernel (SVM), ensemble algorithms (random forests, bagging and boosting), as well as logistic regression.

Various performance metrics are used for the comparison of the classification performance of the obtained FFS identification models, constructed with the above ML methods. The metrics can be defined through the classification matrix shown in Table 4.

- $\text{Sensitivity} = \dfrac{a}{a+c}$
- $\text{Specificity} = \dfrac{d}{b+d}$
- $\text{Precision} = \dfrac{a}{a+b}$
- $\text{Overall accuracy} = \dfrac{a+d}{a+b+c+d}$
- $\text{Average accuracy} = \dfrac{1}{2}(\text{Sensitivity} + \text{Specificity})$

Moreover, we also consider the area under the receiver operating characteristic curve (AUC), which is a popular metric for assessing the performance of binary classification models.

Table 4: Classification matrix.

		Estimated Status	
		Non-FFS	**FFS**
Actual status	**Non-FFS**	a	c
	FFS	b	d

Table 5: Accuracy evaluation in each applied method.

Methods	Sensitivity	Specificity	Precision	Overall Accuracy	Average Accuracy	AUC
Logistic regression	0.94	0.52	0.89	0.86	0.73	0.86
MLP	0.92	0.80	0.96	0.90	0.86	0.91
Decision trees	0.89	0.61	0.90	0.83	0.75	0.85
SVM	0.94	0.52	0.89	0.86	0.73	0.88
Random forests	0.91	0.61	0.90	0.85	0.76	0.93
Bagging	0.97	0.57	0.90	0.88	0.77	0.88
AdaBoost	0.92	0.74	0.93	0.88	0.83	0.89

Table 5 presents the obtained results for the above metrics. It is evident that MLP provides the most consistent results on most metrics, outperforming all methods in terms of overall and average accuracy, as well as in terms of specificity and precision. It also performs very well in AUC, yielding the second-best result behind the random forests algorithm. MLP is followed by the three ensemble algorithms, among which AdaBoost provides the best results on most metrics. On the other hand, the worst results are obtained by logistic regression, decision trees and SVM. Moreover, it is worth noting that the performance of all methods is consistently lower for the FFS group (i.e. low specificity), thus indicating that more information and deeper analysis is required for the accurate identification of FFS cases.

4. Conclusion and Future Research

Nowadays, the complexity of the financial fraud, the plethora of incentives for individuals within a company to carry out fraud, and of course, the lapse of ability to caught fraudulent behavior before it causes enormous cost, in the economy, make it imperative to examine if the corporate governance guidelines are properly followed.

Because CG has a lot of aspects, the financial fraud diamond can cover this field studying the motivation, opportunity, capability of the fraudster and the rationalization of this action. Using these indicators that describe all aspect of financial fraud in the context of the fraud diamond, in combination with financial data, can be valuable for the detection of financial fraud. The results reported in this study provided evidence supporting this research direction, using data from Greece.

For future research, it would be very interesting to further enrich the indicators related to CG based on the fraud diamond aspect and to compare the results with existing previous studies. For instance, it would be useful to use the Crowe fraud pentagon (pressure, opportunity, rationalization, capability and arrogance; Crowe, 2011; Sari *et al.*, 2020) in Greek companies to examine more factors that lead to fraudulent actions and then, to compare the accuracy levels with the existing studies. Further empirical testing on international data would also provide important insights on the validity of the proposed approach.

References

Abdulahi, R. and Mansor, N. (2015). Fraud triangle theory and fraud diamond theory: Understanding the convergent and divergent for future research, *International Journal of Academic Research in Accounting, Finance and Management Sciences*, 5(4), 38–45.

Albeksh, H.M. (2016). The crisis of the ethics of audit profession: Collapse of Enron company and the lessons learned, *Open Access Library Journal (OALib)*, 3(11), 1–18.

Albrecht, W. St., Wernz, G.W. and Williams, T.L. (1995). *Fraud: Bringing Light to the Dark Side of Business*. Burr Ridge, Ill: Irwin Professional Pub.

Amani, A. and Fadlalla, M. (2017). Data mining applications in accounting: A review of the literature and organizing framework, *International Journal of Accounting Information Systems*, 24, 32–58.

Association of Certified Fraud Examiners (2010). Report to the Nations on Occupational Fraud. https://bit.ly/3iBedT9 (Accessed 5 October 2021).

Association of Certified Fraud Examiners (2018). Global Study on Occupational Fraud and Abuse. Available at: https://bit.ly/3iyip6c (Accessed 5 October 2021).

Basilico, E., Grove, H. and Patelli, L. (2012). Asia's Enron: Satyam (Sanskrit Word for Truth), *Journal of Forensic & Investigative Accounting*, 4(2), 142–160.

Baesens, B., Vlasselaer, V. and Verbeke, W. (2015). *Fraud Analytics Using Descriptive, Predictive, and Social Network Techniques: A Guide to Data Science for Fraud Detection*, Wiley: New York.

Behn, B.K., Choi, J.H. and Kang, T. (2008). Audit quality and properties of analyst earnings forecasts, *The Accounting Review*, 83(2), 327–349.

Bierstaker, J.L., Brody, R.G. and Pacini, C. (2006). Accountants' perceptions regarding fraud detection and prevention methods, *Managerial Auditing Journal*, 21(5), 520–535.

Bressler, M. and Bressler, L. (2007). A model for prevention and detection of criminal activity impacting small business, *Entrepreneurial Executive*, 12, 23–36.

Brink, A., Lowe, D. and Victoravich, L. (2013). The effect of evidence strength and internal rewards on intentions to report fraud in the Dodd–Frank regulatory environment, *Auditing: A Journal of Practice and Theory*, 32(3), 87–104.

Carnegie, G.D. and Napier, C.J. (2010). Traditional accountants and business professionals: Portraying the accounting profession after Enron, *Accounting, Organizations and Society*, 35(3), 360–376.

Chow, C. and Rice, S. (1982). Qualified audit opinions and auditor switching, *The Accounting Review*, 57(2), 326–335.

Craswell, A. (1988). The association between qualified opinions and auditor switches, *Accounting and Business Research*, 19(3), 23–31.

Cressey, D. (1953). *Other People's Money: A Study in the Social Psychology of Embezzlement*. Free Press: Glencoe.

Cressey, D. (1973). *Other People's Money*. Montclair: Patterson Smith.

Crowe, H. (2011). *Putting the Freud in Freud: Why the Fraud Triangle is No Longer Enough*. Horwath: Illinois.

Dechow, P.M., Ge, W., Larson, C.R. and Sloan, R.G. (2011). Predicting material accounting misstatements, *Contemporary Accounting Research*, 28(1), 17–82.

Dorminey, J., Fleming, S., Kranacher, M. and Riley, R. (2012), The evolution of fraud theory, *Issues in Accounting Education*, 27(2), 555–579.

Gabbioneta, C., Greenwood, R., Mazzolad, P. and Minoja, M. (2013). The influence of the institutional context on corporate illegality, *Accounting, Organizations and Society*, 38(6–7), 484–504.

Humpherys, S.L., Moffitt, K.C., Burns, M.B., Burgoon, J.K. and Felix, W.F. (2011). Identification of fraudulent financial statements using linguistic credibility analysis, *Decision Support Systems*, 50(3), 585–594.

Jennings, M.M. (2004). Incorporating ethics and professionalism into accounting education and research: A discussion of the voids and advocacy for training in seminal works in business ethics, *Issues in Accounting Education*, 19(1), 7–26.

Indarto, S.L. and Ghozali, I. (2016). Fraud diamond: Detection analysis on the fraudulent financial reporting, *Risk Governance & Control: Financial Markets & Institutions*, 6(4), 116–123.

Kamarudin, K.A., Ismail, W.A.W. and Mustapha, W.A.H.W. (2012). Aggressive financial reporting and corporate fraud, *Procedia Social and Behavioral Sciences*, 65, 638–643.

Karacaer, S. and Ozek, P. (2011). The relationship between the audit firm and earnings management: An empirical study in Istanbul Stock Exchange, *The Journal of Accounting and Finance*, 48, 60–74.

Karpoff, J.M. and J.R. Lott, Jr. (1993). The reputational penalty firms bear from committing criminal fraud, *Journal of Law and Economics*, 36, 757–802.

Karpoff, J.M., Lee, S.D. and Martin, G.S. (2008). The cost to firms of cooking the books, *Journal of Financial and Quantitative Analysis*, 43(3), 581–611.

Kirkos, E., Spathis, C. and Manolopoulos, Y. (2007). Data mining techniques for the detection of fraudulent financial statements, *Expert Systems with Applications*, 32(4), 995–1003.

Kotsiantis, S., Koumanakos, E. and Tzelepis, D. (2006). Forecasting fraudulent financial statements using data mining, *International Journal of Computational Intelligence*, 3, 104–110.

Lin, J.W., Hwang, M.I. and Becker, J.D. (2003). A fuzzy neural network for assessing the risk of fraudulent financial reporting, *Managerial Auditing Journal*, 18(8), 657–665.

Lou, Y. and Wang, M.L. (2009). Fraud risk factor of the fraud triangle assessing the likelihood of fraudulent financial reporting, *Journal of Business and Economics Research*, 7(1), 61–78.

MacLean, B. and Elkind, P. (2003). *Smartest Guys in the Room: The Amazing Rise and Scandalous Fall of Enron*. Portfolio: New York.

Mayhew, B. and Murphy, P. (2014). The impact of authority on reporting behavior, rationalization and affect, *Contemporary Accounting Research*, 31(2), 420–443.

Manurung, D. and Hadian, N. (2013). Detection fraud of financial statement with fraud triangle. *Proceedings of 23rd International Business Research Conference November 2013 Australia.*

Ngai, E.W.T., Hu, Y., Wong, Y.H., Chen, Y. and Sun, X. (2011). The application of data mining techniques in financial fraud detection: a classification framework and an academic review of literature, *Decision Support Systems*, 50(3), 559–569.

Ozcelik, H. (2020). An analysis of fraudulent financial reporting using the fraud diamond theory perspective: An empirical study on the manufacturing sector companies listed on the Borsa Istanbul, *Contemporary Issues in Audit Management and Forensic Accounting*, 102, 131–153.

Peterson, B.K. and Buckhoff, T.A. (2004). Anti-fraud education in academia. Advances in accounting education, *Teaching and Curriculum Innovations*, 6, 45–67.

Price, R.A., Sharp, N.Y. and Wood, D.A. (2011). Detecting and predicting accounting irregularities: A comparison of commercial and academic risk measures, *Accounting Horizons*, 25(4), 755–780.

Reiner, R. (2017). Political economy, crime and criminal justice. In Liebling, A., Maruna, S. and McAra, L. (eds.), *The Oxford Handbook of Criminology*. Oxford University Press: Oxford, pp. 116–137.

Rezaee, Z. (2002). *Financial Statement Fraud: Prevention and Detection*. John Wiley and Sons, Inc.: New York.

Rezaee, Z., Crumbley, D.L. and Elmore, R.C. (2004). Forensic accounting education. Advances in Accounting Education, *Teaching and Curriculum Innovations*, 6, 193–231.

Rudewicz, F. (2011). The fraud diamond: Use of investigative due diligence to identify the "capability element of fraud", *Turnaround Management Association*, IV(1), 1–3.

Sari, M.P., Pramasheilla, N., Fachurrizie, Suryarini, T. and Pamungkas, I.D. (2020). Analysis of fraudulent financial reporting with the role of KAP big four as a moderation variable: Crowe's Fraud's Pentagon Theory, *International Journal of Financial Research*, 11(5), 180–190.

Schilit, H.M. (2002). *Financial Shenanigans*, 2nd edition. New York: McGraw-Hill.

Skousen, C.J., Smith, K.R. and Wright, C.J. (2008). Detecting and predicting financial statement fraud: The effectiveness of the fraud triangle and SAS No. 99 (SSRN Scholarly Paper Sy ID 1295494). Social Science Research Network.

Spathis, Ch. Doumpos, M. and Zopounidis, C. (2002). Detecting falsified financial statements: A comparative study using multicriteria analysis and multivariate statistical techniques, *The European Accounting Review*, 11(3), 509–535.

Statement on Auditing Standards No. 99. (2002). Consideration of Fraud in a Financial Statement Audit, Auditing Standards Board of the American Institute of Certified Public Accountants (AICPA).

Sunardi, S. and Amin, M.N. (2018). Fraud detection of financial statement by using fraud diamond perspective, *European Journal of Business and Management*, 7(3), 878–891.

Supri, Z., Rura, Y. and Pontoh, G.T. (2018). Detection of fraudulent financial statements with fraud diamond, *Journal of Research in Business and Management*, 6(5), 39–45.

Troy, C.J, Domino, M.A. and Landry, St. P. (2009). Exploring accounting fraud in the subsidiary environment, *Journal of Business & Economics Research*, 7(1), 13–22.

Verriest, A.J.M. (2013). Auditor governance, institutions and analyst forecast properties: International evidence, *Journal of International Accounting Research*, 13(1), 1–32.

Westhausen, H.-U. (2017). The escalating relevance of internal auditing as anti-fraud control, *Journal of Financial Crime*, 24, 322–328.

Williams, M. (2010). *Uncontrolled Risk*. McGraw-Hill Education: New York.

Wolfe, D. and Hermanson, D.R. (2004). The fraud diamond: Considering four elements of fraud, *The CPA Journal*, 74(12), 38–42.

Yeh, C.C., Chi, D.J. and Hsu, M.F. (2010). A hybrid approach of DEA, rough set and support vector machines for business failure prediction, *Expert Systems with Applications*, 37(2), 1535–1541.

Zerban, A.M. (2018). Enron of Saudi Arabia: Corporate accounting and auditing failures, *Open Journal of Accounting*, 7, 1–18.

Part III

CG and Externalities

https://doi.org/10.1142/9789811260506_0009

Chapter 9

Governance and Corporate Control around the World

Panagiotis Kyriakogkonas[*,¶], Panagiotis Giannopoulos[†,||], Alexandros Garefalakis[‡,], and Andreas Koutoupis[§,††]**

[*]*Neapolis University, School of Economics, Business and Computer Science,*

Paphos, Pafos, Cyprus

[†]*Department of Public Administration, Panteion University of Political and Social Sciences*

Vice president, Hellenic Accounting and Auditing Standards, Oversight Board, Athens, Greece

[‡]*Hellenic Mediterranean University, Department of Business Administration & Tourism, Operations Research and Management Audit Laboratory, Heraklion, Crete & Neapolis University Pafos, Cyprus*

[§]*University of Thessaly, Department of Accounting and Finance, Volos, Greece*

[¶]*kyrpanos80@hotmail.com*

[||]*pannos@gmail.com*

[**]*agarefalakis@hmu.gr*

[††]*andreas_koutoupis@yahoo.gr*

Abstract

Corporate control, within the context of the capitalism, could take many forms that might make communication among various groups, such as academics, public authorities or employees of any level, difficult and complicated. In the US and other developed countries, capitalism is formed through a large number of corporations of any size who compete with each other, while monopolies are prohibited. Owners of those corporations, the shareholders, especially the minor ones, are usually disorganized and powerless, while other corporations or even state-owned corporations act as shareholders of other corporations and promote their interests through active participation in management with, among others, the selection and the influence of Board members. CEOs, as the heads of management of such corporations, even audited and controlled by many mechanisms in place, could affect decision-making of those corporations by incorporating their personal beliefs and mindsets, cultural influences and political beliefs in their decision-making process. In less developed countries, capitalism is formed through the creation of corporations by wealthy families, with limited number of shareholders, and there are many cases that members of the family possess the vast majority of shareholders' voting rights. The owners of such corporations might sometimes have the power to affect governments' decision-making in order to gain advantage over their competitors, so even though monopolies are prohibited, the actual situation is far away from the terms of perfect competition.

Within this economic context, historically, the evolution of corporate governance has been affected by several factors and events that took place during financial history. Those factors and events not only contributed to the evolution of corporate governance but also differentiated its content among countries with different corporate control types, different cultures, economic power, etc. Emergency events at countries' history like wars, changes in political systems, etc., along with major economic crises due to corporate collapses led corporate governance to emerge and to evolve. Reinforcement of concentration of corporations by wealthy families in some countries, along with the decline of power of some wealthy families in other countries and the corresponding corporate failures, created discrepancies among countries to the applicable legislation for corporate governance. The formation of big business groups, through mergers, acquisitions and creation of new corporations as a response to cope with competition, created new risks for shareholders and stakeholders that had to deal with effectively by legislative authorities, within the context of corporate governance and the established mechanisms of corporate control. The rapid evolution of technology in recent years that had massive impact on privacy issues led to the creation of relevant legislation that had also impact on the governance model of the corporations and on elements of control of corporations. Legislation itself is a factor that not only is affected by the evolution of corporate governance but also affects and triggers its revolution. Capital markets legislation, for example, affects the behavior of shareholders, especially of controlling shareholders who might set up their strategy extending from passive block holders to active participants with diversified portfolios of investments.

This chapter presents basic corporate control types and their influences on their formation by cultural and other factors. Also, this chapter presents basic corporate governance types and their relationship with corporate control types at various countries around the world, based on 2019 recent studies by OECD.

Keywords: Corporate control, corporate governance, shareholders, legislation

1. Introduction

Any system that dominated during the previous century, like the Japanese *keiretsu* structure which promoted the idea of mutual monitoring, the Korean Chaebol, the German bank-centered capital market which promoted the adoption of long-term strategies by managers through debt creation, or the general European concentrated ownership model, faced challenges that accelerated its reform and modification. During recent years, we observe financialization of the global economy and efforts toward its convergence, at least at some parts of it. The established and dominant Anglo-American governance system faced two major crises, that of Enron's collapse back in 2002 and that of the debt crisis of 2008 which originated from the US financial industry sector. Those financial crises, that their consequences were widespread worldwide, brought at the forefront the need for major reformations of corporate governance. In particular, in order to avoid similar circumstances and to gain investors, of any type and size, confidence back, legal changes took place and Codes of corporate governance were adopted. The aforementioned financial uncertainty is accompanied with convergence strategies and the question is whether we are moving toward a convergence to the Anglo-American governance model or to governance systems that combine local regulatory frameworks with practices from other countries. Convergence strategies are illustrated at two major categories. First, at financial market integration with some indicators of convergence efforts to be cross-listings, increased foreign portfolio investments, cross-border mergers and acquisitions and no restrictions at capital flows across countries-continents. Second, at corporate governance efforts and especially at the level of establishment an adoption of corporate governance codes. Codes of corporate governance have the characteristic of motivating corporations not only to fulfill the minimum requirements the law dictates but also to go beyond and comply with best practices that are proposed and adopted at international level. Several researches have pointed out that corporations that adopt corporate governance codes mostly comply with their recommendations, which are, at most cases, beyond legal requirements. Especially during post-Enron period, corporations were under pressure of publicity lights to adopt and comply with corporate governance codes.

Corporate governance includes a number of policies, codes, processes and laws that dictate corporations' direction, administration and control and defines the relationship between corporations and various stakeholders among which are the shareholders of any size. Consequently, a well-organized corporate governance structure contributes to the fair treatment of every stakeholder and of every shareholders regardless of their size, economic power, political lobbying, abilities, etc., and it must include accountability aspects, economic efficiency aspects, strategic efficiency aspects and stakeholder management aspects. According to Cadbury Committee (1992), corporate governance is the system by which corporations are directed and controlled and manage their relationships with the stakeholders. The context within which corporate governance practices are applied must not be underestimated. Different political systems, different cultures, different priorities of corporate governance legislations across countries dictate different stipulations at legal frameworks regarding corporate governance and at their respective codes. Within this context, established corporate governance across countries are attempting to cope with agency problem, as the latter is expressed at contemporary corporations due to the separation between ownership and control.

2. Agency Problem

Traditionally, corporate governance was researched in close association with agency problem as a response to cope with managerial freedom to take decision for corporations in which risk bearing shareholders exist. Shareholders pursuit maximization of their investments within the boundaries of a reasonable risk while managers might pursuit growth of profits as a prerequisite for their salaries' (associated with performance related bonuses) maximization. Agency problems exist when shareholders do not possess the ability to monitor and limit management actions since information might not be perfect and available to them and since it is difficult to pose contractual boundaries to managerial decisions and actions (Eisenhardt, 1989).

A typical listed corporation represents a legal entity with limited liability, transferable shares, delegated management under a board structure, and investor ownership (Hansmann and Kraakman, 2004). The aforementioned type of corporation is the most common and attractive form of corporation. A major disadvantage of such corporations is the agency problem which is illustrated by conflicts of interest between management and shareholders which frequently arise in corporations with a dispersed ownership structure. In such corporations, minority shareholders cannot effectively manage and influence the firm due to coordination and communication problems, so they delegate the control of the corporations to professional managers. Such delegation leads to a divergence of interests between the managers and shareholders (Berle and Means, 1932). Professional managers might pursuit the maximization of their personal interests against shareholders' wealth maximization objective through maximization of the value of the corporation. A major attribute for the reduction of agency problem is accountability of managers for their actions against major and minor shareholders. Such accountability is further enhanced through the existence of an independent, from the major shareholder, Board of Directors which oversees and controls management actions, along with clearly defined responsibilities, through job descriptions, for managers and directors.

Shareholders could align managerial interests and corporation's interests through the deployment of executive compensation contracts (Goergen and Renneboog, 2011; Kulich *et al*., 2011) or through the establishment of mechanisms that effectively monitor managerial actions for their alignment with corporation's objectives (Becht *et al*., 2003; Crespi and Renneboog, 2010; Goergen *et al*., 2008a; Grossman and Hart, 1980; Shleifer and Vishny, 1986). For the latter, and especially for minority shareholders, coordination problems do not allow them to effectively control management actions, so they usually rely on external monitoring mechanisms provided by markets (Fama and Jensen, 1983; Jensen, 1988).

In corporations with concentrated ownership structures, conflicts of interest between shareholders and management are less frequent, since controlling shareholders have strong incentives to monitor management and even replace it when their performance, aligned with corporation's objectives is not satisfactory (Franks *et al.*, 2001). However, in such cases, the presence of a controlling shareholder may modify agency problem since controlling shareholders might adopt an opportunistic behavior against minority shareholders (Faccio and Stolin, 2006). That kind of agency problem, according to La Porta *et al.* (1999) makes controlling blockholders to gain advantages at the expense of minority shareholders. According to various researches throughout the years, ownership structure of corporations tends to vary across countries. Back in 1999, Becht and Roell (1999) researched ownership structure of corporations in Austria, Belgium, France, Germany, Italy, Spain and The Netherlands, and found that the largest shareholder-voting stake exceeded 50%. Also, in a 1999 study conducted by La Porta *et al.*, in 20 largest corporations of each country, it was found that 36% of them were widely held, 30% family owned and controlled (which represented the 25% of the value of the largest 20 corporations per country on average), 18% were state controlled and 15% of them used some other form of ownership structure. It is important that pyramidal ownership structure deployed the 26% of the corporations. In 2003, Claessens, Djankov and Lang found that 75% of corporations of their sample consisting of 7 East Asia countries were associated with business groups, while Valadares and Leal (2000) found concentrated ownership structure of approximately 41% of the equity capital in Brazil. Within corporate governance context, differences in ownership structures and in legislation could affect proposed and applied corporate governance mechanisms. In Italy for example, Brunello *et al.* (2003), found that such arrangements (i.e. concentrated ownership, limited shareholder consideration about corporate governance and lack of banks' monitoring) could affect well-established corporate governance mechanisms such as the existence of independent directors since Boards of Directors, with members influenced by major shareholders, could act as monitoring mechanisms through inside information knowledge. Finally, important elements that must be taken into consideration are the dynamics and the power that large shareholder groups possess. In Japan for example, back in 1992 top five shareholders owned 30% of shares of all listed companies (Prowse, 1992).

Another form might take the agency problem is that between shareholders and creditors, due to the legal formation of the corporation, that of limited liability. The characteristics of such corporation's formation, is that creditors presume the first claim on the corporation's assets while the shareholders are residual claimants. Limited liability implies that the shareholders are not personally liable for the debt obligations of the corporation. Within this context, managers could maximize corporation's wealth, by simply directing shareholders' investments to risky projects, thereby transferring risk to creditors. Creditors, in order to cope with such arrangements should be able to monitor adequately and effectively corporation's activities (Martynova and Renneboog, 2011). There are several cases where in the Board of Directors of a corporation include members who are representatives of the creditors that have lent the corporation. Such arrangements are mostly implemented to companies that face financial difficulties. In such cases, a two-way risk exists. First, existing members of the Board of Directors might pose difficulties to the participation of a new member outside of the corporation member into the Board. Second, the new member might create a new type of agency problem since he will pursuit each assignee interests, i.e. the recovery of the biggest possible percentage of borrowed money, which might be in contrast with corporation's objectives, especially in the short term.

Countries like the UK and the US whose corporations are characterized by dispersed ownership agency problem is mainly addressed through legal regulation along with contractual obligations for managers. In corporations at countries of continental Europe major blockholders might be banks, other financial institutions and wealthy families which have the power to influence the selection of managers along with their decisions, so the intervention of the state through the establishment of relevant legal frameworks is limited. Based on the differences on actions employed by various corporations among various countries in order to mitigate agency problem adverse consequences, we highlight three points: First, corporate governance has been evolved during past decades so as to incorporate, apart from shareholders, other groups, not only financially associated with the corporation like society, competitors, environment, etc. Each corporation with each one of the aforementioned groups could face an agency problem, the magnitude of which will be among others associated with levels of power, levels of influence and levels of interaction. Second, each analysis must take into consideration the fact that, among shareholders, each group might pursuit different goals, which collectively are different from those of the corporation. Banks acting as shareholders of a corporation, for example, might be interested in cash-realized strategies while a wealthy family might be interested on gaining more power to influence not only corporation's decisions but also governmental decisions, especially when the corporation is big and capable of political lobbying. Aguilera and Jackson (2003) provide a categorization of shareholders based on their interests by their participation in a corporation. First, those shareholders who are interested in financial interests. In these cases, shareholders pursuit return from their investments so, irrespective of their size, they implement an investment strategy in order to maximize the market share of their investments (Dore, 2000; O'Sullivan, 2000). Second, those shareholders who are interested in strategic interests as expressed by technological dependencies, securing markets and influencing by selecting or excluding managers to the management of the corporation. Third, those shareholders who balance between liquidity of their investments and commitment, and more specifically between exit and voice (Becht and Rbel, 1999). Exit strategies of shareholders focus on selling their shares of corporations to prices equal or higher than buying price, which implies dispersed and diversified portfolios, along with the existence and operation of mature markets. Commitment strategies of shareholders usually involve large percentages of ownership which can affect the decision for an investment and its return (Lazonick and O'Sullivan, 1996). Finally, those shareholders who are debt or equity shareholders. Debt shareholders usually do not have the ability to influence management until bankruptcy phase of a corporation where they could even undertake management of the corporation. Also, debt shareholders are more risk averse than equity shareholders who possess greater level of control and could influence management actions. Equity shareholders prefer debt to be increased as a way to leverage their earnings in terms of stable number of shares issued, so there is the point where a kind of agency problem might occur. Finally, a structural characteristic of agency problem is its duality, i.e. the fact that focuses on the relationship between two parties, ignoring the interrelations either between parties or either between those parties and other parties. For example, the fact that shareholders of a corporation might be shareholders to other companies might favor corporate competition, networking and innovation (Whitley, 1999).

3. Corporate Control Realization Strategies

The principle of "one share one vote" is important for the allocation of corporate ownership and corporate control (Easterbrook and Fischel, 1991). This principle implies that shareholders with more shares than others exert more control over corporation's actions. In practice, in listed corporations worldwide, this principle might not be applied and powerful shareholders (even while possessing a small percentage of shares) exert control over corporations through mechanisms like dual class shares, pyramidal ownership and cross-shareholding (Bebchuk *et al.*, 2000).

Dual class shares setup, at its simplest form, requires a single corporation which decides to apply different voting rights to categories of stocks. In such a setup, some shareholders gain voting rights so they can influence management actions either by assigning it or by influencing their decisions. The remaining shareholders (usually shareholders who possess shares through stock exchanges) have no voting rights and no power to influence management. Legal frameworks in some countries restrict either the voting ratio by setting up upper and lower boundaries, or the percentage of shares that entail voting rights. An illustrative example is the Swedish Wallenberg Group. The owners of the Group possessed 40% of voting rights and only 20% of the shares of the holding corporation of the Group. In turn, the Group possessed 95% of voting rights of Electrolux and only 7% of the shares. Similar examples exist in South Africa (Bebchuk *et al.*, 2000). Golden shares are a differentiation of dual class shares. Golden shares setup is usually used by governments in order to preserve special control rights. Governments use such arrangements when they consider potential harm of their interests from outside shareholders.

Pyramidal ownership structure for controlling management actions does not require two categories of shares with different voting rights attached. Instead, in such a setup a minority shareholder holds a significant number of shares with voting rights, so the power to influence management of a holding corporation, which in turn, holds a significant number of shares with voting rights, thus having the power to influence management of other companies. It is illustrative that in a 3-level pyramid structure, where a shareholder possesses a minimum for controlling purposes of 50% of shares of the first corporation, ends up in controlling the third-tier corporation by holding 12.5% of the shares (Bebchuk *et al.*, 2000). Within this context, La Porta *et al.* (1999) researched an Asian wealthy family, the Li Ka-shing. Li Ka-shing family possessed 35% of

Cheung Kong public corporation, which in turn possessed 44% of Hutcheson Wampoa, which in turn owned Hong Kong's electricity corporation, Cavendish International.

A subcategory of pyramidal ownership and in particular, of allocation of resources according to the direction of the flow is tunneling and propping. Tunneling refers to the allocation of resources from a low-level corporation of the pyramidal structure to a higher one, while propping refers to the allocation of resources from a high-level corporation to a lower one, with the intention, usually, to save it from financial shortages or bankruptcy (Riyanto and Toolsema, 2008). Real life examples of resources that are transferable include internal asset sales, equity sales, transfer pricing and contracts. The aforementioned statement apply to expropriation mechanisms, which refer to the deployment of mechanisms that allocate resources between wealthy and minority shareholders, usually in favor of the wealthy ones who possess power to influence management. In practice, such allocation of resources between corporations of a business group are legal at many jurisdictions related-party transactions, which as long as they fulfill the obligations of disclosure and approval are legitimate, even when the nature of those transactions harms minority shareholders.

Cross-shareholding structure is similar to pyramidal ownership but ownership and control structures are formed through horizontal cross-holding of shares that create the basis for controlling management. In particular, the difference between pyramidal ownership structure and cross-shareholding structure is that voting rights that entail control power over management actions are distributed horizontally between participating companies rather than to the owner corporation. Riady family offers an illustrative example of cross-shareholding ownership through the investment group of Lippo that is consisted, mainly, of three companies, Lippo Bank, Lippo Life and Lippo Securities. In 1996, Riady family decided to divest from Lippo Bank and Lippo Life but continued to control them, since they were the major shareholder of Lippo Securities which in turn possessed 27% of Lippo Life, which in turn possessed 40% of Lippo Bank (Solomon, 1996).

Another setup used for the exertion of corporate control by shareholders is partnership limited by shares. Such an arrangement requires a small number of unlimited liability partners who exert control and the majority of shareholders who provide the necessary capital but have no influence on control and strategic direction issues. Finally, two further arrangements are corporate charter provisions and some embedded defense mechanisms. As far as the former is concerned, its primary purpose is to secure the corporation, through corporate charter provisions, from outsiders and hostile takeover bids (in US, such arrangements are referred as sharks repellent). Common provisions include voting caps, staggered Boards of Directors and poison pills which allow the placement of newly issued shares to friendly shareholders in order to avoid hostile takeover bids. As far as the latter is concerned, those include specific provisions regarding control in leases, licenses, joint ventures, employment contracts and debt instruments.

A study of 2007 presents interesting points regarding the allocation of the aforementioned. Within 464 corporations of the European Union member states, 44% of them had in place a mechanism of control, with the most common mechanisms to be pyramidal structure and multiple voting rights shares (ISS *et al.*, 2007). Countries like Italy, Finland, Sweden and Switzerland deploy dual class shares mechanism for control leverage (Faccio and Lang, 2002). In another continent, and specifically in East Asian countries, corporations deploy pyramidal structures, while dual class shares mechanism of leveraging control is prohibited in some states (Claessens *et al.*, 2000).

More analytically, in Germany there are three types of shares: ordinary, restricted and preferred shares, with the latter being issued with or without voting rights but with priority on dividends distribution. Listed companies in Germany utilize dual class shares. Also, according to Gibbs (2002), some listed corporations' shares with voting rights were not publicly available but possessed by wealthy families and corporations. Golden shares exist in German corporate environment but the most obvious control setups are pyramidal ownership and cross-shareholding. Back in 2000, JP Morgan estimated that 31% of market capitalization was possessed by strategic shareholders and cross-shareholding (Harris, 2000).

In UK, researches regarding the existence of dual class shares are controversial. Gibbs (2002), for example, indicated that at the sample, used only 3 corporations utilized dual class shares, while Bennedsen and Nielsen (2001), found that 500 corporations of the sample used utilized dual class shares (even though the sample used consisted of corporations belonging to small and medium capitalization). As far as the existence of non-voting shares is concerned, even though the issuance of new non-voting rights is rare, non-voting shares still exist even though the corporation-issuer might be merged or acquired by other corporation.

Cross-shareholding and pyramidal ownership are also utilized in UK in order to be protected against hostile takeovers.

In Spain, even though dual class shares setup is permitted under Spanish law, few corporations utilize that option (Gibbs, 2002; Bennedsen and Nielsen, 2001). On the contrary, golden share setup is utilized by the state at many cases, as privatization programs have commenced since last decade. Also, dual class shares setup and pyramidal ownership are not so frequently utilized by listed Spanish corporations. Instead, those corporations prefer to deploy some other tools we mentioned before, like staggered boards and voting rights ceilings, but as a way to protect management rather than to acquire control of the corporation (Grant and Kirchmaier, 2005).

In Italy, there are three types of shares, ordinary shares, preference shares and voting shares. Preference shares even though do not possess voting rights, they have some priority during earnings distribution or liquidation. Saving shares also have no voting rights but a fixed percentage of yield and the same prioritization with preference shares. As a logical consequence of the aforementioned, Italian listed corporations utilize to a great extent dual class shares (Gibbs, 2002; Bennedsen and Nielsen, 2001; Nenova, 2000). The Italian state deploys golden shares setup for its participation at privatized corporations along with ownership ceilings. Also, pyramidal structure is a common setup in Italian listed corporations due to tax status under which tax is imposed only once independent of the chains of controls through shares. Cross-shareholding and especially circular cross-shareholding appears quite often in Italy. In particular, under such a setup each corporation might possess a percentage of shares of each other corporation of the group.

4. Corporate Control and Governance around the World

As discussed above, ownership structures are affected by the nature of the investors, the goals they pursuit and respectively their investment strategy. As ownership structures differ, there are accordingly differences on resources allocation, monitoring mechanisms and decision-making processes. A 2019 study by OECD of the 10,000 largest corporations around the world of a total of 41,000 listed corporations, which represent US$75.6 trillion market capitalization, classifies owners–shareholders at

5 distinct categories: private corporations and holding companies, i.e. listed and unlisted corporations, their subsidiaries, their operating divisions, etc. Public sector includes central governments, local governments, public pension funds, state-owned corporations and sovereign wealth funds; strategic individuals and families which might be controlling owners, members of a controlling group or family etc.; institutional investors like insurance companies, pension funds, mutual funds, hedge funds, etc.; retail investors that refers to persons that have no obligation to disclose their holdings.

According to the aforementioned study, institutional investors possess more than US$31 trillion of ownership, public sector possesses US$10 trillion of ownership, and the broadly defined category of retail investors possess around US$22 trillion of ownership but mostly includes investments by institutional investors that are below disclosures threshold. Among others, an interesting part of this study is the effect of the internationalization of the equity market. Within this context, we observe that in Hong Kong, Netherlands, UK and Brazil, non-domestic investments represent around 60%, 50%, 40% and 40%, respectively, of the market capitalization of each country. On the contrary, in Philippines, US, China and Saudi Arabia's non-domestic investments represent less than 10% of the market capitalization of each country.

A different view of the aforementioned study, which affects corporate governance and control issues is that of ownership structure of the largest corporations around the world, in terms of control exercise. Nearly 85% of the corporations of the sample have one shareholder who possesses more than 10% of the equity, while at 75% of the corporations, the 3 major shareholders possess more than 30% of the equity. More analytically, in countries' level, corporations in Argentina, Russia and Indonesia have a shareholder who possesses around 70% of the equity of the corporations, while at corporations in Finland, Japan, the UK and the US, the major's shareholder percentage of equity is around 5%.

As we presented previously, the role of institutional investors has evolved during the last decades. The reason that promoted the enhancement of their roles is the strengthening of both public and pension funds whose assets have reach almost 51% of GDP of OECD countries. Moreover, risk diversification strategies led to pool assets ready for diversified investments by institutional investors. Finally, technology, as a driver for many evolutions nowadays, promoted the aforementioned pooling of assets and the new, diversified-driven, investment products and strategies. A major consequence, related with corporate governance, is the emergence of the role of the intermediaries in investments. In particular, the relationship between household and pensions' savings and investment market has been modified and acquired another one part, that of institutional investors which, in most cases, act as intermediaries of investments. Such a modification created new challenges, in terms of corporate governance, which has to do with the alignment of the interests of the ultimate beneficiaries with those of profit maximized-driven intermediaries (institutional investors). As a response, many countries have either modified their respective regulatory frameworks so as to apply different measures regarding the involvement of institutional investors to corporate governance according to their investment strategy, or adopted related codes.

An evidence of the aforementioned statement is the fact that in US corporations the percentage of ownership by institutional investors is divided into two major categories: 60% of institutional investors' ownership is held by domestic investors, while the remaining is held by foreign investors. In the UK, around 30% of the total ownership held by institutional investors is held by domestic investors, 10% by foreign-non-US investors and around 25% is held by the US investors. In Argentina, on the contrary, around 8% of the total ownership held by institutional investors is held by foreign-non-US investors, and around 15% is held by US investors while domestic investors possess no percentage of ownership. In terms of ownership concentration by institutional investors, in US the largest three institutional investors per corporation held around 20% of total equity, while in Saudi Arabia largest three institutional shareholders possess less than 5% of the ownership. If we elaborate more on the aforementioned and focus on the 10 largest corporations per sector, OECD study indicates that in airline industry the largest 3 institutional investors possess 10% of ownership, in online services industry the largest 3 institutional investors possess 15% of ownership while in telecommunications industry the largest 3 institutional investors possess 6% of ownership across the 10 largest corporations of the sector.

Despite the wave of privatizations of public corporations during the previous decade, public sector through the evolution of sovereign wealth funds and the emerging role of public pension funds, managed to preserve control at many corporations around world. In particular, public sector ownership is realized through investments of governments in listed corporations, public pension funds which manage retirement savings of civil servants, organizations owned by governments and sovereign wealth funds which also hold shares of listed corporations. It is worth to mention that ~33% of the total cross-countries ownerships comes from the investor US, which directs its investments mostly in Japan and UK.

Also, in the aforementioned study it was found that 800 corporations have over 50% public sector ownership, and in another 1,160 corporations public sector possesses between 10% and 49% of the equity of the listed corporations. About 56% of all public sector ownership is held by governments, 24% is held by sovereign wealth funds, 11% is held by public pension funds and the remaining 9% is held by state-owned corporations.

An interesting point of the aforementioned study is the allocation of public sector ownership across countries. Saudi Arabia, Malaysia, Hong Kong and China hold between 38% and 46% of public sector ownership, while in Canada, Netherlands, US, Philippines, Israel, Mexico and Chile public sector ownership does not exceed 5%. A further breakdown of the study in sectors focused on public sector produces interesting inferences. At basic materials sector Saudi Arabia and Malaysia's public sector holds over 60% and 40% respectively of ownership, while in UK, Sri Lanka and Japan public sector holds less than 5% of ownership at respective corporations. Accordingly, in China and Hong Kong public sector possesses 77% and 75% of energy sector corporations while in Greece, South Africa and Sweden public sector ownership percentages are around 20%. Finally, at telecommunications sector Pakistan and Saudi Arabia hold over 70% of ownership at respective corporations, while in Greece, Finland and Korea public sector ownership is around 10%.

In the US, in the first half of the 20th century, shareholders were not involved in management monitoring and usually they preserved diversified portfolios (Berle and Means, 1932). Management, on the other hand, had the freedom to adopt high-risk strategies with no monitoring mechanisms in place. Such a scheme allowed the creation of possible sources for conflicts of interest, especially since investors had dispersed their resources by owing small percentages of shares at many corporations. Such a diversification of ownership on behalf of shareholders made Board and management monitoring difficult since shareholders had no unified actions. Corporate governance served a dual purpose: as a protection agency for shareholders and as a control mechanism for management (Mizruchi, 2004). During the last decades of the 20th century in the US, the ownership of corporations changed hands, within different categories of shareholders. Dispersed shareholders now share ownership of corporations along with institutional shareholders, while the state possesses only a small portion of ownership, especially in comparison with European countries (Tonello and Rabimov, 2010).

Before we move on, we consider it important to clarify the nature of institutional investors. According to Gilson and Gordon (2013), there are three major categories of institutional shareholders. First mutual funds, which take the form of a corporation and is subject to strict regulation by the SEC. Such regulation dictates easy implemented exit strategies, along with the implementation of divesting strategies at certain occasions, which in turn links fund managers' performance with short-term profitability and successful liquidity strategies. Second pension funds, whose characteristics are similar to those of mutual funds. Managers of pension funds are pursuing high returns, especially in comparison with related competition. Because pension funds' success is linked to private gains of shareholders along with the accomplishment of high returns in comparison with competition, shareholders have no incentive to be involved in the improvement of management of the pension fund (Gilson and Gordon, 2013). Consequently, mutual fund managers have no incentive, direct or indirect, to actively allocate resources so as to improve the governance of the mutual fund, and are interested in portfolio management in order to maximize returns. Third, hedge funds whose operation is not governed by strict regulation from SEC like the two previous categories of institutional shareholders. Hedge funds clients are usually wealthy investors, who enter in a hedge fund investment usually through private offerings and demand high returns in a longer period. Because of the longer period of investments, hedge funds have the time to consider long-term investment strategies which entail the acquisition of big blocks of shares at certain target-corporations and are actively involved in the improvement of governance and related business practices (Goodwin, 2015).

In the US, directors are responsible for their actions against shareholders through the application of fiduciary duties. In addition, shareholders, in particular the controlling ones, might be responsible for governance decisions they took, against minority shareholders and other stakeholders, through the application of the fiduciary duties of loyalty and care. More specifically, controlling shareholders cannot, in favor of their personal gains, implement governance and other strategies that harm the potential interests of other shareholders and of the corporation itself. Besides that type of responsibility, shareholders presume no other responsibility toward other stakeholders, especially because they are not considered responsible for the direction and the implementation of corporate governance practices (Anabtawi and Stout, 2008). Also, the belief that minority shareholders whose interests might be aligned among them and with those of controlling shareholders care more about corporate governance is a factor that influences the lack of provisions on corporate governance about the relationship between shareholders. Activist shareholders and investors who focus on certain characteristics of corporate governance, through their investment decisions, have questioned the aforementioned absence of provisions of corporate governance about the relationship between shareholders.

Also, an important dimension of the relationship between major corporate governance players is that of the relationship between corporate governance regulation and stakeholders, other than shareholders. Stakeholders secure their interests through contract law, which despite the fact that seems to be of lesser importance than related regulation, stakeholders reinforce its importance through stricter binding rules and corresponding exit strategies (Dai and Helfrich, 2016). A corporation, for example, that pursuits short-term maximization of profits might engage in actions that promote its goals but undermine the goals of its stakeholders, like the goals of creditors, suppliers, etc., since capital management might be a second priority for the corporation.

By 1990 in the US, insurance companies, banks and mutual funds became active and expressed interest on corporate governance matters. However, law prohibited banks from possessing shares, while such prohibitions were not present at legal systems of other countries like Germany or Japan. The aforementioned situation changed when US government agencies and especially the Labor Department encouraged pension funds to be more active for corporate governance matters in terms of monitoring and communicating when such support increases the value of their funds. During that period, pension funds and especially public pension funds exercised the second aspect of the aforementioned regulation, the communications, by submitting proposals to corporations either individually or in cooperation with other pension funds. A second step was to negotiate corporate governance matters directly with management and there were instances where either private or public pension funds could influence decisions for top management replacement and for the improvement of poor corporate governance structures.

During the last decades in the US corporate governance received considerable attention due to high-level corporate scandals and collapses (Enron, Worldcom, Tyco, Adelphi, etc.) which triggered legislative authorities. Sarbanes–Oxley Act in 2002 and Dodd–Frank Act in 2010 were the two legislative frameworks which affected the operations of the corporations in multiple levels. Main provisions of Sarbanes–Oxley Act required from listed in NYSE corporations the majority of Board members to be independent, members of the compensation, audit, and nomination committees to be independent, non-employee directors to have the ability to meet separately and CEOs to be evaluated along with procedures for the selection of Board members (Chaaochharia and Grinstein, 2009). Dodd–Frank Act of 2010 adds two more important provisions that affect shareholder democracy and influence corporate ownership structures: the proxy access and the say-on-pay provisions. Proxy access provision dictates that nominations of one-quarter of the Board could be set by shareholders who possess at least 3% of ownership for 3 years. Additionally, say-on-pay provision gives shareholders the ability to vote against executive compensation schemes.

Also, shareholders' empowerment, as a response to enhance investors' trust that had been injured by the global crisis of 2008, was further enhanced through the introduction of Shareholders' Bill of Rights of 2009. According to its preamble, this Bill of Rights was intended to enhance the authority of shareholders to matters like nomination, election and compensation of public companies' executives. Despite its revolutionary nature, due to the created external conditions, Shareholders' Bill of Rights did not manage to survive in the long term. The aforementioned Dodd–Frank Act of 2010 came as a successor of Bill of Rights but the content was modest in comparison with its predecessor. Some of the stipulations of the Bill of Rights simply disappeared from the Dodd–Frank Act like majority voting, etc. Also, some other stipulations of Bill of Rights were diluted showing that the forthcoming and advertised enhanced shareholder governance rights were possibly a victim of political lobbying that often begins prior to legislative enactment (Coffee, 2012). Section 971 of the Dodd–Frank Act, for example, recognized to the SEC the authority to draw rules regarding the rights of shareholders to nominate directors (see above). The original stipulation in the Bill of Rights was referring not to the authority of the SEC but to the obligation of SEC to draw rules regarding the rights of shareholders to nominate directors. In conjunction with the aforementioned, the proxy access rule of the Dodd–Frank Act generates rights to shareholders of at least 3% of the ownership for the previous 3 years, while the Bill of Rights defined the commencement of proxy access to at least 1% of ownership for the previous 2 years.

Corporate governance in China is defined by Clarke (2006) as a set of rules and practices that regulates the relationships among participants in post-traditional Chinese corporations and govern decision-making processes. In 2001, China issued the first corporate governance code for listed firms (its latest update took place in 2018) which aimed at the protection of shareholders' interests and set the acceptable rules of conduct for directors and managers of listed companies. Few years later, a corporate governance code especially for security companies was issued which regulated and set the acceptable rules toward the protection of shareholders and all other stakeholders that had direct or indirect interests. Both codes established the standards of compliance with corporate governance practices and, they and their modifications thereafter, used as metrics of corporate governance implementation levels. Codes included chapters for controlling shareholders, Board of Directors, General Meetings for shareholders, performance assessment and incentives, stakeholders and information disclosure and transparency. As far as the first is concerned, i.e. the controlling shareholders, code refers to the obligation of controlling shareholders to comply with laws and regulations, to avoid any actions that harm corporations or other shareholders or stakeholders interests. Also, codes provide to controlling shareholders with the right to nominate candidate for director positions as long as they possess a certain minimum level of education, skills and experience. Finally, this chapter of code highlights the fact that decision-making process of corporations belongs to annual general meeting and the Board and controlling shareholders must have no interference on aspects like personnel, assets and financial affairs (Li *et al.*, 2008).

Highly concentrated ownerships are a characteristic of Chinese corporations which in turn affect corporate governance-established practices. Irrespectively if the major shareholder is the state or a private sector investor, those shareholders might pursuit their own interests which affect the interests of other shareholders whose interests in fact are not protected in terms of regulation (Hess *et al.*, 2008). Furthermore, the existence of major shareholders affects market liquidity since, especially at cases when the major shareholder is the state, regulatory restrictions, along with the reluctance of the shareholders to disinvest due to the selected investment strategy, might limit market efficiency. Apart from the aforementioned statement highly concentrated ownerships affect the levels of insider trading, collusion and market manipulation. The cause of this issue is related to corporate governance mechanisms and has to do with monitoring mechanisms in place. The lack of such monitoring mechanisms refers to the lack in monitoring the actions of the corporations by their Board and by regulatory authorities. Also, the temper for incentives' generation to establish effective monitoring mechanisms is low since the perpetrator of insider trading and market manipulation is often the major stakeholder, i.e. the state.

Moreover, the ineffective, in terms of objective set pursuit, operation of Board of Directors and related governing bodies, has its roots in highly concentrated ownership structures. In particular, major shareholders have the power to affect Boards' composition by the application of one share one vote principle. Apart from that, at many cases, a Board member of a corporation where the state is the major shareholder, might be a politician who affects the policymaking process. As a result of the aforementioned factors, members of Board who are influenced by the major shareholders might pursuit their own interests or those of their principal against those of minority shareholders. A research conducted in 2002 by Chen *et al.* found that 80% of the Board members in Chinese corporations are related with the government.

Finally, a major factor that affects the effectiveness of corporate governance mechanisms on ownership structures within the Chinese context is the nature of its legal system. In particular, it is interesting to note the difference between law enforcement and the existence of strong regulation. In China, according to Lin (2004), there exists four major inefficiencies of corporate governance mechanisms: lack of information transparency, weak law enforcement, absence of monitoring mechanisms and weak private small shareholders.

In the UK and US, the notion of corporate control has been associated with takeovers, while in the rest of the world this association does not seem to be so clear (Jekinson and Mayer, 1992). The reasons behind this might be the applied legal frameworks regarding the form the corporations takes among countries, the applicable takeover codes among countries and the organized market rules such as Stock exchange rules, etc. Also, the embedded purpose of takeovers, i.e. reallocation of scarce resources from inefficient operations to the most productive ones could explain this association and applicable differences among various countries, because even if a takeover will not be successfully completed the underlined threat for managers could motivate them toward more effective actions. In any case, it is widely accepted that successfully completed takeovers result in the replacement of ineffective management, which in turn could lead to conflicts of interest between shareholders and managers of targets. Internal mechanisms of corporate governance include size and composition of the Board, the duality of positions of the CEO and Chairman of the Board, ownership of stocks by managers and members of the Board, managerial compensation structure and the power of CEO. In such circumstances, the role of independent directors within the context of corporate governance mechanisms becomes important (Jensen and Ruback, 1983; Stulz, 1988; Bange and Mazzeo, 2004). Independent directors resist to such cases of conflict of interest and develop strategies in order to improve shareholder wealth (Cotter *et al.*, 1997) or to oppose to full merger offers (Bange and Mazzeo, 2004). Closely related to the above is the dimension of CEO's power of the target firm within the context of conflicts of interest. On the one hand is the process of takeover and control of the target firm that the CEO has to serve and on the other hand the risk of losing his/her job. Allen and Phillips (2000), Fee *et al.* (2006), Bargeron *et al.* (2009), Ouimet (2013), and Jenter and Lewellen (2015) state that in such cases, an opportunistic behavior might rise which will possibly result in the resistance of a full-acquisition bid, and in some cases, when the bidder will provide a position to the CEO at the post-takeover period, he/she will probably approve a full merger offer (Hartzell *et al.*, 2004; Moeller, 2005). Finally, the effect of blockholding on cases of conflicts of interest is of crucial importance. Blockholding contributes to the improvement of the monitoring environment for the timely set up of effective preventive measures against conflicts of interests between shareholders and management in cases of takeovers (Demsetz and Lehn, 1985; Shleifer and Vishny, 1986; Hartzell and Starks, 2003). Furthermore, blockholders' power can influence entire takeover process through the influence of Board members and management of the target firm (Paul, 2007; Matvos and Ostrovsky, 2008; Ye, 2014), and can affect the decision-making process prior to the takeover (Gaspar *et al.*, 2005; Greenwood and Schor, 2009; Cooney *et al.*, 2009).

As far as the aforementioned study is concerned, i.e. the related takeover bid rules, a recent OECD study at corporations of 49 jurisdictions including all OECD countries, G20 countries and Financial Stability Board member-countries provides useful insights. About 46 out of 49 countries studied, have mandatory legal frameworks regarding the takeover bid process which either enforced *ex post* (37 countries), i.e. the bidder is required to initiate a takeover bid after acquiring shares exceeding the defined threshold or *ex ante* (9 countries), i.e. the bidder is required to initiate a takeover bid for acquiring shares which would exceed the defined threshold. Moreover, in countries with a regulated takeover bid process, the minimum bid price is set either by the price paid by the offer, or by the average market price or by a combination of both.

From all the aforementioned, it is obvious that ownership structures are constantly evolving around the world, which in turn affect corporate control issues. Since concentrated ownership is a major global trend around the world, prominent in emerging countries as well, which takes many forms as we discussed above, traditional patterns of corporate governance associated with either concentrated of dispersed ownership cannot effectively operate at every situation or context. It is profound that good corporate governance practices are essential for the creation on an environment of confidence among members, of confidence to capital market that supports business development through access to equity capital and consequently of business integrity. In countries' level, good corporate governance practices are attributed through corporate governance legal and regulatory framework which supports and contributes to the competitiveness and to the development of countries' corporations.

An recent study of OECD 2019 on corporations of 49 jurisdictions including all OECD countries, G20 countries and Financial Stability Board member countries found that 84% of the countries have amended either their corporation law or securities law since 2015 and around half of all countries have revised their national corporate governance code during the past 2 years. Also, it is interesting that 83% of countries' corporate governance codes follow the "comply or explain" approach. Only three countries, such as the US, India and China do not apply the "comply or explain" approach. Countries adopt corporate governance practices either through legal and regulatory instruments or through codes and principles or through a combination of all. Legal and regulatory instruments are further divided at companies' law and securities law. Supervision of corporate governance practices applied by listed corporations along with the authority to impose law enforcement measures relies on financial and securities regulators or at a combination of both at 82% of the countries studied by OECD, while 12% of the countries have delegated such duties at their Central Banks. An important extension of the aforementioned that affects independence issues is the funding source of the regulators. Around 70% of the regulators are partially of fully funded by fees (fees or fines) from regulated corporations, and around 25% of regulators are fully financed by the government budget. Within the context of independence, regulators of 86% of the countries studied by OECD have established a governing body the size of which ranges between 2 and 17 members, that are given fixed terms of appointment ranging from 2 to 8 years. An important point of discussion is which authority retains the custody of corporate governance codes across countries. National authorities are the custodians of corporate governance codes at 29% of the countries studied by OECD, while stock exchanges remain the custodians at 19% of the countries studied, and at another 19% of the countries private associations remain the custodians of corporate governance codes. Publication of a periodic report summarizing key findings regarding the adoption of "comply or explain" approach, as a means for supporting effective disclosure and implementation processes is issued in 33 countries, and at almost 66% of them such reports are issued annually by either stock exchanges (10 countries) or the national regulatory authority (12 countries).

We now proceed by further elaborating on core corporate governance practices related with ownership structures, corporate control and shareholders' rights. The related practices are early notification of annual general meetings, shareholders' rights to request a meeting or to place a meeting on the agenda, shareholders' voting issues and predefined roles and responsibilities of institutional investors of any type. At almost 65% (32 countries) of countries researched by OECD, shareholders are directly contacted by corporations for the forthcoming annual general meetings. As far as the notice period is concerned, almost 70% of the countries studied require from corporations to issue a notice between 15 and 21 days before the annual general meeting, and a notice of more than 21 days is required by the remaining 30% of countries studied. Proxy materials follow the same logic as previously, i.e. are sent to shareholders at the same day or right after the aforementioned notice. As far as the publicity methods are concerned, 65% of the countries require from listed corporations to notify shareholders either via stock exchanges' platforms or websites, or the governments' gazettes. Same common publication method is that of uploading the notification of annual general meeting at corporations' websites (61%).

Shareholders can request a special meeting at almost 40 countries up to 60 days after their request is filed. In the UK, Russia and Saudi Arabia, for example, shareholders have to request a meeting 31–60 days before, while in China and Brazil shareholders can request a meeting before 15 days or less. The US, South Africa and Switzerland have not applied any specific deadlines for requests on behalf of shareholders. Although, it is interesting to note how the aforementioned privilege of the shareholders is realized in terms of percentage of ownership, such percentages differ from country to country and, in fact differ when the request is for a special meeting or for the placement of a topic in the agenda of a meeting. Countries like Denmark and Norway set a threshold of 5% for requesting a special meeting and set no threshold for the placement of a topic in the agenda of a meeting. The US, Italy and Russia set threshold of 10% for requesting a special meeting and up to 2.5% threshold for the placement of a topic in the agenda of a meeting. China sets threshold of 10% for requesting a special meeting and 3% threshold for the placement of a topic in the agenda of a meeting. On the other extreme, Chile, India and Mexico set threshold of 10% for requesting a special meeting and for the placement of a topic in the agenda of a meeting.

Previously mentioned in this chapter is the ability, given by legislation of many countries, of the corporations to issue shares with different voting rights. However, it is worth to note that, according to the OECD study, 38 countries allow the issuance of shares with limited voting rights, 26 countries allow the issuance of shares with no voting rights but with preferential rights to dividends and 19 countries allow the issuance of shares with no voting rights and without preferential rights to dividends. Objectivity of the annual general meeting process requires objectivity of the counting process. More than 80% of countries in the OECD study require the disclosure of voting decisions on each item of the agenda and at 59% of the countries, it is obligatory to publicize results within the next 5 days. An interesting point is that in the US, under the Delaware Law, votes' count must be held, for big listed corporations, by independent inspectors.

As far as the role and the responsibilities of institutional investors is concerned, we have already noted the fact that effective corporate governance practices are affected by the objectives and the level of involvement of institutional investors. Also, we have already analyzed the role, the objectives and the form of each of the three major categories of institutional investors, i.e. mutual funds, hedge funds and pension funds. Institutional investors adopt different strategies regarding their interest and level of involvement in corporate governance practices. There are institutional investors who do not allocate resources on engagements regarding corporate governance and there are others in which effective corporate governance practices are high on their priorities' list and are embedded in their business model. OECD's principles for corporate governance state, for the latter category of institutional investors, that legal provisions for the implementation of effective corporate governance practices are simply a tick in the box approach, since no real interest for the promotion of effective corporate governance practices exists. In alignment with the aforementioned, many countries either impose different requirements for different types of institutional investors, or impose different requirements for different percentages of ownership by institutional investors. A problem that arises is when the institutional investor (the investors) comes from a country other than the investee is operating. In such cases, legislation of the country of the investee about institutional investors might not be applicable for foreign investors. Also, if the investor comes from a developed country and the investee is based on a developing country, legislation regarding corporate governance engagements on behalf of institutional investors might be too weak for the institutional investors. For these reasons, many countries have adopted stewardship codes, on a voluntary basis, in order to promote corporate governance practices either by domestic or by foreign institutional investors. Such initiatives for the implementation of stewardship codes are usually driven either by legislative authorities, or by investors' associations or by public sector bodies.

Disclosure of the voting policies of institutional investors is either obligatory or recommended at 75% in the 49 countries studied by OECD and 47% of the countries require the disclosure of the actual voting records. Conflicts of interest policies are required to have corporations at all but two of the countries studied by OECD, even though only 57% of the countries studied require by corporations to disclose policies for managing cases related with conflict of interest. A very important element of sound corporate governance practices that comes from related internal control systems methodology is the monitoring and communicating aspect. Within this context, 33 countries require or recommend to institutional investors to monitor investee corporations, either broadly or explicitly in matters like ESG activities, strategy, performance and capital structure. However, engagements like direct dialogue with the Board is either recommended or required in only 20 countries, like the effectiveness of monitoring of partners enforced with voting rights is either recommended or required in 30 countries (including UK and Japan).

As far as the Board is concerned, matters like its composition, its independence, its embedded committees, its members' remunerations are of major importance for effective corporate governance practices. A total of 10 countries, according to OECD study have set maximum limit on Boards' members (from 15 to 21 members). On the contrary, 40 countries have set a minimum number of members of Boards (to 3 until 5 members). Term of office for Board members varies between 1 and 6 years at all countries. The US, China, India and Italy, for example, have adopted a 3-year office term while Greece and France have a 6-year office term for Board members. More specifically, in terms of Board members duties, most of the countries have established, either a minimum ratio (average around 50% for countries like US, Italy and India) or a minimum number of independent members of the Board (average 2–3 members for countries like Greece, Saudi Arabia and China), consistent with corporate governance best practices. It is worth to mention that there are countries that set this practice of independence on a "comply or explain" basis, and in Japan in particular, they have further tightened such rule by justifying the reasons why such arrangement is inappropriate. Also, the link between corporate control and corporate governance is obvious in countries like the US and Israel, where corporations with concentrated ownership structures are subject to less stringent-related requirements.

Another major and effective corporate governance mechanism is that of the separation of the role of the Chairman of the Board with that of the CEO. Around 30% of the countries studied by OECD require such separation; 40% of them propose such arrangements through relevant codes' stipulations. It is interesting to note that some countries, like India attempt to limit the adverse effects of non-separation by legislating independent members serving on the Board, or countries like Israel where the separation could be waived as long as is approved by majority of minority shareholders. Another one corporate governance practice that enhances independence are the requirements that must be met in order for a member of the Board to be considered as an independent member. Among the typical characteristics that a member of the Board should have, is also its non-relationship with substantial shareholders. Thresholds for the characterization of a shareholder as substantial, within the independence of Board's members context, vary across countries. About 10 out of 49 countries studied by OECD consider substantial a shareholder with 5% ownership, 11 countries with 10% ownership and there are extremes like no threshold set by 6 countries and 4 countries with 50% of ownership. If we connect stakeholder perspective of corporate governance with Board composition and, in particular, with the participation of an employees' representative at Board as member, no country prohibits such arrangement. On the contrary, 12 European countries and China have established legally binding requirements for the participation of employees' representatives at corporations' Boards.

The existence and the effective composition and operation of audit committees is a corporate governance mechanism of major importance. According to EU Directive (2006/43/EC) audit committees have to monitor the financial reporting process, monitor the effectiveness of the corporation's internal control, internal audit where applicable, and risk management systems, monitor the statutory audit of the annual and consolidated accounts and to review and monitor the independence of the statutory auditor or audit firm. Same roles for audit committees are also prescribed in Sarbanes–Oxley Act of 2002 in US, accompanied with the responsibilities of the appointment, compensation, retention and oversight of the work of external auditors engaged in preparing or issuing an audit report. A total of 45 out of 49 countries, according to OECD, require by their legislation from listed corporations to establish audit committees while the remaining 4 countries stipulate such arrangement through corporate governance codes. As far as their composition is concerned, full or majority independent membership is required or recommended by almost all of the 49 countries. The existence of committees within the Board of Directors, other than the audit committee is also common. Around 41 and 45 respectively out of 49 countries of OECD study require or recommend the existence of nomination and remuneration committees. The difference with the case of audit committees is that such requirements or recommendations comes, in majority, not from related legislation but from corporate governance codes' stipulations. What is interesting to note is that, after recent financial crisis, risk management approach has been evolved and was further embedded in the mindset of management of corporations. Countries around the world attempted to support such shift either by incorporating duties or requiring or recommending the existence of independent risk committees at Board level of corporations. About 36 out of 49 countries studied by OECD require or recommend either by Law or by their related corporate governance codes audit committees to be assigned with risk management responsibilities, while 16 countries require or recommend either by law or by their related corporate governance codes the existence of an independent Board level risk management committee.

The matter of Board members nomination and election is directly linked with corporate ownership. In almost all countries, shareholders can propose a candidate for member at the Board. Specific thresholds apply at some countries which are almost similar with those that apply when a shareholder desires to place a new topic at the general assembly meeting. Majority voting is the most common method for the election of Board (31 out of 49 countries). Some specific circumstances regarding Board members election in order to enhance minority shareholders power exist at some countries. In Italy for example, at least one board member must be elected from the slate of candidates presented by shareholders owning a minimum threshold of the corporation's equity. In Israel, a recommendation exists for the initial appointment and a requirement for re-election, that all outside directors be appointed by the majority of the minority shareholders. In the UK a legal rule requires independent directors to be separately approved both by the shareholders as a whole and the independent shareholders as a separate class. Moreover, initial appointments must be approved by the majority of the minority shareholders. As far as the balance between the genders at Boards' composition, many countries, in alignment with G20/OECD Principles, have adopted measures so as to promote women's participation at Boards, by inserting either specific quotas or voluntary targets. Around 18% of the countries studied by OECD have adopted mandatory quotas for listed corporations requiring a certain percentage of board seats to be filled by women. Also, 16% of countries studied rely on voluntary goals or targets while 6% deploy a combination of both. In terms of quantification of the specific quotas or voluntary targets, countries like Denmark, France, Iceland, Norway and Spain require 40% participation of the least represented gender at Board seats. Also, 3 countries require listed corporations to have "at least one" female director on their boards. In the US, different State regulations apply. California listed corporations are required to have at least one woman on the board by the end of 2019, and two by 2021 and other States while they do not require, they encourage and propose to listed corporations to have women on the Board. Another measure for the promotion of such arrangements is the disclosure of the specific aforementioned metrics. About 49% of the countries studied by OECD a legal obligation for such disclosures exists whereas 23% of the countries presume no such obligation or any other kind of recommendation.

5. Conclusion

In the recent decades the importance and domination of financial markets are prevalent. Also prevalent is the academic interconnectedness of corporate governance theory with agency theory and with corporate ownership and corporate control issues (Davis, 2005; Clarke, 2016). Moreover, the role of corporations in societies is dominant, and their power toward globalization tends to be incremental in comparison with previous decades. As a consequence, the obvious different cultures between continents and countries that affect domestic corporations' operations have been weakened (Aguilera and Jackson, 2003, 2010). Countries in Europe and Asia have shifted the legislation related with corporate governance toward the Anglo-American view, either by adopting corporate governance codes or by converging to capital markets operations. Stakeholder model of governance remains contemporary and its importance tends to be incremental while the major cornerstones of corporate governance and relevant legislation still acknowledge the value of shareholder model of corporate governance which focuses mostly on Board issues (composition, remuneration, committees embedded, etc.), CEOs and shareholders. Such approach strengthens the role of shareholders and their interests and weakens other stakeholders' objectives and, as a result, academic research and in particular bibliometric analysis focuses mostly on agency theory and country-specific samples (mostly the US and UK) (Kumar and Zattoni, 2015), rather than on other corporate governance systems like the relationship based on corporate governance system in Asia (mostly Asia-Pacific) and Europe or any other corporate governance system that is applied on emerging countries.

The aforementioned cultural differences and historical origins among countries could be drivers for policy makers and legislators in order to establish or amend corporate governance frameworks that involve and acknowledge different values and objectives of corporations of any sector (Clarke, 2017). Such corporate governance frameworks should be flexible enough to meet the different objectives and expectations of different stakeholders and corporations that operate at different environments, while placing the related internal controls and basic stipulations that protect shareholders and mitigate the adverse effects of the agency problem. Only then, policy makers and legislators will support market participants of any type and size to create value through the efficient use of their capitals. Such process, within the context of globalized and dynamic business environment, should be dynamic enough in order to facilitate radical changes and to accommodate emerging business practices.

References

Aguilera, R.V. and Jackson, G. (2003). The cross-national diversity of corporate governance: Dimensions and determinants, *The Academy of Management Review*, 28(3), 447–465.

Aguilera, R.V. and Jackson, G. (2010). Comparative and international corporate governance, *Academy of Management Annals*, 4(1), 485–556.

Allen, J.W. and Phillips, G.M. (2000). Corporate equity ownership, strategic alliances, and product market relationships, *Journal of Finance*, 55, 2791–2815.

Anabtawi, I. and Stout, L.A. (2008). Fiduciary duties for activist shareholders. *Cornell Law Faculty Publications. Paper 718*. http://scholarship.law.cornell.edu/facpub/718.

Bange, M.M. and Mazzeo, M.A. (2004). Board composition, board effectiveness, and the observed form of takeover bids, *Review of Financial Studies*, 17, 1185–1215.

Bargeron, L.L., Schlingemann, F.P., Stulz, R.M. and Zutter, C.J. (2009). Do target CEO's sell out their shareholders to keep their job in a merger? Fisher College of Business Working Paper No. 2009-03-002, Charles A. Dice Center Working Paper No. 2009-2, ECGI — Finance Working Paper No. 236/2009. https://ssrn.com/abstract=1337226 or http://dx.doi.org/10.2139/ssrn.1337226.

Bebchuk, A.L., Kraakman, R. and Triantis, G. (2000). Stock pyramids, cross-ownership, and dual class equity: The mechanisms and agency costs of separating control from cash-flow rights, in Randall K. Morck (ed.), *Concentrated Corporate Ownership*. The University of Chicago Press, pp. 445–460.

Becht, M. and Rodl, A. (1999). Blockholding in Europe: An international comparison, *European Economic Review*, 43, 10–49.

Becht, M., Bolton, P. and Röell, A. (2003). Corporate governance and control, in G. Constantinides, M. Harris and R. Stulz (eds.), *The Handbook of the Economics of Finance*. Elsevier: North-Holland.

Bennedsen, M. and Nielsen, K. (2001). The impact of the breakthrough rule on European firms, *European Journal of Law and Economics*, 17(3), 259–283.

Berle, A. and Means, A. (1932). *The Modern Corporation and Private Property*. Harcourt, Brace & World: New York.

Brunello, G., Graziano, C. and Parigi, B.M. (2003). CEO turnover in insider-dominated boards: The Italian case, *Journal of Banking & Finance*, 27(6), 1027–1051.

The Cadbury Committee (1992). Report of the Committee on the financial aspects of corporate governance, https://ecgi.global/sites/default/files//codes/documents/cadbury.pdf.

Chen, D.H., Fan, J.P.H. and Wong, T.J. (2002). Do politicians jeopardize professionalism? Decentralization and the structure of Chinese corporate boards. https://www.researchgate.net/publication/228820884_Do_politicians_jeopardize_professionalism_Decentralization_and_the_structure_of_Chinese_corporate_boards.

Chhaochharia, V. and Grinstein, Y. (2009). CEO compensation and board structure, *The Journal of Finance*, 64(1), 231–261. https://doi.org/10.1111/j.1540-6261.2008.01433.x.

Claessens, S., Djankov, S. and Lang, L. (2000). The separation of ownership and control in East Asian Corporations, *Journal of Financial Economics*, 81, 92–93.

Clarke, D.C. (2006). The independent director in Chinese corporate governance, *Delaware Journal of Corporate Law*, 31(1), 125–228.

Clarke, T. (2016). The continuing diversity of corporate governance: Theories of convergence and diversity, *Ephemera*, 16(1), 19–52.

Clarke, T. (2017). *International Corporate Governance: A Comparative Approach*. Routledge Second Edition: London and New York.

Coffee, J.C. Jr. (2012). The political economy of Dodd–Frank: Why financial reform tends to be frustrated and systemic risk perpetuated, *Cornell L. Review*, 97, 1019. https://scholarship.law.columbia.edu/faculty_scholarship/517.

Cooney, J.W., Moeller, T. and Stegemoller, M. (2009). The underpricing of private targets, *Journal of Financial Economics*, 93, 51–66.

Cotter, J.F., Shivdasani, A. and Zenner, M. (1997). Do independent directors enhance target shareholder wealth during tender offers? *Journal of Financial Economics*, 43, pp. 195–218.

Crespi, R. and Renneboog, L. (2010). Is (institutional) shareholder activism new? Evidence from UK shareholder coalitions in the pre-Cadbury era, *Corporate Governance: An International Review*, 18, 274–295.

Dai, S. and Helfrich, C. (2016). The structure of corporate ownership and control, *Comparative Corporate Governance and Financial Regulation*, 9, https://scholarship.law.upenn.edu/fisch_2016/9. (Accessed 11 November 2020).

Dang, M. and Henry, D. (2015). Partial-control versus full-control acquisitions: Does target corporate governance matter? Evidence from eight East and Southeast Asian countries, *Pacific-Basin Finance Journal*, http://dx.doi.org/10.1016/j.pacfin.2015.12.011.

Davis, G. (2005). New directions in corporate governance, *Annual Review of Sociology*, 31, 143–162.

De la Cruz, A., Medina, A. and Tang, Y. (2019). Ownership of listed companies around the world. *OECD Capital Market Series*, Paris, www.oecd.org/corporate/Ownership-of-ListedCompanies-Around-the-World.htm.

Demsetz, H. and Lehn, K. (1985). The structure of corporate ownership: Causes and consequences, *Journal of Political Economy*, 93, 1155–1177.

Dore, R. (2000). *Stock Market Capitalism: Welfare Capitalism. Japan and Germany versus Anglo-Saxons*. Oxford University Press: New York.

Eisenhardt, K.M. (1989). Agency theory: An assessment and review, *Academy of Management Review*, 14, 57–74.

Easterbrook, F.H. and Fischel, D.R. (1991). *The Economic Structure of Corporate Law*. Harvard University Press: Harvard, pp. 67–70.

Faccio, M., Larry, H.P. and Lang, L.H.P. (2002). The ultimate ownership of Western European corporations, *Journal of Financial Economics*, 65(3), 385–387.

Faccio, M. and Stolin, D. (2006). Expropriation vs. proportional sharing in corporate acquisitions, *The Journal of Business*, 79, 1413–1444.

Fama, E. and Jensen, M. (1983). Separation of ownership and control, *Journal of Law and Economics*, 26, 301–325.

Fee, C.E., Hadlock, C.J. and Thomas, S. (2006). Corporate equity ownership and the governance of product market relationships, *Journal of Finance*, 61, 1217–1251.

Franks, J., Mayer, C. and Renneboog, L. (2001). Who disciplines management of poorly performing companies? *Journal of Financial Intermediation*, 10, 209–248.

Gaspar, J.-M., Massa, M. and Matos, P. (2005). Shareholder investment horizons and the market for corporate control, *Journal of Financial Economics*, 76, 135–165.

Gibbs, P. (2002). *Dual-Class Stock: Value of the Vote is Confused with Undervaluation*. JP Morgan Mergers & Acquisitions Research.

Gilson, R.J. and Gordon, J.N. (2013). The agency costs of agency capitalism: Activist investors and the revaluation of governance rights, *Columbia Law Review*, 113(863), 863–928.

Goergen, M. and Renneboog, L. (2008). Contractual corporate governance, *Journal of Corporate Finance*, 14, 166–182.

Goergen, M. and Renneboog, L. (2011). Managerial remuneration, *Journal of Corporate Finance*, 17(4), 1068–1077.

Goodwin, S. (2015). Corporate governance and hedge fund activism. https://ssrn.com/abstract=2646293 or http://dx.doi.org/10.2139/ssrn.2646293.

Grant, J. and Kirchmaier, T. (2005). Corporate control in Europe, *Corporate Ownership and Control*, 2(2), 65–76.

Greenwood, R. and Schor, M. (2009). Investor activism and takeovers, *Journal of Financial Economics*, 92, 362–375.

Grossman, S.J. and Hart, O. (1980). Takeover bids, the free-rider problem, and the theory of the corporation, *Bell Journal of Economics*, 11(1), 42–64.

Hansmann, H. and Kraakman, R., (2004). The basic governance structure, in Kraakman, R., Davies, P., Hansmann, H., Hertig, G., Hopt, K., Kanda, H., and Rock, E. (eds.), *The Anatomy of Corporate Law*. Oxford University Press: Oxford, pp. 33–70.

Harris, T. (2000). *German Capital Gains Tax Reform*. JP Morgan Securities Research.

Hartzell, J.C. and Starks, L.T. (2003). Institutional investors and executive compensation, *Journal of Finance*, 58, 2351–2374.

Hartzell, J.C., Ofek, E. and Yermack, D. (2004). What's in it for me? CEOs whose firms are acquired, *Review of Financial Studies*, 17, 37–61.

Hess, K., Gunasekarage, A. and Hovey, M. (2010). State Dominant and non-state dominant ownership concentration and firm performance: Evidence from China, *International Journal of Managerial Finance*, 6, 264–289.

ISS *et al*. (2007). Report on the proportionality principle in the European Union. https://ec.europa.eu/smart-regulation/impact/ia_carried_out/docs/ia_2007/sec_2007_1705_en.pdf. (Accessed 12 December 2020).

Jekinson, T. and Mayer, C. (1992). The assessment: Corporate governance and corporate control, *Oxford Review of Economic Policy*, 8(3), 1–10.

Jensen, M.C. (1988). Takeovers: Their causes and consequences, *Journal of Economic Perspectives*, 2, 21–48.

Jensen, M.C. and Ruback, R.S. (1983). The market for corporate control: The scientific evidence, *Journal of Financial Economics*, 11, 5–50.

Jenter, D. and Lewellen, K. (2015). CEO preferences and acquisitions, *Journal of Finance*, 70, 2813–2852.

Kulich, C., Haslam, S.A., Renneboog, L., Ryan, M. and Trojanowski, G. (2011). Who gets the carrot and who gets the stick? Evidence of gender disparities in executive remuneration, *Strategic Management Journal*, 32, 301–321.

Kumar, P. and Zattoni, A. (2015). In search of a greater pluralism of theories and methods in governance research, *Corporate Governance: An International Review*, 23(1), 1–2.

La Porta, R., Lopez-de-Silanes, F. and Shleifer, A. (1999). Corporate ownership around the world, *Journal of Finance*, 54, 471–517.

Lazonick, W. and O'Sullivan, M. (1996). Organization, finance and international competition, *Industrial and Corporate Change*, 5, 1–49.

Li, L., Naughton, T. and Hovey, M.T. (2008). A review of corporate governance in China. https://ssrn.com/abstract=1233070 or http://dx.doi.org/10.2139/ssrn.1233070. (Accessed 31 December 2020).

Lin, T.W. (2004). Corporate governance in China: Recent developments, key problems, and solutions, *Journal of Accounting and Corporate Governance*, 1, 1–23.

Martynova, M. and Renneboog, L. (2011). Evidence on the international evolution and convergence of corporate governance regulations, *Journal of Corporate Finance*, 17, 1531–1557.

Matvos, G. and Ostrovsky, M. (2008). Cross-ownership, returns, and voting in mergers, *Journal of Financial Economics*, 89, 391–403.

Mizruchi, M.S. (2004). Berle and Means revisited: The governance and power of large U.S. corporations, *Theory and Society*, 33, 579–617.

Moeller, T. (2005). Let's make a deal! How shareholder control impacts merger payoffs, *Journal of Financial Economics*, 76, 167–190.

Nenova, T. (2000). The value of corporate votes and control benefits: A cross country analysis. https://ssrn.com/abstract=237809 or http://dx.doi.org/10.2139/ssrn.237809.

OECD (2015). *G20/OECD Principles of Corporate Governance*. OECD Publishing: Paris. http://dx.doi.org/10.1787/9789264236882-en.

OECD (2019). OECD Corporate Governance Factbook 2019. www.oecd.org/corporate/corporate-governance-factbook.htm.

Paul, D.L. (2007). Board composition and corrective action: Evidence from corporate responses to bad acquisition bids, *Journal of Financial and Quantitative Analysis*, 42, 759–783.

Porta, R., López-de-Silanes, F., Andrei, S. and Robert V. (1999). Corporate ownership around the world, *Journal of Finance*, 54(2), 471–520.

O'Sullivan, M. (2000). *Contests for Corporate Control. Corporate Governance and Economic Performance in the United States and Germany*. New York: Oxford University Press.

Ouimet, P.P. (2013). What motivates minority acquisitions? The trade-offs between a partial equity stake and complete integration, *Review of Financial Studies*, 26, 1021–1047.

Prowse, S.D. (1992). The structure of corporate ownership in Japan, *The Journal of Finance*, 47(3), 1121–1140.

Riyanto, Y.E. and Toolsema, L.A. (2006). Tunneling and propping: A justification for pyramidal ownership, *Journal of Banking and Finance*, 32, 2178–2187.

Shleifer, A. and Vishny, R.W. (1986). Large shareholders and corporate control, *Journal of Political Economy*, 94, 461–488.

Solomon, J. (1996). Indonesia's Lippo restructuring approved, *Dow Jones International News Service*. (29 September), pp. 11–33.

Stulz, R. (1988). Managerial control of voting rights: Financing policies and the market for corporate control, *Journal of Financial Economics*, 20, 25–54.

Tonello, M. and Rabimov, S.R. (2010). The 2010 Institutional Investment Report: Trends in Ass*et* allocation and Portfolio Composition (11 November 2010). *The Conference Board Research Report*, No. R-1468-10-RR, 2010. https://ssrn.com/abstract=1707512.

Valadares, S.M. and Leal, R.P.C. (2000). Ownership and control structure of Brazilian companies. https://ssrn.com/abstract=213409.

Ye, P. (2014). Does the disposition effect matter in corporate takeovers? Evidence from institutional investors of target companies, *Journal of Financial and Quantitative Analysis*, 49, 221–248.

Whitley, R. (1999). *Divergent Capitalisms: The Social Structuring and Change of Business Systems*. Oxford University Press: Oxford.

https://doi.org/10.1142/9789811260506_0010

Chapter 10

Event Study Methods in Corporate Governance Studies*

Manapol Ekkayokkaya[†,¶], Krishna Paudyal[‡,||] and Poonyawat Sreesing[§,]**

[†]*Chulalongkorn Business School, Chulalongkorn University, Bangkok, Thailand*

[‡]*University of Strathclyde, United Kingdom*

[§]*Assumption University, Thailand*

[¶]*Manapol@cbs.chula.ac.th*

[||]*Krishna.paudyal@strath.ac.uk*

[**]*Poonyawatsrs@au.edu*

Abstract

Our goal in this chapter is to point out potential problems associated with applying conventional event study methodology to corporate governance studies (CG). It can be viewed as a nontechnical reference for those who want to conduct an event study but are not yet familiar with the subject

*We thank Anant Chiarawongse and Sira Suchintabandid for valuable comments on the technical aspect of this chapter. All remaining errors are ours.

matter. To our knowledge, existing works that address the methodological problems of event studies or provide insightful reviews of published methods are highly technical and are suitable mainly for advanced readers. This chapter deals mainly with techniques for examining short-term price changes at the time of the event, while describing methods for analyzing price movements over a long period after the event.

Existing evidence from simulations and empirical studies suggests that the short time horizon tests appear to be more robust to potential statistical problems.

Keywords: Event study, corporate governance, abnormal returns, calendar-time characteristics

1. Introduction

What is an event study? Fundamentally, it is a study that analyzes how security prices adjust to any specific kind of new information. The event study methodology was first developed by Fama, Fisher, Jensen and Roll (FFJR) (1969) to examine how share price reacts to the announcement of a stock-split decision, i.e. how the announcement affects stock price of the firm conducting the split. Since then, there has been a great deal of extensions and refinements made to the methodology developed by FFJR (1969). One of the most (if not the most) widespread applications of FFJR (1969), with further developments in testing methods, has been made in the area of corporate finance. That is, to test the wealth effect of a corporate decision or event. In other words, the FFJR (1969) methodology is commonly employed in addressing the question of how a managerial decision (or, corporate event) affects shareholders' wealth. The methodology has been applied to testing the price changes not only around the event announcement, but also over a much longer period following the time of the event (e.g. 3 or 5 years after the event).

Application of the FFJR (1969) methodology has also gained increasing popularity among studies on corporate governance (CG) issues. These include not only studies on firm-specific CG events, but also studies on CG-related regulations. The FFJR (1969) methodology is a fruitful approach since the market reaction, or share price reaction, to the arrival of new information about a CG event can provide a meaningful indication of the expected effect of the event as assessed by market participants in aggregate. Indeed, CG events by nature can often influence firms' activities in the long run, i.e. have long-term implications on firms. Thus, examination of the effect of CG events over a long horizon may conceivably be viewed by many as desirable.

Our objective in this chapter is to point out to potential issues inherent in application of the conventional event study methodology to CG studies. In doing so, we shall refrain from making reference to any particular studies whose reported findings appear to be attributable to their potentially debatable application of the event study methodology.

Another use of this chapter can also be viewed as non-technical notes for those seeking to conduct an event study, but are not yet familiar with *what it is all about*. To our knowledge, the existing work that addresses methodological problems inherent in event studies or insightfully reviews the published methodologies is highly technical and suitable mostly to advanced readers. Given the nature of the topic itself, this is understandable and the way it has to be. Unfortunately, it leaves novices with a big leap to make by themselves. In relation to the materials currently available in the literature, this chapter can be viewed, hopefully, as a primer that covers the groundwork needed for embarking on the more technical and advanced reading in the literature. Naturally, discussion of highly technical issues in fine detail is beyond the scope of this chapter.

This chapter essentially has two main parts. The first part is on the techniques for testing the price changes (more precisely, abnormal return) in the short run (i.e. days) around the time of the event. The second part describes the methods for analyzing price movements during a long period (e.g. 5 years) following the event. The first part of this chapter is largely self-contained so that the second part is optional to those who need to examine only short-term abnormal return. However, it is advisable that those with the research objective of examining long-term abnormal return first familiarize themselves with the tests of short-term abnormal return in order to install an understanding of the rationale underlying an event study. Such an understanding is essential because the tests of long-term abnormal return are fundamentally an outgrowth of the methodology fundamentally designed for a short window.

The first part of this chapter consists of Sections 2 and 3. Sections 4 and 5 constitute the second part. In Section 2, the process of measuring short-term abnormal return is described. This includes identification of an event date, definition of an event window and the common procedures in estimating the price reaction to an event announcement.

Section 3 provides notes on hypothesis testing, which is necessary for assessing statistical reliability of the observed abnormal returns. The common statistical issues are also discussed in this section. The common approaches to measuring abnormal return in the long run after the event are presented in Section 4. In Section 5, the methodological issues surrounding tests of long-term abnormal return and a perspective on these issues are discussed. This chapter ends with take-home messages offered in Section 6.

2. Measuring Announcement-Period Abnormal Return

The process of measuring abnormal return begins by correctly identifying an event date, which is followed by defining the length of the event window. As discussed below, the event window should be as short as possible. Once the appropriate window length is defined, abnormal return can be meaningfully estimated against the benchmark or expected return with reference to the *correctly* identified event date.

2.1 *Identifying the event date*

Great care must be taken when identifying the event date. In most event studies, the event date is referred to as the *announcement* date. This is the date on which firms conducting an event under investigation publicly announce for the *first time* their decision to conduct the event, e.g. an acquisition, equity offering, CEO appointments and capital expenditure. Hence, an event date is the day on which the market learns information about the event for the first time. That is, an event date must be the date of a *surprise*. There are other dates related to the announcement date, for example, the date on which a firm files with the SEC its intention to make an equity offering. The filing date cannot be considered as an event date. This is simply because issuers usually do not publicly announce when they make the filing although the filing date is kept as a public record. There is no arrival of new information in the market on the filing date.

The utmost importance of accurately identifying the date of a surprise also applies to CG studies. The official public announcement date for several CG-related events are not always the date of a surprise as such. One example is the date on which an institutional investor publicly announces for the first time its decision to place a firm on its watch list for a substandard governance practice. If such a decision by some protocol is made following publicly disclosed communications between the investor and the firm, the observed or recorded public announcement date of the decision should not be treated as an event date. Much of the information about the decision is already transmitted into the public domain through the preceding public disclosure of the discourse.

In an attempt to gauge the valuation effects of changes in firms' governance mechanisms and/or practice, a number of studies examine how firms' share prices react to the introduction of, or change in, CG-related regulations. While this is a fruitful empirical strategy as regulatory changes are exogenous to firms, accurate identification of the event date remains challenging. In most cases, the official enactment date or the date on which the regulation comes into effect should not be taken as the date of a surprise. The enactment or effective date of regulatory changes is usually known, or at least well anticipated, in advance. Thus, any regulatory effect is likely to be impounded into share prices before the date identified as the event date. To ensure an accurate regulatory event date, researchers can consider the path taken by Larcker *et al.* (2011). These authors collect *both* the date on which each regulation they examine was officially introduced and the date on which it first appeared in the news media, and see whether the two dates are the same. The date on which a regulatory change is reported in a newspaper in and of itself is not always an accurate event date. For studies examining firms experiencing a change in their CG rating, similarly, the date on which an updated rating table is uploaded on the rating agency's website, or the website of some other organization, is not necessarily the date of a surprise. When extracting an event date from a website, it is crucial to ensure at least that the ratings are updated in a systematic pattern, e.g. always updated on a certain trading day of each month.

The obvious consequence of mis-identifying the true event date is a measurement error that predictably pushes the statistical result, i.e. the average market reaction or abnormal return, towards being insignificant. Assuming that investors significantly react to an observed change in CG (as would be implicitly assumed by researchers in formulating their hypothesis), studies adopting a wrong event date will systematically miss the significant market reaction. To this extent, one inference typically ensues: the effect of the CG change is not important, or the market fails to react to the CG change.

One useful way to analyze the valuation effects of CG attributes of firms is to employ as a laboratory some corporate decisions with an event date that can be accurately identified. Among several decisions, one popular candidate is corporate acquisitions. For instance, one may examine how the market reaction to the acquisition announcement differs across acquirers with various CG attributes (see, e.g. Masulis *et al.*, 2007; Wang and Xie, 2009; Cai and Sevilir, 2012; Schmidt, 2015; Masulis and Zhang, 2019). Within the framework of the conventional event study setup, one may also analyze the relation between event firms' CG attributes (including CEO attributes) and deal characteristics (see, e.g. Grinstein and Hribar, 2004; Harford *et al.*, 2012; Jenter and Lewellen, 2015). It is also possible and fruitful to employ these approaches to announcements of securities issuances (e.g. Di Giuli and Laux, 2021).

2.2 *The event window*

Suppose the true event date has been accurately identified. An abnormal price movement or return due to, as a proxy for the wealth effect of, the event should *ideally* be measured on this date. An event study is all about precision in measuring a price response, or how the market reacts, to a surprise. Traditionally, announcement dates are collected from a newspaper, e.g. the *Wall Street Journal*. The section in a newspaper dedicated to reporting public announcements by firms usually lists the announcements made on the stock exchange on the *previous* day. Hence, the actual event date is the day preceding the press date. In reality, not all investors actually go to the stock exchange every day to observe announcements made by firms.

However, it is conceivable that investors on average read newspapers to see if there is any corporate announcement that may be relevant to their portfolio. As a result, studies employing data collected from a newspaper or press document, which are usually the earlier studies, measure abnormal return over a 2-day period or window covering the press date and the previous day. Such a period is commonly referred to as the announcement period, and in this case, would be specified as the event window (−1, 0) where day 0 is the press date. This is why abnormal return is measured over a multiple-day window even though an event is announced only once on a particular date. The event window may be widened to include days before day −1 in order to capture the effect of information leakage, e.g. (−10, 0). Considering the importance of CG mechanisms to firms' stakeholders, it would be difficult to rule out the possibility of information leakage of CG-related events. That is, the nature of the CG event being analyzed needs to be taken into account when selecting the window length. Due to strong belief in market efficiency, as we should also note, an event window covering days after day 0 has traditionally been uncommon.

Announcement dates are also often collected a periodic magazine, e.g. *Acquisitions Monthly*. The announcement date reported in such a source would be the date on which the announcement is made on the stock exchange. In this case, a reasonable event window may be (−1, +1) or (−5, +5) in order to allow for human errors in entering data into the source. Such symmetric event windows have become common among recent studies. Since the late 1990s, an electronic database such as the Securities Data Company (SDC) database and Bureau van Dike (BvD), have become increasingly available to authors. An electronic database, too, is subject to human errors alike. For example, Masulis *et al.* (2007) point out that the vast majority of acquisition announcement dates recorded by the SDC are correct: the recorded announcement dates that are inaccurate are usually off by no more than two trading days. Owing to this note, subsequent studies of corporate acquisitions using the SDC database tend to adopt the (−2,+2) window, which is reasonable.[1] Of course, one may decide to adopt the (−10,+10) window to reduce the chances of missing the true announcement date. However, a longer window may come with a material cost. The longer the window, the noisier the estimate of abnormal return becomes.

Unless there is a specific reason or economic issue to investigate, an event window should be as short as possible. For the reasons discussed above, nevertheless, a realistic event window is longer than one day.

2.3 *Estimating benchmark return and abnormal return*

There are several alternative ways to measure abnormal return to a firm that conducts a corporate event, or is involved in an event. That is, one can assume a number of alternative return-generating processes in estimating benchmark or expected return. The most commonly adopted expected

---

[1]For the BvD, we know of no authors that have made a similar note. But then again, to the best of our knowledge, the BvD has been nowhere near as popular as the SDC for announcements of corporate acquisitions or securities offerings.

return model is the OLS-based *statistical* model in Equation (1), also known as the market model:

$$r_{it} = \alpha_i + \beta_i r_{mt} + \varepsilon_{it} \tag{1}$$

Where r_{it} is return to event firm i observed on day t and r_{mt} return on a market-wide index (as a proxy for market return) observed on day t. As a proxy for the market-wide index, the value-weighted index and equally weighted index are equally common. ε_{it} is the regression error term, which is assumed to be normally identically and serially uncorrelated with a mean of zero and homoscedastic variance of $\sigma^2_{\varepsilon_i}$ (this assumption is commonly referred to as the i.i.d. assumption). Both r_{it} and r_{mt} are calculated as continuously compounded return, which is compatible with the classical linear regression model framework. Using continuously compounded return is also intuitively appealing in the sense that an economy works continuously, and hence, reinvestment of output made accordingly. Return calculation should include not only the price change, but also dividends.[2]

By running Equation (1) using data from the period *preceding* the event window, abnormal return can be estimated as a *forecast* error or regression error calculated out of sample:

$$ar_{i\tau} = \hat{\varepsilon}_{i\tau} = r_{i\tau} - \left(\hat{\alpha}_i + \hat{\beta}_i r_{m\tau}\right) \tag{2}$$

where $r_{i\tau}$ and $r_{m\tau}$ are, respectively, return on firm i and the market return observed on day τ during the event window. Conceptually, the term $(\hat{\alpha}_i + \hat{\beta}_i r_{m\tau})$ represents the return firm i would be expected to achieve if there was no event, i.e. the benchmark or expected return. Therefore, $ar_{i\tau}$ is a measure of abnormal return to (i.e. abnormal share price movement of) firm i on event day τ.

For example, let us define the announcement date (i.e. event date) for a firm's inclusion in the good CG index as day 0, and the announcement

---

[2]This is because the total return to shareholders or equity investors can be divided into the capital-gain and income components. Although failing to include dividends in the return calculation may not materially affect the results based on a short window, it is obviously important to include dividends if one is to analyze long-term abnormal returns.

period as a 5-day window (−2, +2).[3] The terms $\hat{\alpha}_i$ and $\hat{\beta}_i$ can be estimated by running Equation (1) using r_{it} and r_{mt} observed on day −255 through day −6, i.e. days during the period before the event. This period can be referred to as the estimation window (−255, −6). Abnormal return to firm i on each day τ during the 5-day event window can then be calculated using Equation (2). It should be noted that, by definition, the estimation window is assumed to be a quiet period or period of *normal return*.

Unfortunately, there is no theoretical guidance on how long the estimation window should be. In practice, the window should be long enough so that there are sufficient observations to get a stable estimate for $\hat{\alpha}_i$ as well as $\hat{\beta}_i$. Also, the longer the estimation window the statistically more precise $\hat{\alpha}_i$ and $\hat{\beta}_i$ become (see also Section 3.2). However, use of a very long estimation window may come at a cost. If the nature of the firm's business operations has recently changed, $\hat{\alpha}_i$ and $\hat{\beta}_i$ estimated using a long pre-event window will represent not only the firm's current business profile but also outdated information about its risk-return characteristics. To the extent that corporate events reflect firms' response to fundamental change in their business environment or product market, it is possible that the risk-return characteristic of typical event firms is materially different from what it was, say 5 or 6 years, earlier. A long estimation window may also cover an earlier event. In studies of new CEO appointments, for example, a long estimation window may well contain the announcement of a previous CEO announcement. As discussed below, this can render the estimation of the model parameters problematic.

Considering the efficiency gains and potential costs of a long estimation window, the length of 1 or 2 years of daily data seems a reasonable balance for several types of events. Since the choice of the estimation window length is admittedly arbitrary, one useful way to assess the impact of the window length on quality of the results is to employ alternative window lengths and see if the results based on different lengths lead to the same or different conclusions.

[3]The inclusion in such an index would typically be hypothesized to convey new information to the market that the true quality of the firm's CG mechanism is good, or better than what investors had expected based on the information set publicly available prior to the announcement of the inclusion.

Due to the ease of estimation and practicality, the market-adjusted model has recently become increasingly popular. In this model, abnormal return to firm *i* is measured as:

$$ar_{i\tau} = r_{i\tau} - r_{m\tau} \tag{3}$$

Here, the market return is therefore the assumed benchmark return for all event firms in the sample. While Equation (2) allows the beta risk to vary across event firms, the market-adjusted model in Equation (3) assumes that the beta risk is unity across firms. Despite this challenging assumption, the simulation results of Brown and Warner (1980) show that, for short event windows, adjusting for the systematic (beta) risk does not improve the quality of abnormal return estimates.

Though appearing to be a lazy man's approach, this low-cost model has additional merit. Many firms repeatedly conduct an event within a given period of time (e.g. 1 or 2 years). For instance, several recent merger studies report that many firms in their samples make multiple acquisitions within a period of 3 years (e.g. for US, Fuller *et al.*, 2002; Ekkayokkaya and Paudyal, 2015; for UK, Ekkayokkaya *et al.*, 2009b). In such studies, there is no an estimation window that is free from the event under analysis for a large portion of the sample firms. Studies of CG events are also prone to a similar problem. Given its nature, a CG event may not occur in isolation. The inclusion in the good CG index, for example, is obviously an outcome of economically significant wealth-maximizing decisions observed in the recent past.[4] As a result, it is clearly possible that the estimation window in a CG-related event study covers important events with a predictable valuation effect. That is, the estimation window may well be a period of predictable abnormal return, which in turn would bias $\hat{\alpha}_i$.

Because abnormal return in Equation (3) is estimated directly from the event window, the market-adjusted model does not suffer from this problem. In large part due to its practicality, the model has been widely adopted as a return benchmark in recent event studies.

---

[4]A CG event can also be systematically followed by subsequent material events. To the extent that the good CG index inclusion reduces information asymmetry about firms, for example firms may well raise capital following their index inclusion. As discussed in Section 4, subsequent events have an important implication on tests of post-event long-term abnormal return.

3. Hypothesis Testing

Once abnormal return is measured for each event firm in the sample, statistical or hypothesis testing is needed to objectively determine whether the event under investigation produces any economically meaningful and statistically reliable value impact on the sample firms. The first step in hypothesis testing is to calculate the average, or median, abnormal return for the sample, i.e. to form an event portfolio and calculate the abnormal return on the portfolio. The next step is to assess the statistical significance of the point estimate (i.e. average or median abnormal return). In doing so, assessment of the economic significance is often overlooked even though we are interested in corporate events primarily because such events are expected (for good theoretical reasons) to produce *material* wealth effects on shareholders. Section 3.1 describes the event-portfolio formation and discusses related issues. In Section 3.2, the commonly applicable test statistics are discussed. A perspective on statistical significance in coexistence with economic significance is then offered in Section 3.3.

3.1 *Aggregation of abnormal returns and forming an event portfolio*

For reasons discussed in Section 2.2, the wealth effect of corporate events is typically measured over an event window, e.g. a 5-day (–2, +2) window. Thus, $ar_{i\tau}$ needs to be summed across T days during the event window to yield *cumulative abnormal return* (CAR):

$$CAR_i = \sum_{\tau=1}^{T} ar_{i\tau} \tag{4}$$

In order to draw a meaningful inference about the general value impact of the event, we need to aggregate CAR_i's across firms in the sample. That is, we need to form an event portfolio or calculate an average percentage CAR for the sample of n event firms:

$$\overline{CAR} = \frac{1}{n}\sum_{i=1}^{n} CAR_i \tag{5}$$

Obviously, Equation (5) assumes that an equal amount is invested across firms in the sample. In other words, all of the sample firms are given equal importance or weight regardless of their size. An equal weighting scheme, i.e. forming an equally weighted portfolio, is reasonable if the research objective is to measure the *typical* value impact of an event, e.g. how the market assesses the value impact of the good GC index inclusion for a typical firm. When the objective is to measure the *aggregate* wealth effect of an event, on the other hand, calculating an average abnormal *dollar* return ($\overline{CAR_D}$) is appropriate[5]:

$$\overline{CAR_D} = \frac{1}{n}\sum_{i=1}^{n}[V_i CAR_i] \tag{6}$$

where V_i is the market capitalization (or, market value) of common equity of firm *i* observed on the day *prior to* the event window, e.g. day −3. Since abnormal return is estimated in event time, it is important, especially when the sample period is long, that V_i is standardized at each point in time using an appropriate deflator. One commonly used deflator is the price level of a value-weighted market index.[6] Importantly, standardization helps ensure that V_i is comparable in real term across time. Estimating abnormal dollar return is equivalent to estimating CAR for a value-weighted portfolio. Percentage CAR for a value-weighted portfolio ($\overline{CAR_{VW}}$) can be calculated as:

$$\overline{CAR_{VW}} = \sum_{i=1}^{n} w_i CAR_i \tag{7}$$

where $w_i = \frac{V_i}{\sum_{i=1}^{n} V_i}$. It should be noted that while it is possible to calculate a median abnormal dollar return with equal weighting, it is not possible to do so meaningfully with value weighting.

[5]For an insightful discussion on the economics of abnormal dollar return as a measure of wealth effects, see Malatesta (1983).

[6]See, for example, Mitchell and Stafford (2000), Boehme and Sorescu (2002) and Ekkayokkaya *et al.* (2009a, 2009b).

3.2 *Statistical properties and test statistics*

The objective of testing whether an event in general has any statistically reliable value impact on the sample firms implies the null hypothesis that the average (or, median) CAR is zero. Therefore, one is to test whether the average CAR significantly differs from zero, and as a result, needs to estimate the variance of the estimated CAR. The statistical assessment of the CAR based on the market model in Equation (2) is first described, and then followed by the description of the assessment of the CAR based on the market-adjusted model in Equation (3). Given the assumption of the beta of unity across firms underlying the use of the market-adjusted model, an alternative approach to test the null of hypothesis of zero abnormal return is also described.

3.2.1 *The market model*

When $ar_{i\tau}$ is measured using the market model and the equal weighting scheme adopted as in Equation (5), the variance of $\overline{CAR}$ ($\overline{\sigma}^2$) can be calculated as:

$$\overline{\sigma}^2 = \frac{1}{n^2}\sum_{i=1}^{n}\sigma_i^2 \qquad (8)$$

where σ_i^2 is the variance of each CAR_i (again, over an event window of T days) and estimated as:

$$\sigma_i^2 = \sum_{\tau=1}^{T}\left[\hat{\sigma}^2_{\varepsilon_i} + \hat{\sigma}^2_{\varepsilon_i}\left(\frac{1}{d} + \frac{\left(r_{m\tau} - \bar{r}_m\right)^2}{\sum_{t=1}^{d}\left(r_{mt} - \bar{r}_m\right)^2}\right)\right] \qquad (9)$$

The bracketed is the term the variance of an individual $ar_{i\tau}$, where $\bar{r}_m$ is the simple average of market returns observed during the estimation window of d days. The term $\hat{\sigma}^2_{\varepsilon_i}$ is the variance of the market-model regression in Equation (1) for firm i and estimated using the return observations in the d-day estimation window:

$$\hat{\sigma}^2_{\varepsilon_i} = \frac{1}{d-k}\sum_{t=1}^{d}\left(r_{it} - \hat{\alpha}_i + \hat{\beta}_i r_{mt}\right)^2 \qquad (10)$$

Since there are two parameters in the market model, $k = 2$. As can be seen from both Equations (1) and (9), the larger the value of d, i.e. the longer is the estimation window, the smaller $\hat{\sigma}^2_{\varepsilon_i}$ and σ_i^2 become, ceteris paribus. Thus, one statistical benefit of using a long estimation window is an increase in the precision of $ar_{i\tau}$. As discussed in Section 2.3, nevertheless, the potential problems associated with a very long estimation period should not be ignored.

For a large sample of event firms, the equally weighted $\overline{CAR}$ from Equation (5) under the null hypothesis of zero abnormal return is distributed as: $\overline{CAR} \sim N\left(0, \overline{\sigma}^2\right)$. A test of the null can be conducted using the following test statistic:

$$t = \overline{CAR} / \overline{\sigma} \tag{11}$$

In practice, it is safe to assume that this test statistic, t, follows Student's t distribution because it approximates the normal distribution for a large number of observations, e.g. 120 or more. Here, it is useful to note that a two-tailed test is generally preferred to a one-tailed test since it is easier to reject the null using the later. For this reason, results reported based on a one-tailed test without strong priors on the direction of the event's impact are often viewed as weak.

Often, a theoretical hypothesis predicts that $\overline{CAR}$ for one group of firms is larger or smaller than that for the other group, e.g. between firms that adopt a pay-for-performance compensation scheme and those that do not. A test statistic for assessing the difference between the CAR for group 1 ($\overline{CAR}_1$) and the CAR for group 2 ($\overline{CAR}_2$) can be calculated as:

$$t_{diff} = \left(\overline{CAR}_1 - \overline{CAR}_2\right) / \sqrt{\overline{\sigma}_1^2 + \overline{\sigma}_2^2} \tag{12}$$

where $\overline{\sigma}_1^2$ and $\overline{\sigma}_2^2$ are, respectively, the variance of $(\overline{CAR}_1)$ and $(\overline{CAR}_2)$. As with Equation (11), the test statistic t_{diff} can be assumed to follow Student's t distribution.

As mentioned in Section 3.1, measuring dollar CAR $(\overline{CAR}_D)$ in Equation (6) or value-weighted percentage CAR $(\overline{CAR}_{VW})$ in Equation (7) can be desirable from some theoretical point of view. The variance of $(\overline{CAR}_D)$ $(\overline{\sigma}_D^2)$ can be calculated as:

$$\overline{\sigma}_D^2 = \frac{1}{n^2}\sum_{i=1}^{n}\left(\sigma_i^2 V_i^2\right) \tag{13}$$

Similar to the case of *CAR*, the null hypothesis of zero abnormal dollar return can be conducted using the test statistic:

$$t_D = \overline{CAR}_D / \bar{\sigma}_D \tag{14}$$

Using the same structure, the variance of $\overline{CAR}_{VW}$ $(\bar{\sigma}^2_{VW})$ can be calculated as:

$$\bar{\sigma}^2_{VW} = \sum_{i=1}^{n} \left(\sigma_i^2 w_i^2\right) \tag{15}$$

and the null of hypothesis of zero value-weighted percentage abnormal return can be conducted using the test statistic:

$$t_{VW} = \overline{CAR}_{VW} / \bar{\sigma}_{VW} \tag{16}$$

Both t_D and t_{VW} can also be assumed to follow Student's *t* distribution.

To test the difference in abnormal return between two groups of firms, the test statistics in Equations (17) and (18) can be employed for the difference in $\overline{CAR}_D$ and CAR_{VW}, respectively:

$$t_{D,diff} = \left(\overline{CAR}_{D,1} - \overline{CAR}_{D,2}\right) / \sqrt{\bar{\sigma}^2_{D,1} + \bar{\sigma}^2_{D,2}} \tag{17}$$

and

$$t_{VW,diff} = \left(\overline{CAR}_{VW,1} - \overline{CAR}_{VW,2}\right) / \sqrt{\bar{\sigma}^2_{VW,1} + \bar{\sigma}^2_{VW,2}} \tag{18}$$

where subscripts 1 and 2 denote groups 1 and 2, respectively. These test statistics can also be assumed to follow Student's *t* distribution.

When the sample is relatively small, it is useful to assess the median CAR in addition to $\overline{CAR}$ from Equation (5). The average of a small sample can be sensitive to the presence of outliers, if any. The statistical significance of a median CAR can be assessed using the Wilcoxon signed-rank test. The non-parametric equivalent for Equations (12), (17) and (18) is the Mann–Whitney U test, also known as Wilcoxon rank-sum test. Since non-parametric tests are essentially tests of location, the only required input for these tests is CAR_i from Equation (4). Options for these nonparametric tests are regularly available in most statistical/

econometrics software packages. As mentioned in Section 3.1, a median value-weighted CAR is not economically meaningful. For technical details and estimation procedure of these tests, readers are referred to Brown and Warner (1980) and Hollander and Wolfe (1999). These non-parametric tests are also applicable to the estimation of CAR based on the market-adjusted model in Equation (3).

3.2.2 *The market-adjusted model*

With an equal weighting scheme, the only way to estimate the variance of $\overline{CAR}$ calculated using $ar_{i\tau}$ from Equation (3) ($\sigma^2_{\overline{CAR}}$) is to estimate it as a cross-sectional sample variance:

$$\sigma^2_{\overline{CAR}} = \frac{\sum_{i=1}^{n}\left(CAR_i - \overline{CAR}\right)^2}{n-1} \quad \text{and} \tag{19}$$

the null hypothesis of zero percentage abnormal return can be conducted using the test statistic commonly known as the simple t-test:

$$t_{simple} = \overline{CAR} / \sigma_{\overline{CAR}} \cdot \sqrt{n} \tag{20}$$

To test the difference between two groups of firms, it is appropriate to use the independent-samples t-test which has the same structure as the test statistic in Equation (12). Both the simple t-test and independent-samples t-test are readily available in virtually all statistical software packages. These test statistics and the ones below in this subsection follow Student's t distribution.

If one is to test the null hypothesis of zero abnormal dollar return, the following test statistic can be used:

$$t_{D,simple} = \overline{CAR_D} \Bigg/ \left(\sigma_{\overline{CAR}} \sqrt{\sum_{i=1}^{n} V_i^2}\right)(n) \tag{21}$$

It should be noted here that it would be incorrect to test the null of $\overline{CAR_D} = 0$ by directly applying the simple t-test. This is because, unlike CAR_i, V_i is predetermined rather than being a random variable. Similar reasoning holds for the null of $\overline{CAR}_{VW} = 0$. The test statistic below can be used to test the null of zero value-weighted percentage abnormal return:

$$t_{VW,simple} = \overline{CAR}_{VW} \bigg/ \left(\sigma_{\overline{CAR}} \sqrt{\sum_{i=1}^{n} w_i^2} \right) \tag{22}$$

To test the difference in $\overline{CAR}_D$ and $\overline{CAR}_{VW}$ between two groups of firms, a test statistic of the same structure as those in Equations (17) and (18), respectively, can be employed. It is also worth noting that the test statistics described in this subsection can be viewed as implicitly assuming that the variance of individual CAR_i's is constant and equal to $\sigma^2_{\overline{CAR}}$.[7]

3.2.3 *The cross-sectional regression approach*

As mentioned in Section 2.3, although the market-adjusted model does not require use of the estimation window, it assumes that the beta risk is unity across firms. It is possible to address, in part, this assumption and still avoid using the estimation window by allowing the benchmark return model to reflect the average beta risk (as well as other risk factors) of the sample firms. In a nutshell, this approach employs a cross-section of data and measures average abnormal return in the regression framework of Jensen's alpha. Here, the statistical significance of abnormal return can be obtained as part of the regular regression routine. Assuming the CAPM as the return generating process, average abnormal return for the sample firms can be estimated by running the following regression[8]:

$$\left(r_{i\mathrm{T}} - r_{f\mathrm{T}}\right) = \alpha_{\mathrm{T}} + \beta_{\mathrm{T}}\left(r_{m\mathrm{T}} - r_{f\mathrm{T}}\right) + \varepsilon_{i\mathrm{T}} \tag{23}$$

---

[7] Therefore, these test statistics are different from their counterparts based on the market model in Equation (2), which by structure take account of individual variances of CAR_i observations which may be heteroscedastic.

[8] This cross-sectional regression approach to testing the null of zero abnormal return has been adopted by Draper and Paudyal (2006) and Ekkayokkaya *et al.* (2009b). In the light of the recent evidence that the size effect, book-to-market effect as well as return persistence explain a cross-section of stock returns above and beyond the beta (systematic) risk (e.g. Fama and French, 1996), one can directly extend Equation (23) to include these additional priced risk factors.

where r_{iT} is return to firm i observed over the T-day event window and calculated as: $r_{iT} = \sum_{\tau=1}^{T} r_{i\tau}$. If return is calculated as continuously compounded return, r_{iT} represents buy-and-hold return to firm i over a T-day period. r_{fT} and r_{mT} are the corresponding risk-free return and market return: both of which are calculated in the same fashion as r_{iT}. Technically speaking, the market return can be calculated from either an equally weighted or value-weighted market index. Since the theoretically optimal market portfolio is a value-weighted portfolio, use of a value-weighted market index is advocated here.

In Equation (23), the estimated intercept $(\hat{\alpha}_T)$ is a measure of equally weighted average abnormal return to the sample firms over the T-day event window (Jensen's alpha). The standard error for testing the significance of $\hat{\alpha}_T$ is readily provided by the regression procedure. The potential impact of non-constant variances of event firm returns on the statistical significance of all model parameters (including $\hat{\alpha}_T$) can then be conveniently accounted for by employing the White heteroscedasticity-consistent standard error, which is nowadays a standard built-in option in practically all of the available econometric software packages. The average systematic risk of the sample firms is captured by the estimated slope coefficient $(\hat{\beta}_T)$.

A test of there being a statistically significant difference in abnormal return between two groups of firms can be carried out by adding to Equation (23) an indicator variable for the grouping and an interaction term between the indicator variable and the risk factor. This is to run the following regression model:

$$\left(r_{iT} - r_{fT}\right) = \alpha_T + \beta_T\left(r_{mT} - r_{fT}\right) + \gamma_T(G) + \delta_T\left(\left(r_{mT} - r_{fT}\right) \bullet G\right) + \varepsilon_{iT} \qquad (24)$$

where G is the indicator variable taking the value of 1 when the term $(r_{iT} - r_{fT})$ is observed for firm group 1 (or, group 2) and zero otherwise. The estimated coefficient $\hat{\gamma}_T$ measures the difference in abnormal return (i.e. Jensen's alpha) between the two groups of firms. The interaction term is incorporated to account for the difference in the slope coefficient, i.e. average systematic risk, between the firm groups. Omitting the interaction term when such a difference is important would be to load on G not only the difference in abnormal return but also the difference in risk, making $\hat{\gamma}_T$ of little use in practice.[9] To the extent there are theoretical priors to warrant a statistical test of the difference in abnormal return between firm groups, it is likely that the groups also have materially different risk-return characteristics. For example, the risk-return combination of investments is likely to vary between firms that adopt a pay-for-performance compensation scheme and those that do not.

Equation (23) can be adjusted to test the null hypothesis of zero abnormal dollar return over a T-day event window. To do so, following Eckbo and Thorburn (2000), the terms $(r_{iT} - r_{fT})$ and $(r_{mT} - r_{fT})$ are pre-multiplied by V_i. The regression model can then be re-run. The resulting intercept provides a measure of an equally weighted average abnormal dollar return. The structure of Equation (24) can be directly applied should one have theoretical priors to expect a difference in abnormal dollar return between firm groups. It is noted here that it is not feasible to estimate value-weighted average percentage abnormal return using the framework of Equations (23) and (24).

3.3 *Interpretation of results — Statistical and economic significance*

For most of the times, statistically significant results are also economically significant or meaningful. This is because a point estimate generally has to be economically sizeable for it to be statistically significant. Often enough, however, a statistically significant abnormal return is very small in magnitude. A small, and yet significant, point estimate can easily arise from a large sample.

As an illustration, consider an equally weighted $\overline{CAR}$ of 0.3% for a sample of 250 observations with the standard deviation of 2.99. This would not be statistically significant, based on the simple *t*-test, at the conventional levels as the test statistic would be 1.59 with the *p*-value of 0.114. Note here that sample size of 250 observations is not small, and indeed, is more than enough for Student's *t* distribution to approximate the

[9]The statistical importance of the difference in the slope coefficient can be assessed from the significance of the estimated interaction term coefficient ($\hat{\delta}_T$).

Normal distribution. Now, suppose with an electronic database, the available sample size becomes substantially larger (which is empirically desirable), say 950. With this sample size, *other things constant*, the test statistic for this 0.3% $\overline{CAR}$ would mechanically become 3.09 with the *p*-value of 0.002, thereby making the same $\overline{CAR}$ significant at the 0.01 level. This pattern tends to be observed more often among recent studies as the sample size employed typically gets larger and larger, thanks to the burgeoning availability of electronic databases. Though naïve, this simple illustration offers another important message. In a large sample, weak statistical significance, e.g. at the 0.10 level, is unlikely to be viewed as sufficiently reliable evidence to reject the null of zero abnormal return. This message is compatible with a number of event studies in the mainstream journals interpreting their results as statistically significant if the *p*-value is 0.05 or less.

A large number of authors condition their interpretation of results primarily on statistical significance. While focusing on statistical significance yields objectivity and is the right thing to do, it is also equally important to pay attention to the economic significance of the point estimate(s). When we are empirically interested in analyzing a given corporate event, we are so because we have theoretical reasons to expect the event to produce an economically meaningful value impact, e.g. to destroy shareholders' wealth in a material fashion. In the above illustration, an appropriate inference that can be drawn assuming the sample size of 950 observations is that the event can be expected to systematically affect wealth, but its economic effect is only small. To this extent, focusing solely on statistical significance may well give an incomplete picture of the wealth effect of the event.

It is difficult to make a judgment call on what is and is not economically significant. Unfortunately, there exists no hard and fast rule (i.e. theoretical guidance) on how to gauge economic significance. One way to do so is to compare the point estimate, e.g. 0.3% CAR over a 5-day event window, with the results reported by the comparable existing studies. Given this average CAR, another useful way is to compare it with the degree of price movement other strands of the finance literature considers as a large price movement. For example, a 1.5%, 2.0% or 2.5% increase or decrease in the CRSP market index, either equally weighted or value-weighted, is defined in studies of institutions' trading behavior as a large price movement (e.g. Dennis and Strickland, 2002; Lipson and Puckett,

2010). Clearly, a statistically significant $\overline{CAR}$ of 0.3% is far from being economically significant: it would be so if it were, say, 1.1%.

3.4 *Statistical problems*

There are two common problems associated with the inference about the statistical significance of abnormal return estimates. These problems are related to the i.i.d. assumption; namely, heteroscedasticity or varying specific variances, and cross-sectional correlation among abnormal returns. In the following subsections, these problems and their empirical importance are discussed.

3.4.1 *Problem of heteroscedastic variances*

For heteroscedasticity, the conventional practice is to standardize each individual CAR using its own standard deviation, i.e. (CAR_i / σ_i). In this case, the applicable test statistic under the null of hypothesis of zero abnormal return by definition becomes standard normal (also commonly known as the *Z*-statistic):

$$Z = \frac{1}{\sqrt{n}} \sum_{i=1}^{n} \frac{CAR_i}{\sigma_i} \tag{25}$$

This standardization accounts for heteroscedasticity in the estimated abnormal return and can make the test statistic more powerful in detecting abnormal return (Brown and Warner, 1985). Since Equation (25) requires specific variances of individual CARs, it is applicable only when the market model (Equation (2)) is used to estimate CAR_i. Alternatively, one can also account for heteroscedasticity in the variance component of the test statistic. By structure, $\overline{\sigma}^2$ in Equation (8) incorporates a specific variance of CAR_i (σ_i^2). Therefore, the structure of the test statistic in Equation (11) and its variants in Section 3.2.1 accounts for varying specific variances. The key difference between Equations (25) and (11) is that the former assumes that the distribution of the standardized CAR is unit normal whereas the latter makes no such an assumption.

As discussed earlier, the test statistics in Section 3.2.2 make use of a cross-sectional sample variance. Because the market-adjusted $ar_{i\tau}$ from Equation (3) is calculated entirely within the event window, the variance of the resulting average CAR (whether percent or dollar) is by structure the cross-sectional sample variance. Therefore, these test statistics are not subject to the heteroscedastic variances inherent in the case of the abnormal return estimation based on the market model from Equation (2). Since the cross-sectional regression approach in Section 3.2.3 also estimates abnormal return entirely within the event window, it, too, is not subject to such heteroscedastic variances. As mentioned in the section, although this regression approach is still subject to the non-constant variances of event firm returns, the remedy is readily available from the regression procedure.

3.4.2 *Problem of cross-sectional correlation*

A potentially more concerning statistical problem is the cross-sectional correlation among abnormal returns: also known as the cross-dependence problem. This problem arises when individual abnormal returns (i.e. CARs) are contemporaneously, or cross-sectionally, correlated across firms. As has been widely observed, abnormal returns to firms that conduct the same event tend to move together *in event time* in a noticeable manner. That is, the cross-dependence is positive in nature.

While all of the test statistics discussed above assume random sampling, corporate events, as correctly noted by Mitchell and Stafford (2000), are *not* random events. While some firms choose to participate in a certain event (e.g. make an SEO), some others choose not to do so. It is also well documented that M&As do not take place randomly across industries or time. Rather, these activities occur in waves or clusters, exhibit industry clustering and are also systematically associated with macro-economic conditions (e.g. Mitchell and Mulherin, 1996; Harford, 2005). Other corporate events, such as security issues and share repurchases also occur in waves (see Rau and Stouraitis, 2011). A sample of firms involved in a CG event is no exception. Firms that get included in a good CG index, for example, are likely to have chosen to make wealth-maximizing decisions prior to their index inclusion and have been experiencing good performance, either stock price or operating, or both. As another example, firms adopting a pay-for-performance compensation scheme are likely to have chosen to do so for a similar set of reasons. Accordingly, the stock prices of firms in these examples would move in a similar direction during the event window, i.e. would be positively cross-sectionally correlated. Intuitively, firms that choose to conduct an event do so because they expect to benefit from the event. Thus, event firms are bound to be of certain characteristics, and the market is likely to react to event firms *systematically* differently from how it would react to random non-event firms.

One key consequence of cross-dependence is systematic underestimation of the true variance of the estimated average abnormal return, i.e. the mean CAR calculated in Equations (5)–(7). This is because while the cross-dependence is by and large positive in nature, the conventional variance estimation (e.g. that in Section 3.2) assumes zero correlation among abnormal returns. In other words, CAR_i's are assumed to be cross-sectionally independent. Such systematic underestimation of true variance in turn leads to an overstatement of a conventional test statistic, with the upshot being too many rejections of the null of zero abnormal return when it is true.

Cross-dependence is most severe when there are overlapping return-calculation periods. That is when a given sample firm is observed: (i) twice or more in the sample; and (ii) within the time span shorter than the event window. Consider a simple case of a single firm conducting the event twice. During the overlapping period, the firm's abnormal return will be counted, i.e. observed, twice. This is where the problem arises. The average of two identical abnormal returns will be the same as each estimate. This is not the case for variance. Assuming cross-sectional independence, the estimated variance of the average (say, equally weighted) would be only half that of each constituent abnormal return. However, the true variance of this average abnormal return is, as it should be, identical to the variance of the constituent abnormal returns, which are essentially a single abnormal return counted twice in the calculation of the average CAR.

One way to account for cross-dependence is to make the Crude Dependent Adjustment (CDA) suggested by Brown and Warner (1980). With the CDA, the standard deviation of the average abnormal return is calculated as the standard deviation of the event-time series of abnormal returns observed during the pre-event period (see Brown and Warner, 1980, Equations A.4 through A.6). Since the standard deviation is estimated from the average, or portfolio, abnormal returns observed in event time, any cross-dependence among individual abnormal returns is captured in the calculation. Another way to deal with cross-dependence is to form a portfolio of the sample firms in calendar time. Forming the event firm portfolio in calendar time completely eliminates the cross-dependence problem. Since cross-dependence is unlikely to materially affect the statistical inference of abnormal returns estimated from a short event window, the details of the calendar-time portfolio approach are discussed in Section 5 where the tests of long-term abnormal return are discussed.

3.4.3 *Empirical importance of statistical problems*

Both of the heteroscedasticity and cross-dependence problems are important statistical aspects of event studies. Regardless of their observed empirical importance, it is essential that one be aware of these aspects to be able to make judgment on the statistical reliability of abnormal return estimates. Empirically, the findings of the simulation studies by Brown and Warner (1980, 1985) indicate that, for a short event window, neither of the problems appears to affect in an important way the statistical significance or the magnitude of abnormal return estimates. Indeed, the findings of a number of empirical event studies also show that the choice of return benchmark (e.g. market model vs. market-adjusted model) does not materially affect the detection of abnormal return.

For instance, in examining abnormal returns around takeover announcements, Draper and Paudyal (1999) employ the return benchmarks in Brown and Warner (1985) with and without the CDA. Their results show that the abnormal return estimates are insensitive to model specification in terms of statistical significance as well as the magnitude of the estimates. Since Draper and Paudyal (1999) employ test statistics that involve and do not involve the standardization discussed in Section 3.4.1, the insensitivity of their results serves as an empirical indication that the presence of varying specific variances of abnormal returns is unlikely to affect the statistical inferences of abnormal return estimates. Indeed, the insensitivity of their results also provides non-simulation evidence that adjusting for cross-dependence does not affect the quality of abnormal return estimates. In their subsequent large-sample study of takeovers, Draper and Paudyal (2006) employ the cross-sectional regression approach similar to that in Equation (23). They assume three return generating processes: the CAPM; Fama–French three-factor model; and the three-factor model with a variable representing the average past return for the sample firms. Especially for the 3-day window surrounding the announcement date, their abnormal return estimates are notably comparable across the employed benchmarks in both magnitude and statistical significance. This pattern can be viewed as a non-simulation indication that accounting for other risk factors in addition to the market risk factor affects neither the magnitude nor statistical significance of abnormal return estimates.

Employing the market-adjusted model as in Equation (3) and a large sample of takeovers by European firms, Faccio *et al.* (2006) examine whether the announcement-period abnormal returns to acquirers differs between takeovers of listed targets and takeovers of unlisted targets. As part of their empirical analysis, they categorically address the potential problem of cross-dependence using the calendar-time portfolio approach. Their results show that the difference in abnormal return between the two types of takeovers is comparable in both magnitude and statistical significance whether the average CAR is calculated in event time or calendar time. This pattern is also persistently observed across their various sample partitions. Thus, the findings of Faccio *et al.* (2006) serve as an additional non-simulation testimony to the insensitivity of short-window abnormal return estimates to cross-dependence, if any. Given that cross-dependence is severe when there is return overlap, such insensitivity is intuitive. Firms generally do not repeat the same event within a very short period of time, e.g. within 5 or 10 days, thereby making return overlap unlikely.

In sum, it is well documented in the event study literature that neither the choice of return benchmarks nor the statistical problems of heteroscedastic variances and cross-dependence of abnormal returns is a serious concern in conducting tests of abnormal return in a short event window. As discussed below, however, this is not the case for tests of abnormal return in a long event window, e.g. a 3-year post-event window.

4. Measuring Long-Term Abnormal Return

In addition to testing the announcement-period or short-term abnormal return, event studies often include, as material part, examination of abnormal return over a long period of time following the event. For an analysis of post-event abnormal return, this period is essentially the event window. As with the short-horizon analysis, there is no theoretical guidance on how long the event window in the post-event analysis should be. Almost all of the existing studies employ 1-, 2- and 3-year post-event windows with several also focusing on the 5-year window. Obviously, the key difference between tests of short-term and long-term abnormal return is simply the length of the event window.

An attempt to measure an event-induced value impact over a very long period of time exposes tests of long-term abnormal return to contamination. This is so regardless of the statistical approaches, and CG-related event studies are no exception. For instance, a successfully implemented change in firms' CG mechanism can pave the way for subsequent corporate activities. That is, it is clearly possible that a CG event is systematically followed by other events that are of substance to firms. To this extent, the abnormal return detected during the post-event window, if any, is attributable not only to the CG event being studied but also to the subsequent activity(ies).

For the long window analysis, moreover, there are several issues and complications — both conceptual and statistical — that appear to remain debatable. In Section 4.1, a brief background of the literature on tests of post-event long-term abnormal return is introduced. In the remaining subsections, the commonly adopted approaches to measuring long-term abnormal return are described.

4.1 *Background*

Much of the empirical event study literature has, and still does, primarily focused on tests of announcement-period abnormal return (i.e. short-term abnormal return). Such a focus on short-term abnormal return is primarily due to "the strong belief in market efficiency" (Agrawal and Jaffe, 2000, p. 8; see also Masulis *et al*., 2007, footnote 9), which would dictate zero abnormal return in the period following the event outcome. As an illustration, Jensen and Ruback (1983, p. 20) remark that negative post-event abnormal returns are "unsettling because they are inconsistent with market efficiency and suggest that changes in stock prices overestimate the future efficiency gains from mergers". Especially during the 1990s, the literature saw a burgeoning interest in tests of post-event long-term abnormal return. Not surprisingly, the typical motivation or discussion of results given in a number of long-term abnormal return studies alludes to market inefficiency, or investors suffering from a behavioral bias(es) one way or another.[10]

[10]For example, Loughran and Ritter (1995), Loughran and Vijh (1997), Rau and Vermaelen (1998), and Boehme and Sorescu (2002). For theoretical arguments predicting patterns of long-term abnormal return, see Shleifer and Vishny (2003).

Several intuitively and statistically appealing empirical approaches have been put forward in the literature. In the main, these approaches can be categorized into the *event-time* and *calendar-time* approaches, and for both approaches, the benchmark return can be estimated using a *k*-factor asset pricing model or return to a characteristic-based control firm/portfolio. Yet, each of these approaches is plagued with methodological problems one way or another. Unsurprisingly, there appears to be no consensus on the fool-proof way to measure long-term abnormal return. Based on the existing evidence, it would indeed be safe to generalize that long-term abnormal return estimates are sensitive to model specification. Such sensitivity is, at least in part, attributable to the length of the window itself, and yet, the objective is to measure abnormal return during a long window. Since the conventionally adopted windows in a long-horizon test are extremely long, considerable noise is inevitable. To the contrary, the event study methodology is fundamentally designed to capture an abnormal price reaction to the new information, or surprise, that arrives at the market at *a very specific point in time*.[11] In other words, the methodology is not designed to isolate noise from the valuation effect of new information.

Because there are a number of methodological issues surrounding tests of long-term abnormal return, it is worthwhile to briefly mention here the central message of this part of the chapter, in the hope of maintaining tractability of the discussion. Different approaches address different aspects abnormal return measurement. It is important for researchers to contemplate both the economic and statistical properties of abnormal return estimates. Given the known sensitivity of the estimates of long-term abnormal return to model specification, one useful empirical strategy is to employ at least one event-time specification and one calendar-time specification, and then compare the results.

4.2 *Firm-specific Fama–French three-factor model*

One intuitive way to measure long-term abnormal return earned by an average event firm in the sample is to use a *k*-factor asset pricing model as a return benchmark as in Barber and Lyon (1997a). Here, abnormal

[11] As discussed in Section 2.1, it is crucial to identify the true event date, or the precise time at which the market first learns about the event.

return to event firm *i* during the *T*-month window following the month of the event outcome can be estimated in the regression framework of Jensen's alpha. One important implicit assumption underlying the choice of window length is that the value impact of an event under the alternative hypothesis lasts for the length of the window. Due to the findings of Fama and French (1992, 1993), subsequent studies of corporate events commonly control for the size and book-to-market (BM) effects when formulating an expected-return benchmark.[12]

$$R_{it} - R_{ft} = \alpha_i + \beta_i\left(R_{mt} - R_{ft}\right) + s_i SMB_t + h_i HML_t + \varepsilon_{it}\ ^{13} \qquad (26)$$

R_{it} is return to firm *i* observed in month *t* during the *T*-month event window. R_{ft} and R_{mt} are the corresponding risk-free return and market return. SMB_t and HML_t are the return spreads observed in month *t* between small and big firms, and between firms with high and low book-to-market ratios, respectively. In other words, these spreads are the size and book-to-market risk factors as in Fama and French (1993).

The estimated intercept ($\hat{\alpha}_i$) is a measure of abnormal return firm *i* earns *per month* during the *T*-month event window.[14] Here, one could get a sense of per-annum or holding-period return by multiplying $\hat{\alpha}_i$ by 12 or the number of months in the window, respectively. The average, equally weighted or value-weighted, abnormal return can then be calculated by averaging $\hat{\alpha}_i$'s across the sample in the fashion similar to Equation (5) or (7), respectively. Similarly, the average monthly dollar abnormal return can be calculated following Equation (6). Because each $\hat{\alpha}_i$ is estimated relative to the event month, this approach measures abnormal return in *event time*.

---

[12] Fama and French (1992) find that firm size and the BM ratio are important and the most robust factors in explaining the cross-section of expected stock returns for the US non-financial firms. A subsequent study by Barber and Lyon (1997b) documents that these relations also hold for financial firms in the US market. In the UK market, the size and BM factors have also been found as important risk factors (see, e.g. Davies *et al.*, 1999; Gregory *et al.*, 2013).

[13] The subscripts used from this point onwards are not related to and not to be confused with those used in the discussion of tests of short-term abnormal return. Subscripts 't' and 'T' are used in this part simply to maintain compatibility with the convention.

[14] If abnormal return is to be measured during a 3-year window, for example, the number of monthly returns to be included in the regression model is 36.

Employing the cross-sectional sample variance as in Barber and Lyon (1997a), the null hypothesis of zero monthly abnormal return can be tested using the test statistic similar to Equation (20) or (22) for equally weighted or value-weighted average percentage abnormal return, respectively. The structure of Equation (21) is applicable to the null of zero monthly abnormal dollar return. To account for varying specific variances, the test statistics in Equations (27)–(29) can be used to test the null of zero equally weighted and value-weighted percentage monthly abnormal return, and monthly abnormal dollar return, respectively:

$$t_{EW} = \left(\frac{\frac{1}{n}\sum_{i=1}^{n} \hat{\alpha}_i}{\sqrt{\sum_{i=1}^{n} se_i^2}} \right) \bullet n \tag{27}$$

$$t_{VW} = \left(\frac{\sum_{i=1}^{n} w_i \hat{\alpha}_i}{\sqrt{\sum_{i=1}^{n} w_i^2 se_i^2}} \right) \tag{28}$$

$$t_{dollar} = \left(\frac{\frac{1}{n}\sum_{i=1}^{n} V_i \hat{\alpha}_i}{\sqrt{\sum_{i=1}^{n} V_i^2 se_i^2}} \right) \bullet n \tag{29}$$

where se_i is the regression standard error for $\hat{\alpha}_i$. The terms n, V_i, and w_i are defined as in Section 3. These test statistics follow Student's t distribution. Alternatively, one may choose to assume that the distribution of standardized $\hat{\alpha}_i$, i.e. $(\hat{\alpha}_i/se_i)$, is unit normal in testing the relevant null hypothesis of zero abnormal return. To test the difference in average abnormal return between two groups of firms, the structure of the test statistics in Equations (12), (17) or (18) can be adopted.

To ensure that the regression estimates are reasonably stable, firms are typically required to have a minimum of 12 or 24 valid returns. Such requirement clearly gives rise to the survivorship bias as only firms that have survived the required minimum post-event period are included in the analysis. One way to avoid this survivorship bias is to adopt the regression framework of Equation (23). To enter Equation (23), firms need to have only 1 month of valid return following the month of the event outcome.

4.3 *Event-time characteristic-based return benchmark*

Due to the bad model problem (for a more detailed discussion, see Section 5.1), a number of studies measure buy-and-hold abnormal return (BHAR) against a characteristic-based return benchmark over a period of T months following the month of the event outcome:

$$BHAR_{iT} = \prod_{t=1}^{T}\left[1 + R_{it}\right] - \prod_{t=1}^{T}\left[1 + \mathrm{E}\left(R_{it}\right)\right] \tag{30}$$

As mentioned earlier, the commonly adopted window length (T) is 12, 24, 36 or 60 months. R_{it} is return to firm i observed in month t during the T-month event window. $\mathrm{E}(R_{it})$ is the return firm i is expected to earn during month t, i.e. its benchmark return. For estimation purposes, a number of studies calculate return as a simple return. It is also possible to use continuously compounded return as an input to Equation (30) — in which case, the right-hand side of the equation becomes: $\left(\sum_{t=1}^{T} R_{it}^{L}\right) - \left(\sum_{t=1}^{T} \mathrm{E}\left(R_{it}^{L}\right)\right)$, where superscript L denotes continuous compounding.[15]

$\mathrm{E}(R_{it})$ can be estimated as return to the characteristic-based *control firm* or *control portfolio*. Due to the Fama–French findings as mentioned above, most studies select a control firm or firms to constitute a control portfolio that are comparable to event firm i in terms of size (market capitalization of common equity) and book-to-market ratio. As with the window length, there is no theoretical guidance on how to do

[15] Several authors advocate the use of simple return as it is not subject to a downward bias due to Jensen's inequality. More simply, for a given increase (decrease) in price, continuously compounded return is always less positive (more negative) than simple return. The magnitude of this effect can be of some concern if a sample contains a big number of large price changes, e.g. changes larger than 15 percentage points per calculation interval. For small price changes, however, simple and continuous return calculations should yield results that lead to the same conclusion.

the size and book-to-market matching. Here, the rule of the day is common sense, and one can follow the widely adopted sequential sorting method in Barber and Lyon (1997a). Loughran and Vijh (1997) employ a slightly different sorting method as well as the Barber–Lyon sequential sorting, and report that their results are qualitatively similar between the two methods.

Unfortunately, there is a bit more to the process of identifying control firms. By definition, a control firm must not conduct the event under analysis at any time during: (i) the event window and (ii) the pre-event period of the same length. This requirement also applies to firms to enter a control portfolio. Due to the assumption that the value impact of an event during a T-month window under the alternative hypothesis lasts for T months, it is *not* enough that control firms are a non-event firm only during the event window. It is this requirement that can call the reality of this approach into question in terms of both costs of tracing the activities by the candidate control firms and finding firms that qualify as control firms.

As in the case of tests of short-term abnormal return, $BHAR_{iT}$'s can be averaged with equal or value-weighting, or as an equally weighted average abnormal dollar return. Because $BHAR_{iT}$ is calculated within the event window, the feasible test statistics necessarily rely on the cross-sectional sample variance. The test statistics in Section 3.2.2 are therefore applicable to testing an average BHAR. To address the impact of outliers on the abnormal return estimates, the non-parametric tests described in Section 3.2.1 can be employed. These non-parametric tests are also applicable to the approach discussed in Section 4.5.

4.4 *Calendar-time Fama–French three-factor model*

In response to the cross-dependence problem, many studies estimate the Fama–French three-factor model in calendar time. That is, a portfolio of event firms is formed in calendar time, and the time series of portfolio returns is regressed on the corresponding time series of the three risk factors. For each calendar month, return is calculated for a portfolio of firms that conduct the event within the previous T months (T = 12, 24, 36 or 60 months). The portfolio is *rebalanced* (or, reformed) monthly to drop all firms that reach the end of their period of T months and to add all firms that have just conducted the event.[16] This portfolio formation yields a time series of monthly portfolio returns (R_{pt}). Also importantly, it gives only *one* return for any given calendar month, and as a result, there is *no* cross-correlation at any given point in time. For each portfolio, the Fama–French three-factor model can be estimated in the following regression framework:

$$R_{pt} - R_{ft} = \alpha_p + \beta_p \left(R_{mt} - R_{ft} \right) + s_p SMB_t + h_p HML_t + \varepsilon_{pt} \tag{31}$$

In this *time-series* regression model, R_{pt} is the return to the event-firm portfolio observed in month t, and can be equally weighted or value-weighted. All other variables are defined similarly to those in Equation (26). Accordingly, $\hat{\alpha}_p$ is a measure of average monthly abnormal return to the event-firm portfolio during the T-month window following the event. The heteroscedasticity-autocorrelation-consistent (HAC) standard error readily provided by the regression procedure can be used to assess the statistical significance of $\hat{\alpha}_p$.

In correcting for heteroscedasticity, several authors employ the weighted least square (WLS) estimator, instead of the OLS estimator. Commonly, the weights are set proportional to $\sqrt{j}$, where j is the number of firms in each monthly portfolio (see Mitchell and Stafford, 2000). As Mitchell and Stafford show, this weighting assumes that individual-firm residuals are uncorrelated, and hence, "completely defeats the purpose of forming calendar-time portfolios, which is to account for the fact that individual-firm residuals are cross-sectionally correlated" (p. 317). Because heteroscedasticity is a problem of inference common in regression analysis, not just the calendar-time Fama–French three-factor model, it will be reasonable to resort to the readily provided HAC standard error.

To examine whether there is a statistically significant difference in the average monthly abnormal return between two groups of firms, one can apply the dummy variable technique in Equation (24). Since the data used in Equation (31) is time-series data, however, the observations must be stacked in a chronological order (i.e. time order) for the estimated auto-correlation-consistent standard error to be meaningful.

[16] In this procedure, firms that become delisted before the end of the window are automatically dropped out of the portfolio at the beginning of the month of delisting.

4.5 *Calendar-time characteristic-based return benchmark*

Alternative to the calendar-time Fama–French three-factor model is to apply the characteristic-based return benchmark in calendar time. This approach is also known as the calendar-time rolling portfolio approach, first employed by Jaffe (1974) and Mandelker (1974). As its main appeal, it is free from the assumption of parameter stability over time which underlies a k-factor asset pricing model. Here, the formation of an event-firm portfolio is similar to that in Section 4.4, i.e. assumes monthly rebalancing. For each calendar month t and firm i that conducts the event within the previous T months, abnormal return (AR_{it}) can first be measured against a characteristic-based return benchmark where:

$$AR_{it} = R_{it} - \mathrm{E}\left(R_{it}\right) \tag{32}$$

As with its event-time counterpart in Section 4.3, $\mathrm{E}(R_{it})$ can be return on the *control firm* or *control portfolio*. Following Lyon *et al.* (1999), each month t, abnormal return on the event-firm portfolio (MAR_t) can then be calculated as:

$$MAR_t = \sum_{i=1}^{j} w_{it} AR_{it} \tag{33}$$

where j is the number of event firms with valid return in month t. With an equal weighting scheme, $w_{it} = \frac{1}{j}$, and $w_{it} = \frac{V_{it-1}}{\sum_{i=1}^{j} V_{it-1}}$ for a value-weighting scheme. The average monthly portfolio abnormal return for the sample is:

$$\overline{MAR} = \frac{1}{m}\sum_{t=1}^{m} MAR_t \tag{34}$$

where m is the number of months in the time series of MAR_t. Also note that Equation (34) applies whether MAR_t is equally weighted or value-weighted. This is because the weighting takes place when a portfolio is formed in each month, i.e. in Equation (33). Naturally, Equation (34) weights monthly returns equally across the sample period.

The null of zero $\overline{MAR}$ can be conducted using the simple t-test as follows:

$$t_{\overline{MAR}} = \left(\frac{\overline{MAR}}{\hat{\sigma}_{\overline{MAR}}}\right) \bullet \sqrt{m} \tag{35}$$

where $\hat{\sigma}_{\overline{MAR}}$ is the intertemporal sample standard deviation of $\overline{MAR}$ calculated within the sample using the time series of MAR_t. At variance with Equation (35), Fama (1998) advocates the method of standardizing MAR_t by its time-series standard deviation, which is normally calculated using a series of between 50 and 60 lagged values of MAR_t (e.g. Jaffe, 1974; Mandelker, 1974; Spiess and Affleck-Graves, 1999). While doing so helps address the problem of heteroscedasticity due to the varying number of firms that enter the monthly portfolios (i.e. j varying across months t), many observations from the early part of the sample period will be lost. This standardization therefore introduces an inadvertent selection bias in the sample, which will be of great concern when the sample period is relatively short, e.g. 10-years.

5. Issues Surrounding Tests of Long-Term Abnormal Return

The dispute over the best model of expected stock return is far from settled. A test of long-term abnormal return is essentially a joint test of market efficiency and the effect of the event. If one assumes that the adopted return generating process is correctly specified, the observation of statistically significant long-term abnormal return can be interpreted as evidence against market efficiency. With the assumption of market efficiency, alternatively, significant long-term abnormal return implies that the expected return model is mis-specified, or a bad model. Apparent from Section 4 is that several attempts have been made to address various problems inherent in tests of long-term abnormal return. Naturally, different approaches give different pictures of abnormal return. It is important to understand what the adopted model(s) does and does not do, and be aware of the potential problem that comes with the chosen test method(s).

This section reviews the known methodological problems surrounding tests of long-term abnormal return. The remedies offered in the existing literature are also discussed in this section. The measurement issues are discussed in Section 5.1, and statistical issues in Section 5.2. Section 5.3 attempts to draw a perspective on the methodological issues as one's research objective may call for an analysis of long-term abnormal return.

5.1 *Measurement issues*

Central to the measurement of abnormal return is that the estimate actually represents the true abnormal return earned by investors and is unbiased. When an asset pricing model is used, e.g. as in Sections 4.2 and 4.4, it is implicitly assumed that the model is a correct return generating process. As pointed out by Fama (1998, p. 292), however, "any asset pricing model is just a model and so does not completely describe expected returns". This conclusion was drawn from extensive evidence of significant long-term abnormal return following several corporate events. As Fama and French (1993) themselves observe, their *three-factor model* is designed to price stocks on the size and book-to-market dimensions, and even so, it still misprices small high-growth (i.e. low book-to-market) firms. Moreover, Fama and French (1996) report that the return persistence or momentum documented in Jegadeesh and Titman (1993) is not explained by their three-factor model. These empirical observations on the performance of the Fama–French three-factor model may well be the reason why several subsequent studies of long-term abnormal return employ the Fama–French three-factor model plus the Carhart (1997) momentum factor (see, e.g. Moeller *et al.*, 2004; Bouwman *et al.*, 2009). Whether or not this four-factor model completely describes the return generating process is not obvious. To this end, it should also be noted that while the CAPM is a theoretically founded asset pricing model, the size and book-to-market as well as momentum factors are originally motivated by empirics.

The use of an asset pricing model has also been criticized for the regular rebalancing of the event firm portfolio. That is, the portfolio is mechanically rebalanced at the end of every return calculation interval. For the methods described in Sections 4.2 and 4.4, for instance, the portfolio is rebalanced every month. Such a regular rebalancing strategy is likely to incur substantial transaction costs for investors, and is hence, an unlikely description of typical investors' portfolio strategy (also Loughran and Vijh, 1997). The punchline of this criticism is that using an asset pricing model as a return benchmark leads to a measure of abnormal return that is inconsistent with investors' experience. As advocated by many, especially Barber and Lyon (1997a) and Lyon *et al.* (1999), long-term abnormal return should be measured as *buy-and-hold* return as it does not assume such regular rebalancing and allows for compounding. Because the event window is typically very long, it is conceptually important to incorporate compounding in measuring long-term abnormal return earned on a portfolio of event firms.

Apparently, the buy-and-hold return calculation is intuitively appealing. However, the compounding itself poses a serious problem of artificial abnormal return. As pointed out by Mitchell and Stafford (2000), as long as abnormal return exists in any portion of the return series, BHAR can artificially grow even in the absence of true abnormal return, and this artificial BHAR grows in the length of the window, i.e. the holding period.[17] In a nutshell, such artificial BHAR growth is caused by the reinvesting of abnormal return in period(s) of zero abnormal return at the rate of normal return. To correct for the artificial BHAR problem, one can adopt the wealth relative measure (practically, a variant of BHAR) as in Loughran and Ritter (1995). For firm *i*, a wealth relative measure over a period of T months (WR_{iT}) can be calculated as:

$$WR_{iT} = \frac{\prod_{t=1}^{T}[1+R_{it}]}{\prod_{t=1}^{T}[1+\mathrm{E}(R_{it})]} \tag{36}$$

Because WR_{iT} is a ratio of the end of period wealth in an event-firm to the end of period expected (benchmark) wealth, this measure of long-term abnormal return takes account of compounding but does not grow in the length of the holding period.

In response to the bad model problem and regular rebalancing, several authors sidestep the use of an asset pricing model altogether, and adopt a characteristic-based return benchmark described in Section 4.3. Both control-firm and control-portfolio returns are commonly employed as a proxy for expected return. However, this approach is not trouble-free. In relation to the use of a control portfolio, Barber and Lyon (1997a) identify three biases: namely; new listing bias, rebalancing bias and skewness bias. The *new listing bias* is expected to systematically drive the abnormal return estimate upward. This is because the control portfolio includes not only seasoned firms, but also newly listed firms which generally underperform market averages. It is the inclusion of newly listed firms that systematically drives the control portfolio return downward. Compounding gives rise to the *rebalancing bias* when constituent returns in the control

[17] Fama (1998, p. 294) illustrates a simple example of this artificial BHAR problem.

portfolio reverse.[18,19] While the control portfolio effectively gets rebalanced periodically in order to maintain equal weights, there is no rebalancing for the sample firm.[20] With return reversal, periodic rebalancing of the control portfolio translates into the purchase (sale) of stocks that perform well (badly) in the next period, inflating the long-term return earned by the portfolio. If the control portfolio is value-weighted, however, periodic rebalancing does not lead to the rebalancing bias. The *skewness bias* arises from the dissimilarity in distribution between long-term return to a sample firm and long-term return to the control portfolio. Because returns on an individual stock can be very large whereas portfolio returns typically are relatively small, the resulting abnormal return is generally skewed. Since the risk factor(s) in an asset pricing model is essentially a spread in portfolio returns, these biases are also present when using an asset pricing model as a return benchmark. The outcome of these biases is misspecification of test statistics, i.e. rejection of the null hypothesis of zero abnormal return when it is true.

Barber and Lyon (1997a) show that the use of control-firm return eliminates the new listing and rebalancing biases, and largely alleviates the skewness bias. First, the identified control firm must be listed at the beginning of the event period of interest. Second, there is no portfolio rebalancing when the benchmark is a control firm. Finally, the random chances of both individual sample firms and their respective control firm experiencing large positive return are equally likely. Nevertheless, one question remains. Is it empirically possible to find a true control firm as such? As explained in Section 3.4.2, firms conducting the same event are likely to share similar characteristics. To this extent, it is highly likely that the available pool of candidate control firms (or, firms to enter a control portfolio) is much smaller than what one would expect on the surface. In reality, moreover, there is no such a thing as a single firm (or, even a portfolio) that represents an *exact* match for a given event firm. This may

[18]Note that this rebalancing bias is not the same problem as the problem of regular rebalancing discussed above, which pertains to the event-firm or sample-firm portfolio.

[19]Barber and Lyon (1997a) note that the observed return reversals in the control portfolio are not necessarily sufficient for profit making since these reversals may well be the outcome of a bid-ask bounce.

[20]Although the control-portfolio return may be measured as buy-and-hold return, rebalancing still mechanically occurs with the use of interval returns (e.g. monthly returns) as an input.

explain why significant long-term abnormal return, as reported in many studies, still survives the characteristic-based return benchmark.

In the interest of completeness, it is worth mentioning the remedies for the new listing and rebalancing biases suggested by Lyon *et al*. (1999). To avoid these biases, Lyon *et al*. calculate long-term return to a control portfolio by first compounding over the event window the returns to individual constituent firms in the portfolio and then averaging across firms. In order to alleviate the skewness bias, Lyon *et al*. advocate the use of bootstrapped skewness-adjusted *t*-statistics and a nonparametric bootstrap approach based on an empirical distribution of returns in a pseudo-portfolio, which contains one randomly selected firm for each sample firm.

The measurement issues also include the controversy over how the event-firm portfolio should be weighted. For tests of long-term abnormal return, the choice of portfolio weighting has an implication further from whether the objective is to measure the typical or aggregate wealth effect of an event. On the one hand, Fama (1998) argues that value-weighting gives an appropriate measurement of abnormal return since it more accurately captures the total wealth effects experienced by investors. On the other hand, Loughran and Ritter (2000) contend that value-weighting leads to low power to detect true abnormal return, particularly when abnormal return is expected to persist among smaller firms, and therefore, advocate the use of equally weighted returns. Employing the Fama–French three-factor model, Brav and Gompers (1997) report that underperformance of IPO firms is much weaker with value-weighting than with equal weighting, and that small high-growth firms earn significantly negative abnormal return whether or not they are issuers. Indeed, Fama (1998) also points out that the significant long-term abnormal return on an equally weighted portfolio, which is found in many studies, shrinks a lot and often disappears when value-weighting is adopted. Given the existing empirical patterns, it appears that the use of equal weighting can be expected to produce significant abnormal return, especially if the sample is tilted toward small high-growth firms.

5.2 *Statistical issues*

At the heart of an ideal method for measuring abnormal return lie two key statistical properties. First, the method must not reject the null hypothesis of zero abnormal return when it is true. Second, the method must have sufficient power to reject the null when it is false, i.e. to detect abnormal return when it exists. As mentioned earlier, Lyon *et al.* (1999) propose the use of skewness-adjusted *t*-statistics and empirical distribution of pseudo-portfolio returns via bootstrapping as remedies to measurement problems. Lyon *et al.* report that these techniques are well-specified and powerful in detecting abnormal return. However, this result holds only in the random sample situation. In the presence of industry clustering and calendar clustering, these methods yield mis-specified test statistics. Intuitively, the non-random nature of corporate events is likely to violate the two implicit assumptions made by the bootstrapping procedure: (i) the residual variances of sample firms are identical to those of the randomly selected firms; and (ii) the observations are independent of each other (Mitchell and Stafford, 2000).

As Mitchell and Stafford (2000) point out because event firms are clearly different from random non-event firms, an empirical distribution created from characteristic-based matching does not replicate the covariance structure underlying the original event sample, and in this case, an overstatement of statistical significance could result. Indeed, Lyon *et al.* (1999) recognize that the bootstrapping methods do not solve the problem of cross-sectional correlations among abnormal returns. As described in Section 3.4.2, it is possible to adjust for cross-dependence by using Brown and Warner's (1980) CDA. However, the CDA requires the use of pre-event data, which would exacerbate the new listing bias.

As explained in Section 4, forming the portfolio of event firms in calendar time *eliminates* the cross-dependence problem. In fact, this is the only way to eliminate cross-sectional correlation among abnormal returns. In Section 4, two alternative calendar-time approaches are described. Lyon *et al.* (1999) report that the calendar-time Fama–French three-factor model yields well-specified statistics in random samples although it is generally mis-specified in situations of extreme sample biases. More importantly, this approach yields well-specified statistics in the case of return overlap: the sample situation in which cross-dependence is most severe. This result is observed for both equal and value-weighting. As reported by Lyon *et al.*, the characteristic-based benchmark approach such as one described in Section 4.5 is comparably well-specified, but suffers from having lower power than the Fama–French three-factor model. Nevertheless, whether or not even the three-factor model with value-weighting is sufficiently powerful remains debatable. Loughran and Ritter (2000) report that, on a value-weighted basis, the three-factor model captures only half of the true abnormal returns. Taking an alternative perspective, Mitchell and Stafford (2000) observe high R^2 values (generally in excess of 0.90) for their value-weighted Fama–French three-factor regressions, and thereby argue that the model has "considerable power" (p. 315). Mitchell and Stafford also report that the evidence of statistically significant BHAR practically disappears once the average covariance and correlation of individual BHARs are controlled for, and on this basis, argue that a calendar-time approach is more powerful than BHAR (i.e. an event-time approach) after controlling for cross-sectional correlation. On balance, empirical evidence on the relative power of the calendar-time approaches to tests of long-term abnormal return on balance remains inconclusive.

5.3 *Taking perspective on the methodological problems*

In terms of guidance on what to do exactly when conducting tests of long-term abnormal return, the above two sections are far from encouraging. Again, it is crucial to be fully aware of what the adopted test method(s) does and does not do, and what problem is likely to come with it. As Lyon *et al.* (1999) emphasize in their abstract, "analysis of long-run abnormal returns is treacherous". This is true, and the testimony is provided by Masulis *et al.* (2007, footnote 9): "given the serious methodological concerns that long-run stock return studies raise and the controversial nature of the evidence they produce (see Mitchell and Stafford, 2000; Andrade *et al.*, 2001[21] for detailed discussions of the evidence for acquisition activity), we choose to focus on short-run stock price reactions instead."

For many, unfortunately, a formal test of long-term abnormal return is called for by the orientation of their research objective. Given the problems discussed above and a lack of definite solution, robustness checks are of absolute necessity. To obtain any empirical standing, results must be strong enough to show that they stand up to both the measurement and statistical problems.

It is economically important that the abnormal return estimates to be reported are compatible with a real-world strategy for investors. To many, it is more realistic to expect investors to invest in event time and demand interest on interest than to invest in calendar time with monthly rebalancing. In terms of the choice of return benchmark, the question is whether

[21] Cited in Masulis *et al.* (2007).

or not one can accept the price of identifying ideal control firms or portfolios. If one is to view, and can justify, that a true control firm/portfolio exists, then an approach that utilizes a characteristic-based return benchmark is a plausible test method. Otherwise, a k-factor asset pricing model provides a more definite return benchmark. In event time, it should not be too time-consuming or costly to implement the approach in Equation (26) and apply the setup of Equation (23).

It is of equal importance that abnormal return estimates are statistically reliable. For instance, Fama (1998) contends that formal tests of abnormal return should be based on short-interval returns for which normality is a better approximation.[22] It is the cross-dependence problem, which is a serious concern for a long-horizon test, that renders the event-time methods statistically inadequate, and based on the findings of Mitchell and Stafford (2000), powerless in detecting abnormal return. In order to establish statistical reliability of abnormal return estimates, it is therefore crucial to employ a calendar-time approach, using either a formal asset pricing model or characteristic-based return benchmark, or both.

In sum, there is no single fool-proof approach to measuring long-term abnormal return. At the very least, one event-time method and one calendar-time method should be employed. If the two sets of results are similar and lead to the same conclusion, then it may be claimed that there is discernible evidence of event-induced long-term abnormal return. Otherwise, the results are just inconclusive. To this end, another caveat is in order. Inconclusive results may be interpreted as "no finding". Because long-horizon tests are basically plagued with methodological problems, no finding also means (to virtually all of our well experienced and meticulous colleagues) that "your methods are problematic" and/or "there is just a lot of noise in your data". Accordingly, it would inevitably follow as a conclusion that the comprehensive analysis we have just conducted tells us nothing about the event: rather than the event, on balance, empirically having no long-term value impact.

6. Take-Home Messages

Event studies, either short-horizon or long-horizon, all begin with accurate identification of the true event date, or the date of a surprise. In

[22] See Fama (1998, p. 294) for a detailed discussion on this debatable point.

measuring the effect of an event, both the short-term windows and long-term windows are subject to measurement as well as statistical issues. However, the existing insights from simulation and empirical studies consistently indicate that the short-horizon tests appear more robust to the potential statistical problems. To properly conduct long-horizon tests requires a sizable investment. Yet, it is well documented in the literature that these tests remain "treacherous". Understandably, long-horizon tests may appear appealing to the orientation of some research questions. To this extent, it is likely to be useful for one to ponder over the following question. Is an analysis of long-term abnormal return the only meaningful way to answer the research question?

References

Agrawal, A. and Jaffe, J.F. (2000). The post-merger performance puzzle, in Cooper, C. and Gregory, A. (eds.), *Advances in Mergers and Acquisitions*, Vol. 1. Elsevier Science.

Andrade, G., Mitchell, M. and Stafford, E. (2001). New evidence and perspectives on mergers, *Journal of Economic Perspectives*, 15, 103–120.

Barber, B.M. and Lyon, J.D. (1997a). Detecting long-run abnormal stock returns: The empirical power and specification of test statistics, *Journal of Financial Economics*, 43, 341–372.

Barber, B.M. and Lyon, J.D. (1997b). Firm size, book-to-market ratio, and security returns: A holdout sample of financial firms, *Journal of Finance*, 52, 875–883.

Boehme, R.D. and Sorescu, S.M. (2002). The long-run performance following dividend initiations and resumptions: Underreaction or product of chance? *Journal of Finance*, 57, 871–900.

Bouwman, C.H.S., Fuller, K. and Nain A.S. (2009). Market valuation and acquisition quality: Empirical evidence, *Review of Financial Studies*, 22, 633–679.

Brav, A. and Gompers, P.A. (1997). Myth or reality? The long-run underperformance of initial public offerings: Evidence from venture and nonventure capital-backed companies, *Journal of Finance*, 52, 1791–1821.

Brown, S.J. and Warner, J.B. (1980). Measuring security price performance, *Journal of Financial Economics*, 8, 205–258.

Brown, S.J. and Warner, J.B. (1985). Using daily stock returns: the case of event studies, *Journal of Financial Economics*, 14, 3–31.

Cai, Y. and Sevilir, M. (2012). Board connections and M&A transactions, *Journal of Financial Economics*, 103, 327–349.

Carhart, M.M. (1997). On persistence in mutual fund performance, *Journal of Finance*, 52, 57–82.

Davies, J.R., Unni, S., Draper, P. and Paudyal, K. (1999). *The Cost of Equity Capital*. CIMA Publishing: London.

Dennis, P.J. and Strickland, D. (2002). Who blinks in volatile markets, individuals or institutions? *Journal of Finance*, 57, 1923–1949.

Di Giuli, A. and Laux, P.A. (2021). The effect of media-linked directors on financing and external governance, *Journal of Financial Economics*, forthcoming.

Draper, P. and Paudyal, K. (1999). Corporate takeovers: Mode of payment, returns and trading activity, *Journal of Business Finance and Accounting*, 26, 521–558.

Draper, P. and Paudyal, K. (2006). Acquisitions: Private versus public, *European Financial Management*, 12, 57–80.

Eckbo, B.E. and Thorburn, K.S. (2000). Gains to bidder firms revisited: Domestic and foreign acquisitions in Canada, *Journal of Financial and Quantitative Analysis*, 35, 1–25.

Ekkayokkaya, M. and Paudyal, K. (2015). A trade-off in corporate diversification, *Journal of Empirical Finance*, 34, 275–292.

Ekkayokkaya, M., Holmes, P. and Paudyal, K. (2009a). The Euro and the changing face of European banking: Evidence from mergers and acquisitions, *European Financial Management*, 15, 451–476.

Ekkayokkaya, M., Holmes, P. and Paudyal, K. (2009b). Limited information and the sustainability of unlisted target acquirers' returns, *Journal of Business Finance and Accounting*, 36, 1201–1227.

Faccio, M., McConnell, J.J. and Stolin, D. (2006). Returns to acquirers of listed and unlisted targets, *Journal of Financial and Quantitative Analysis*, 41, 197–220.

Fama, E.F. (1998). Market efficiency, long-term returns, and behavioral finance, *Journal of Financial Economics*, 49, 283–306.

Fama, E.F. and French, K.R. (1992). The cross-section of expected stock returns, *Journal of Finance*, 47, 427–465.

Fama, E.F. and French, K.R. (1993). Common risk factors in the returns on stocks and bonds, *Journal of Financial Economics*, 33, 3–56.

Fama, E.F. and French, K.R. (1996). Multifactor explanations of asset pricing anomalies, *Journal of Finance*, 51, 55–84.

Fama, E.F., Fisher, L., Jensen, M.C. and Roll, R. (1969). The adjustment of stock prices to new information, *International Economic Review*, 10, 1–21.

Fuller, K., Netter, J. and Stegemoller, M. (2002). What do returns to acquiring firms tell us? Evidence from firms that make many acquisitions, *Journal of Finance*, 57, 1763–1793.

Gregory, A., Tharyan, R. and Christidis, A. (2013). Constructing and testing alternative versions of the Fama–French and Carhart models in the UK, *Journal of Business Finance and Accounting*, 40, 172–214.

Grinstein, Y. and Hribar, P. (2004). CEO compensation and incentives: Evidence from M&A bonuses, *Journal of Financial Economics*, 73, 119–143.

Harford, J. (2005). What drives merger waves? *Journal of Financial Economics*, 77, 529–560.

Harford, J., Humphery-Jenner, M. and Powell, R. (2012). The sources of value destruction in acquisitions by entrenched managers, *Journal of Financial Economics*, 106, 247–261.

Hollander, M. and Wolfe, D.A. (1999). *Nonparametric Statistical Methods*. Wiley: New York.

Jaffe, J.F. (1974). Special information and insider trading, *Journal of Business*, 47, 410–428.

Jegadeesh, N. and Titman, S. (1993). Returns to buying winners and selling losers: Implications for stock market efficiency, *Journal of Finance*, 48, 65–91.

Jensen, M.C. and Ruback, R.S. (1983). The market for corporate control: The scientific evidence, *Journal of Financial Economics*, 11, 5–50.

Jenter, D. and Lewellen, K. (2015). CEO preferences and acquisitions, *Journal of Finance*, 70, 2813–2851.

Larcker, D.F., Ormazabal, G. and Taylor, D.J. (2011). The market reaction to corporate governance regulation, *Journal of Financial Economics*, 101, 431–448.

Lipson, M. and Puckett, A. (2010). Institutional Trading during Extreme Market Movements. Working Paper, University of Virginia.

Loughran, T. and Ritter, J.R. (1995). The new issues puzzle, *Journal of Finance*, 50, 23–51.

Loughran, T. and Ritter, J.R. (2000). Uniformly least powerful tests of market efficiency, *Journal of Financial Economics*, 55, 361–389.

Loughran, T. and Vijh, A.M. (1997). Do long-term shareholders benefit from corporate acquisitions? *Journal of Finance*, 52, 1765–1790.

Lyon, J.D., Barber, B.M. and Tsai, C.L. (1999). Improved methods for tests of long-run abnormal stock returns, *Journal of Finance*, 54, 165–201.

Malatesta, P.H. (1983). The wealth effect of merger activity and the objective functions of merging firms, *Journal of Financial Economics*, 11, 155–181.

Mandelker, G. (1974). Risk and return: The case of merging firms, *Journal of Financial Economics*, 1, 303–335.

Masulis, R.W. and Zhang, E.J. (2019). How valuable are independent directors? Evidence from external distractions, *Journal of Financial Economics*, 132, 226–256.

Masulis, R.W., Wang, C. and Xie, F. (2007). Corporate governance and acquirer returns, *Journal of Finance*, 62, 1851–1889.

Mitchell, M.L. and Mulherin, J.H. (1996). The impact of industry shocks on takeover and restructuring activity, *Journal of Financial Economics*, 41, 193–229.

Mitchell, M.L. and Stafford, E. (2000). Managerial decisions and long-term stock price performance, *Journal of Business*, 73, 287–329.

Moeller, S.B., Schlingemann, F.P. and Stulz, R.M. (2004). Firm size and gains from acquisitions, *Journal of Financial Economics*, 73, 201–228.

Rau, P.R. and Stouraitis, A. (2011). Patterns in the timing of corporate event waves, *Journal of Financial and Quantitative Analysis*, 46, 209–246.

Rau, P.R. and Vermaelen, T. (1998). Glamour, value and the post-acquisition performance of acquiring firms, *Journal of Financial Economics*, 49, 223–253.

Schmidt, B. (2015). Costs and benefits of friendly boards during mergers and acquisitions, *Journal of Financial Economics*, 117, 424–447.

Shleifer, A. and Vishny, R.W. (2003). Stock market driven acquisitions, *Journal of Financial Economics*, 70, 295–311.

Spiess, D.K. and Affleck-Graves, J. (1999). The long-run performance of stock returns following debt offerings, *Journal of Financial Economics*, 54, 45–73.

Wang, C. and Xie, F. (2009). Corporate governance transfer and synergistic gains from mergers and acquisitions, *Review of Financial Studies*, 22, 829–858.

https://doi.org/10.1142/9789811260506_0011

Chapter 11

CG and Prosperous Investment Decisions — The Paradigm of Mergers and Acquisitions

Paschalis Kagias[*,¶], Markos Kourgiantakis[†,||], Ioannis Passas[†,], Konstantina Ragazou[†,††], and Stauros Bakeas[‡,§§]**

[*]*University of Western Macedonia, Department of Accounting and Finance, Kozani, Greece*

[†]*Hellenic Mediterranean University, Department of Business Administration & Tourism, Heraklion, Crete*

[‡]*Hellenic Mediterranean University, Department of Business Administration & Tourism, Operations Research and Management Audit Laboratory, Heraklion, Crete*

[¶]*paschaliskagias@hotmail.com*

[||]*mkourg@hmu.gr*

[**]*ipassas@hmu.gr*

[††]*kragazou@hmu.gr*

[§§]*staba7@gmail.com*

Abstract

Mergers and acquisitions are business transaction that if occur they have a pervasive effect both to the seller and the buyer and they can derive in substantial benefits or failures. The chapter aims to approach mergers and acquisitions in a spherical way, synthesizing business reasons driving to M&As, the risks, the challenges, the financial aspects and the accounting treatment based on the IFRS's.

Keywords: Investments, decision making, corporate governance, mergers, acquisitions

1. Introduction

Mergers and acquisitions (M&A) do not happen frequently in the life of a business. However, when they happen, they are changing fundamentally the operations of the companies involved. In most cases, M&A will have a pervasive effect in the company affecting its operations, financial reporting, revenues, and capabilities. In this chapter we will discuss why companies take part in those transactions, what the most common steps are and how the financial reporting is affected by the buyer and the seller as well.

2. Types of M&A

There are three types of acquisition structures:

2.1 *Stock acquisition*

In stock acquisition the acquiring company, buys the shares and obtains the control over the acquired company. The acquiring company becomes the parent company, the acquired company becomes subsidiary and both companies continue to exist. In the case of private firms this is can be made by a stock purchase agreement between the buyer and the shareholders of the target company, while in listed companies this is made by a tender offer. It is not infrequent the tender to offer a consideration that it is higher than the market price. The consideration may be paid in cash or through a stock exchange or both.

2.2 *Merger*

In contrast in the cases of mergers the assets and the liabilities of the acquired company pass to the acquiring company and the acquired company ceases to exist. In public companies the merger can be accomplished in one stage (where all shareholders consent and sign the purchase agreement) or two stages (where the acquirer purchases the majority of the shares and then squeezes-out, forcing the minority shareholders to sell their shares) (Miller and Segall, 2017).

2.3 *Asset purchase*

The difference of asset purchase from the merger and the stock acquisition is that in asset purchase the acquiring company buys some or all assets or liabilities of another company, but it does not acquire the whole business. In those transactions the acquirer usually obtains a division of a company. For example, a company that excavates and processes marbles can sell the activity of the processing by selling its property, machinery, and equipment of this operating activity while it will retain the operations of the excavations.

Another cauterization of the M&A is based on the industry in which the acquired company operates.

2.4 *Horizontal acquisitions*

In horizontal acquisitions the acquired company operates in the same industry with the acquirer. For example, when a supermarket chain acquires another to benefit from the economies of sale.

2.4.1 *Vertical acquisitions*

In vertical acquisitions the acquirer moves upper or lower in the supply chain. The primary reason for such acquisitions is to achieve synergies. For example, a company that provides cool storage services might purchase a transportation company.

2.4.2 *Conglomerate acquisitions*

In these acquisitions the acquiring and the acquired companies operate in completely different sectors. The usual reason for such transactions is the diversification of risk.

Another categorization of the M&A's is between friendly and hostile takeovers. In friendly M&A's the acquiring company has the consent of the management while in hostile takeovers the acquiring company obtains the control by aggressive tactics.

3. Advantages and Disadvantages of Expanding through Acquiring Companies

3.1 *Advantages*

The acquisition of a company in the current structure changes significantly the way that the company operates. Through M&A the acquiring company may achieve market, power, efficiency gains and other advantage that may provide competitive advantage. Some these advantages are:

Economies of scale: A company that increases its size may be in position to negotiate better terms with its customers, suppliers, it may have greater access to capital, or funding with better conditions and increased bargaining power against the competitors.

Synergies: Synergies defined as a combination of two firms' assets that are more valuable together than they are separately (Feldman and Hernandez, 2020) and are also referred as: "one plus one, equals three". Actually, is a combined ancient Greek word from the word "syn" that means plus or together and the noun "ergon" or action meaning working together. In businesses, synergies may allow for the two firms to exploit opportunities that they could not while acting on their own. Such a paradigm is the acquisition of Lucasfilm from Disney which allowed Disney the ability to add theme park rides and similar services to its current portfolio. Synergies may also take the form of cost and financial synergies.

Reduction of dependence: In some cases, buying a supplier or a customer can reduce the risk of dependence. For example, a car manufacturing company if acquires a supplier that provides certain parts will obtain the control of the manufacturing process, reducing risks relating to the supply chain.

Access to talent, research and development: Through a business combination a company may acquire human talent that it lacks.

Tax benefits: In some cases, governments may provide incentives for the formation of larger and more competitive business structures. But even if this is not the case the acquisition and the transfer of some operations in a country with lower taxes may increase the profitability of the acquiring company.

Faster strategy implementation: This usually happens when a company intends to enter in new markets, for which it lacks local knowledge. By acquiring an established and reputable local firm the cultural differences may be overcome faster, the local knowledge can also be proven valuable, and the realization of the benefits might become easier and faster.

Diversification of risk: More revenue streams provide a less risk. It is a much safer way of operating than relying in just one product/service or market. Consider the following example. Assume that you own a factory in UK that produces and sell single-use plastic straws in UK. Assume also that you live in the year 2019. In 2020, the single-use plastic straws in UK. Unless your company produces other products or sell the single-use plastic straws in other countries it is highly possible that it will fail.

Adding value: A company may consider that it has the ability to purchase another firm, to enhance its performance and either to re-sell it or obtain the increased cash flows. There are many ways to add value in a company. For example, Miller and Segall (2017) referred to the agency problem and they suggested that in some cases the management may do not act to the interests of the shareholders, to be ineffective or greedy. An acquiring company could add value by correcting the mismanagement.

3.2 *Challenges*

Unfortunately, not all mergers and acquisitions are successful.

Missing the target: If the aim is to achieve consolidation and synergies, the acquisition must take place only of there are sufficient, identifiable and quantitative synergies. If at any point during the negotiations or the due diligence becomes apparent that this is not the case, the buyer must withdraw its interest.

Inadequate due diligence: Due diligence is a process by which the acquiring company estimates the true financial position of the target company (among others). The aim for due diligence is that the acquiring company is to verify what it gets from the transaction and how it will utilize it. If the due diligence is not sufficient the acquirer will lose a valuable opportunity to understand the acquired company.

Overestimating synergies: Managers tend to be optimistic and as a result they may fantasize synergies that they will never be realized or that will be achieved but in a lower extend. Conservatism, due diligence of sufficient quality and risk awareness may be the solution.

Failure to integrate companies: In practice the integration between two companies, with possibly different systems, culture and processes may be proved more difficult than anticipated. Companies must be careful to identify and retain the critical resources and to safeguard that vital products and projects will not be affected negatively.

Lack of cultural fit: Cultural difference exists not only to different countries but also to the same industry and the same country. Cultural clashes will make the integration more difficult. However, the top management can take steps ranging from forceful integration of the two firms or allowing a degree of independence to the local management but with defined and clear goals.

Lack of strategic plan: The acquiring company.

Exogenous risks: Even if everything is planned in the maximum possible detail the possibility of failure due to external factors is always present.

Overpaying: It is one of the most common reasons for the failure of an M&A, destroying the shareholders' value.

Lack of strategic fit: An M&A shall have a good reason. Gaining market share, achieving synergies are good reasons.

Lack of management involvement: If the management in the post-acquisition process will not have an active involvement to implement the M&A and the integration of the two firms the transaction is doomed.

To overcome these challenges Perry and Herd (2004) suggested two simple rules:

(a) to follow the leaders, to imitate what they did correct and avoid their mistakes;
(b) turning the odds in your favor, meaning to make sure that the target organization is a good fit. This can be the case when assumption used for the valuations are realistic, the buyer is considering for changes in the external environment, assessment of all synergies and costs

The ten steps in the M&A deal process.

Identification of the target company	**Development of acquisition strategy** The acquisition strategy involves the objectives setting from the acquiring company, or in simple words what it wants to obtain from the transaction. For example, it is the aim to buy a company with a view to resell it in the future the objective is to identify undervalued businesses.
	Establishment of M&A criteria The establishment of the criteria is the next step of the process. In this step the acquiring company sets objective and measurable criteria to identify potential targets.
	Investigation for potential targets Based on the criteria established in the previous stage the management tries to identify target companies that meet those criteria.
Establishment of the agreement	**Acquisition planning** The acquiring company contacts with the businesses of the previous stage to gather more information, to further validate that they meet the criteria and to prioritize the targets.
	Valuation The valuation of the target company will allow to the acquiring company to determine the amount that is willing to offer for the transaction. For doing so, the acquiring company will need financial data from the target company. For performing the valuation to be feasible the acquiring company establishes initial contacts and conversations.
	Negotiations After the determination of the target company, the two companies enter in negotiations aiming to get the best deal.
	Due diligence Due diligence is a critical process for understanding the target company, verifying the financial, legal and tax position and many other critical aspects. The due diligence process is further analyzed below. It is also relevant to note the process of due diligence and the negotiation is dynamic. As new information arises the acquiring company may adjust the valuation and the consideration that is willing to pay.
	Contractual arrangement If everything has gone as planned, at this stage the two parties include their decisions in a formal and enforceable agreement.
	Financing strategy for the acquisition The financing of the acquisition can be through equity, debt, or a combination of both.
Post-acquisition period	**Integration of the two businesses** In this stage the management of the acquiring company works to complete the merger and the integration of two firms, so that the established criteria set from the begging to be achieved.

objectively, review the business processes of the seller, posterization of key value drivers and risks.

4. The Process

The process of an M&A process, in the buyer's view, can be distinguished in three main stages: (a) the identification of the target company, (b) the procedures for the establishment of an agreement and (c) the post-acquisition process.

However, sometimes the process can start from the acquiring company for many reasons, for example, if it faces economic difficulties, when the shareholders need liquidity, etc. In accordance with Miller and Segall (2017) the acquisition processes of the company's target point of view, includes the following eight stages:

Valuation of the business: The purpose of the valuation is to determine what the acquired company will take from the transaction. In many cases the initial valuation is performed by an investment banker. The value of the business can be estimated using either an income approach, a market approach or an asset approach. With the income approach, the estimated future cash flows are discounted to their present value. Market approaches utilize valuation methods derived from transactions of similar businesses and assets. This will provide the ability for direct comparisons. However, a possible problem could be the absence of similar transactions. With the asset approach, assets and liabilities from the financial statements are revalued based on their fair values. It is also relevant to be noted that the value usually is not expressed at a definite number but as a range due to the estimations involved irrespective of the valuation method. Usually, the valuation of private companies is more difficult because there is no reference in the public trading price. Private companies may also be audited by external auditors or not depending on the jurisdiction and the audit limits. If the financial statements are audited there is a reasonable assurance that the financial statements are free from material errors or omissions. However, even if the financial statements are not audited the buyer will rationally perform due diligence and material irregularities will be exposed.

Investment bank engagement letters: Investment bankers provide valuable services in the transaction, by locating potential buyers, assisting in negotiations, valuing the business, etc. It is a common practice in the professional services for a contractual arrangement to be signed between the service recipient and the service provider that will determine the rights and the liabilities of each party in the transaction and that will not allow misinterpretations. Although the format and the context may vary, the most common elements are:

- Compensation of the service provider (fee). This may be determined by a reference to the consideration, a standard fee or a combination of both. It is also likely that the fee will include reimbursement of expenses.
- Scope of services. In this section the parties will agree in written the nature of the services that will be provided.
- Indemnification provisions. The seller has a strong motive when selling the company to conduct financial statements fraud, securities fraud, etc. The indemnification clauses safeguard the investment banker from such hazards.

Confidentiality agreements: The potential buyer in the course of the due diligence will acquire significant knowledge of the seller, included trading secrets that cannot go public. Confidentiality is crucial. Consider the damage a pharmaceutical company will face if its research and development projects that have not been completed get leaked. Confidentiality agreements are signed by anyone who has access to confidential information. The most common elements in confidentiality agreements are:

(a) Definition of confidential information. This paragraph states exactly what confidential information is and what is not (for example, financial statements are not confidential information because they can be accessed by anyone, since usually these are available or the company's web or the registrar of companies. Instead, the customers list is confidential information). Confidential information usually involves business plans, strategies, existing or proposed bids, costs, technical developments, intellectual property, proprietary information, financial or business projections, investments, marketing plans or training information and materials.
(b) Recipients of Confidential Information. The recipient party shall use or cause the Confidential Information to be used only to evaluate the Transaction and, in a manner consistent with the terms and conditions of this Agreement, and at no time shall the recipient party otherwise use the Confidential Information for the benefit of itself or any other third party or in any manner adverse to, or to the detriment of, the disclosing party or its affiliates or their respective shareholders.

Letters of intent: The letter of intent is a non-binding document. It is a preliminary declaration of one's party's intention to do business with another. Their usefulness lies to the fact that they establish a minimum common understanding on the negotiated transaction before the two parties spend time and money.

Employee retention arrangements: Miller and Segall (2017), also pointed out the significance of the human factor in an acquisition and the need to retain talent. They stated than in many cases, especially in the private companies, the "buyer is buying the people who created the products and run the business". Moreover, the loss of key management personnel may cause difficulty in realizing the planned benefits of the merger and recruitment costs. A merger can lead to uncertainty about the future organizational direction including but not limited to feelings of loss of previous organizational culture, uncertainty about personal job security, perceptions of lack of leadership credibility feelings of confusion due to a lack of communication, survivor guilt due to downsizing of other employees and perceptions of increased job stress and workload Deloitte (2009). To overcome this threat Deloitte (2009) suggested a combination of

- financial remuneration, which will remove the uncertainty at least for a period. However, it may not be adequate on its own since employees may obtain the benefits and leave the company soon after;
- organizational support, so that employees will consider that the organization values their efforts. This can be achieved by credible leadership and sufficient access to information (in order to explain why the M&A is advantageous);
- managerial support. This may involve discussion with the employees for their role in the post-acquisition period, meetings, and performance management.

Business, legal intellectual property and due diligence: Miller and Segall (2017), distinguish business and legal due diligence from the intellectual property due diligence (patterns, copyrights, trade secrets, trademarks). This separation is important for one reason. Companies, from their operations, develop data basis, know-how and other intangible assets. Based on the most financial reporting frameworks, not all these assets are included in the financial statements; they are hidden assets. These assets are valued in a M&A. However, just as the other assets the acquiring company must make sure that it will gain their control after the transaction and economic benefits will be obtain. In some industries the intellectual property may be the most asset (for example in pharmaceutical companies, and computer software companies). Consequently, depending on the nature of the business if the IP is not protected sufficiently, the effect of the value of the business might be very significant. Control can be obtained by the exclusive use and the exclusion of others.

From signing to closing: This stage concerns the bureaucratic process but necessary steps to complete the transaction. Usually this involves the approval by the shareholders of the deal, third-party consents (for example, bank payoff letters) and possibly regulatory clearances.

5. Due Diligence

5.1 *Importance*

Due diligence is one of the most fundamental elements in a business acquisition. Consider that you want to buy a used car. The car dealer will try to get the maximum possible price and he has a strong incentive to hide damages and other aspects that would reduce the price. Due diligence is something similar, in a larger scale. Its value can best be described by the simple words of Perry and Herd (2004) who stated that "anything that can go wrong, it will ... early on the buying company needs to fully understand exactly what it's getting and what it's getting into" and they also remind that about the 50% of the M&As failed to produce returns greater than their competitors.

Due diligence has significant similarities with the audit of financial statements, but its scope is much broader and provides an in-depth understanding of the target-entity. Of course, due diligence has to be completed before the establishment of the agreement.

Due diligence is "a process of verification, investigation, or audit of a potential deal or investment opportunity to confirm all relevant facts and financial information, and to verify anything else that was brought up during an M&A deal or investment process" (BBG, 2019) or "looking under the hood" (Deloitte, 2017). In an M&A deal, hard due diligence is the battlefield of lawyers, accountants and negotiators (Investopedia, 2021).

Due diligence is completed before a deal closes to provide the buyer with an assurance of what they are getting (CFI). It is also relevant to be noted that some matters affecting the buyer's decision and/or the transaction price are not included in the financial statements. For example, in some liabilities known as contingent liabilities are not recognized in the statement of financial position. Contingent liabilities based on IAS 37 are possible obligations depending on whether some uncertain future event occurs or present obligations but payment is not probable or for which the amount cannot be measured reliably. Other usual findings in the due diligence process include inadequate customer arrangements, vague bonuses to employees, covenants not to compete, etc. (Miller and Segall, 2017).

With due diligence the buyer can verify what he gets from the transaction. However, the seller can be also benefit from the due diligence as well by providing trust and revealing the fair market of the company (CFI).

Due diligence is a complex process that can last from some weeks to months, and it needs a special team comprising accountants, lawyers, possibly other professionals and usually is conducted from audit firms.

5.2 *Scope of due diligence*

The scope of an audit of financial statements is to provide assurance that the financial statements provide a true and fair view on the entity's operations or in simple words that the financial statements are free from material errors or omissions. On the other hand, due diligence includes the strategic fit of the target company, technologies, patterns, legal issues, information technology, environmental issues and much more. In accordance with the CFI, the due diligence process includes:

(1) *Understanding of the target company*: This means understanding why the owners sell their business, if there were previous attempts, what are the revenue streams of the company (products, services, main markets, and customers), strategic objectives and long-term prospects. It is also relevant to note that strategies are followed with risks. Many mergers failed as a result of incomplete or absence of considering risks (Perry and Herd, 2004) and therefore it is highly important in this stage to understand what the risks are and how they are managed by the target company.

(2) *Financials*: The financial review involves not only historical but prospective financial information as well. The review of the historical information involves:

- review of key financial ratios over a period of time;
- review of the audit report to ensure that the figures on the financial statements are materially correct. However, it may be appropriate for the acquiring company to engage their auditor to verify significant balances and transactions;
- assessment of the target-entity's financial performance and financial position.

  In respect of the prospective financial information, it should be assessed whether:
- whether the projections are based on reasonable assumptions;
- whether the projections are internally consistent;
- whether the calculations are consistent with those assumptions and
- to estimate the working capital and capital expenditure requirements.

(3) *Tax issues position*: The compliance with taxes is an area with great risk. In tax most things are in the grey zone rather black and white. It is a usual phenomenon, that the taxpayers might see some controversial aspects as light grey while the tax authorities as dark grey. Moreover, in addition non-compliance may be revealed many years after the submission of the tax returns. For example, let us assume that a company submits transfer pricing file to the tax authorities for the year 2020 on 2021. Let is also assume that the tax authorities have the right to conduct tax inspection for 5 years. That means that the non-compliance and the penalties may arise in 2025. For this reason, thorough investigation is needed. The due diligence team shall ensure compliance with:
- timely submission of the tax returns;
- appropriate filling of income taxes, indirect taxes, withheld taxes and payroll contributions;
- transfer pricing;
- overseas taxes.

The acquirer should also consider outcomes of past investigations, for many reasons. For example, if the target firm has a history of considerable fines and tax penalties it is likely that this will be repeated in the future. Moreover, in some jurisdictions the tax authorities have a time limit to conduct tax investigation. The greater is the period of the unaudited fiscal years from the tax authorities, the greatest is the possibility of fines and penalties.

(4) *Legal issues*: In the same logic, the due diligence team shall obtain evidence that the target-company complies with the other laws and legislation, pending or threaten litigations and similar aspects.

(5) *Technology/Patterns*: This step is to ensure the legal ownership and control over the IP rights and their quality. The most common valuation methods for the IP rights are the income method (which is based on the estimated future cash flows) and the market method (which is based on similar transactions to determine the market price). The main difference of the two methods is that the market method is exogenous, while the income method is focused on the business and the cash flows that can generate from the use of the IP rights.

(6) *Strategic fit*: In the first steps the buyer targets companies that it is likely to serve its strategic goals. The due diligence process will confirm or reverse the initial assessment.

(7) *Management/Workforce*: This aspect covers all related employee matters including but not limited to salaries of key management personnel and employees, bonuses, termination and other benefits.

(8) *Information technology*: Information technology concerns include the IT infrastructure of the target company, capacity and investment requirements and maintenance costs.

(9) *Corporate matters*: Corporate matters include any arrangement that it is relevant with the governance of the organization including but not limited to officers, directors, and shareholders, voting arrangements and similar aspects.

(10) *Environmental issues*: It includes the environmental risk exposures of the target firm and how it is managing those risks.

(11) *Production*: The construction includes key suppliers, sub-contractors and materials, capacity, maintenance, and possibly capital expenditure requirements.

(12) *Marketing strategies*: Marketing strategies involve all the marketing strategies and arrangements of the target entity including distribution, representative and franchise arrangements.

6. Tactics Hostile Takeovers and Avoidance Techniques

6.1 *Hostile takeover*

Hostile takeovers occur, when a company tries to take the control of the target company without the consent of its management, in some cases when the negotiations have failed. Hostile takeover can be achieved in three ways (a) toehold acquisition, (b) tender offer and (c) proxy fight.

Toehold acquisition: With this method the one company acquires shares of the target company in the open market. That way it can control the general assembly of the target firm and the majority in the board of directors. Depending on the ownership structure it is likely that this can be achieved with ownership interest less than 50%.

Tender offer: With this method the company acquires offers to buy the shares held by the shareholders of the target company with a premium over the market price.

Proxy fight: That situation involves a group of shareholders to join forces in an attempt to oppose and vote out the current management or board of directors (CFI a).

6.2 *Avoidance tactics*

Own shares: With this tactic the target company buys back its shares from the shareholders in order to avoid dilution of control. However, in some case there may be an upper limit by the corporate law.

Pacman: This tactic is very easy to be understood from those who have played this electronic game. In this game the packman was trying to "eat" as many dots as possible running between corridors, while it was hunted by little ghosts. However, in certain cases the little ghosts were changing color and the packman could "eat" them too. In the context of hostile takeovers, the target-company tries to buy as many shares as possible from the company that makes the takeover attempt.

Crown jewels: The target company trying to become less attractive sells its most valuable assets.

Staggered board: In these types of BODs, also known as classified boards, only a small number of directors is re-elected annually. In contrast, the BOD members have re-election period distinguished in three to five classes, something that discourages takeover due to the reduced returns to the target-company's shareholders.

White knight: This type of defense involves a friendly investor, the "white knight", who acquires the target company at a fair consideration, when it faces hostile takeover attempts, with the consent of the board of directors.

White squire: The logic of this defense is similar to the white knight with the difference that in the case of the white knight the whole company is acquired. In contrast, with the white squire technique the investor acquires only a part of the target-company.

Scorched earth: In the military terminology, scorched earth means that when troops retreat of a battle, they burn corps or destroy infrastructure so that they cannot be used by the enemy and also to make harder for the enemy to be supplied with food and equipment. In mergers, scorched earth is another tactic aiming to make the target company unattractive to the would-be acquirer company. With this tactic the company does everything that it can to become unattractive on its own. For example, it can dispose its most valuable assets.

Poisson pill: With this tactic the target company issues rights to the existing shareholders to buy shares at a discount. That way the control of the potential acquirer is diluted, something that also discourages the taking over of the company.

Leveraged recapitalization: With the leveraged recapitalizations, companies change the capital structure (the mixture between debt and equity) and they use debt to buy back equity. In this process it is likely that senior managers and employees will receive shares. The use of more debt in financing companies has certain advantages such as the tax shield (interests on loans are tax deductible, while the dividends are not). However, more financial gearing means more risk and the would-be buyers may be unwilling to undertake.

Leveraged buyout: With this method the target company issues debt to buy its stock that increases the leverage and the risk of the company substantially.

7. Post-Merger Integration

There is consensus between academics and practitioners that closing the deal of the merger is only the beginning (Steigenberger, 2017; Graebner *et al.*, 2017; Schweiger and Goulet, 2005). There are many cases of M&A failures due to the failure of integration, for example, the merger of Daimler and Chrysler (Monin *et al.*, 2013). If the acquiring and the acquired companies are in the same of complementary industry in most cases the acquiring company will want to integrate the two firms in order to achieve synergies (McKenzie, 2017). Post-merger integration has been defined as "the making of changes in the functional activity arrangements, organizational structures and systems, and cultures of combining organizations to facilitate their consolidation into a functioning whole" (Pablo, 1994). However, this is not always the case. The post-merger (PMI) integration is a dynamic process (McKenzie, 2017), in which the merging firms or their components are combined to form a new organization (Graebner *et al.*, 2017). This process is not a bureaucratic process, even for companies with experience in acquiring and integrating businesses with unpredictability and uncertainty, it is to be considered as something that it is expected. The PMI can be distinguished in three categories:

(a) strategic integration;
(b) sociocultural integration; and
(c) experience and learning;

where strategic integration concerns the amalgamation of resources, while sociocultural integration refers to human, social and cultural factors, and experience and learning refers to the experience that can affect the PMIs performance.

The strategic integration is further distinguished by Graebner *et al.* (2017) in two main categories "interaction, alignment and structural integration" and "reconfiguration and renewal". The first category comprises the activities aiming to integrate the two companies based on standardization, structural absorption of the target and communication (see Figure 1).

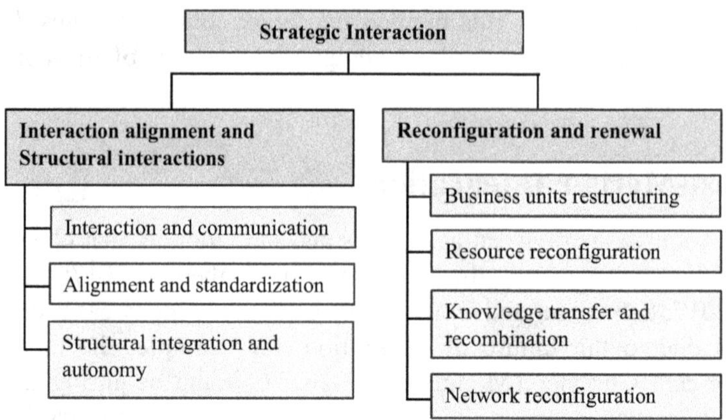

Fig. 1: Strategic interaction components.

Source: Based on Graebner *et al.* (2017).

In accordance with Graebner *et al.* (2017) the interaction and communication will enhance the coordination and the performance between the two companies leading to higher performance. On the other hand, standardization of processes, management, production, and marketing programs allows economies of scale and scope. Other considerations include the level of autonomy or structural integration which relates of the level of control from the buyer to the seller.

Reconfiguration and renewal, concerns the emerging opportunities for value creation such as recombining business units, knowledge and social networks. Graebner *et al.* (2017) found that restructuring results in better performance, while Karim (2006) examining the industry of healthcare and pharmaceutical companies found that the business unit reconfiguration increased the strategic flexibility of the acquired firm.

On the other hand, sociocultural integration and experience and learning refer to the relationship between cultural differences, the conflicts that is possible to arise due to the cultural differences and the effects in performance. Interestingly, Weber *et al.* (1996) found in contrast to the national mergers where organizational cultural differences negatively affected the cooperation and commitment in the international ones, the cultural differences resulted to better cooperation. Graebner *et al.* (2017), attributed this paradox to the greater explanatory power in the explanatory power of national cultural differences.

8. Accounting for Business Combinations

Business combinations and acquisitions in terms of accounting fall in the general category of business combinations and they will significantly affect the financial statements of both parties in the transaction in both their stand-alone and consolidated financial statements. Through business combinations companies may obtain or lose control or significantly influence resulting to changes in the consolidation methods. Moreover, other disclosure standards may become relevant.

9. The Accounting of the Acquired Company

9.1 *Accounting for the acquiring company*

If the negotiations go as planned, and the acquiring company (or the investor in the context of business combinations) will obtain the control over the target (or the investee), the investor shall present consolidated financial statements. In accordance with the IFRS's there are different consolidation methods (and standards) based on the degree of control that the investor obtains over the investee. The control may range from significant influence, control or joint control.

This section is analyzed as follows: first there is an analysis on how the level of control is determined, then there is a presentation of the full consolidation method, the equity method. The relation of the level of control and the accounting standards can be summarized in Figure 2.

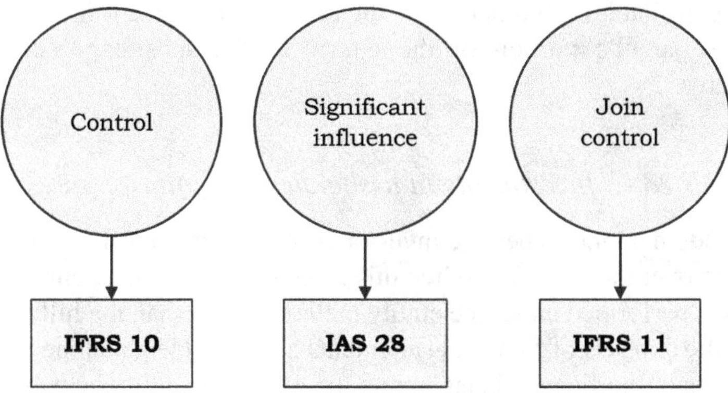

Fig. 2: Relevant IFRSs.

9.1.1 *IFRS 10 — Consolidated financial statements*

The first step to the consolidation process is to assess whether the investor has control over the investee or significant influence. In accordance with IFRS 10 [IFRS 10:7]. An investor controls an investee if and only if the investor has all of the following elements:

- Power over the investee, i.e. the investor has existing rights that give it the ability to direct the relevant activities (the activities that significantly affect the investee's returns).
- Exposure, or rights, to *variable* returns from its involvement with the investee. In other words, the investor will not obtain fixed returns for example preference dividends or loan coupons.
- The ability to use its power over the investee to affect the amount of the investor's returns.

If all the above apply, the parent company has to present consolidated financial statements unless the exceptions are applicable [IFRS 10:4]. Consolidated, financial statements are those that present the separate financial statement of the two entities as if they were one single entity. In cases where the control is achieved jointly by two parties, the standards IFRS 11 and IAS 28 are applied instead. The consolidation requirement begins and ceases at the date when the investor obtains or loses the control over the investee. The standard also describes the accounting policies and the consolidation procedures. In brief, the consolidation process involves the elimination of the intra-group balances and profits, elimination of unrealized profits in inventories, calculation of the goodwill (there are two methods available), elimination of the parent's investment in subsidiary with the parent's portion of the equity to the subsidiary and other procedures.

9.1.2 *IAS 28 — Investments in associates and joint ventures*

This standard applies when the investor applies joint control or significant influence over the investee. When this standard applies, the consolidation process is performed under the equity method, rather than the full consolidation; the two sets of financial statements are not added, and the investor recognizes in the financial statements the costs to acquire the subsidiary.

Subsequently the investment to the subsidiary is increased or decreased to the post-acquisition profits/losses.

In accordance with the standard [IAS 28:4], significant influence is the power to participate (not to form, just to participate) in the financial and operating policy decisions of the investee but cannot control or joint control those policies. For example, when the investor has the ability to appoint one director in a four members BOD, it has a limited power to affect the corporate policies but not to exercise control. The benchmark provided by the standard is 20% meaning that when the investor has less than 20% of the voting rights, it does not have significant influence (or control) and the standard is not applied. The investment will be classified and treated as financial instruments and will be accounted for in accordance with IFRS 9 — financial instruments. Instead, when the investor has between 20% and 50% this standard applies. It is also mentioned that voting rights that can potentially be obtained, for example, through financial instruments with a conversion right the entity shall examine whether they will be exercised or not.

A joint venture is a joint arrangement whereby the parties that have joint control of the arrangement and have rights to the net assets of the arrangement [IAS 28:4].

9.1.3 *IFRS 11 — Joint arrangements*

This standard applies when two or more parties have joint control deriving from a contractual arrangement. When this standard applies the investor will apply either the proportional consolidation method in the case of the joint operators [IFRS 11:20] or the equity method in case of joint ventures [IFRS 11:24], which is the same treatment as the investments in associates. The difference between joint operations and joint ventures is that joint operations require the unanimous consent of the parties sharing control while in the case of the joint ventures the parties have rights to the net assets of the arrangement [IFRS 11: Appendix A].

9.2 *Accounting for the acquired company*

9.2.1 *Going concern — IAS 1*

Based on the IASB conceptual framework: The growing concern is the assumption that the entity will continue its operations in the foreseeable future, meaning that it has neither the intention nor the need to liquidate or to cease trading. If this is not, the financial statements shall be prepared on another basis.

Some mergers will result in the business ceasing to exist as a legal entity. In that case, in accordance with the IAS 1:25, the entity shall disclose the fact that the financial statements have not been prepared on the growing concern basis.

9.2.2 *IFRS 5: Non-current assets held for sale and discontinued operations*

This standard has two components: the classification and the measurement of assets (or group of assets and liabilities) to be disposed and the disclosures, especially in the case of the discontinued operations. In the context of this chapter, it is more relevant when speaking for non-current assets held for sale to consider group of assets or business segments (and possibly related liabilities) rather than individual assets, that they be disposed in a single transaction. Obviously, this standard affects the entity that disposes a business segment rather than the acquiring entity.

9.2.3 *Classification of an asset as held for sale*

In accordance with this standard an asset shall be classified as a non-current asset held for sale if its carrying amount will be recovered principally through a sale transaction rather than through continuing use [IFRS 5:6]. To meet this requirement the asset must be available for immediate sale in its present condition and the sale must be highly possible [IFRS 5:7]. In other words, a non-current asset can be classified as held for sale much before the bidding sale arrangement. For the sale being highly probable the following condition shall apply [IFRS 5:8]:

- the management must be committed to the selling plan;
- there must be an active program to locate a buyer;
- the asset must be marketed at a price that is reasonable in relation to its current fair value; and
- the sale must be expected to be completed within the year from the date of the classification of the asset as held for sale.

Frequently, students and practitioners confuse the classification requirements between non-current assets held for sale with the investment properties. In accordance with IAS 40, investment property is a property (land or a building or part of a building or both) held to earn rentals or for capital appreciation or both [IAS 40.5]. By comparing the two definitions it is apparent that:

- Investment property does not include assets other than property, for example, equipment, intangible assets, inventories, etc.
- Investment property does not include liabilities (for example, when a lease asset is disposed the seller disposes simultaneously both the asset and the liability).
- Non-current assets held for sale does not include assets held to gain rentals.
- However, what confuses most is the element of the disposal. Investment properties include properties that it will be disposed at some point in the future when its value will be appreciated. In contrast in order to classify an asset as held for sale, the strict conditions already mentioned must apply.

9.2.4 *Measurement*

Property plant and equipment, in accordance with the IAS 16 can be measured either under the fair value model or under the cost model. When the cost model is applied the value of the asset is the lower of the book value and the recoverable amount which is the highest of the value in use and the fair value costs less to sell. However, when an asset is planned to be disposed the value in use, becomes nil (or minimal). For this reason, IFRS 5:18 requires impairment testing, in accordance with IAS 36 — impairment, immediately before the classification as held for sale in accordance with the standard applicable before the classification. After, the classification of the asset (or the disposal group of assets and liabilities) as held for sale, the measurement is based on the fair value less cost to sell [IFRS 5:15], for the simple reason that value in use does not exist (or it is minimal). After the classification as held for sale no depreciation or amortization is attributed to the asset [IFRS 5:25] and any additional impairment is recognized in the profit or loss [IFRS 5:20].

9.2.5 *Discontinued operations*

IFRS 5, defined discontinued operations as: a component of an entity that either has been disposed of or is classified as held for sale and:

(a) represents a separate major line of business or geographical area of operations;
(b) is part of a single co-ordinated plan to dispose of a separate major line of business or geographical area of operations;
(c) is a subsidiary acquired exclusively with a view to resale.

For example, if Coca Cola decides to dispose its operation in Europe, this will be a discontinued operation since it represents a major line of business and geographic area.

The provisions for discontinued operations do not affect elements in the statement of financial position but the disclosures. The aim to increase the predictive value of the financial statements allowing users to make assessments for the future prospects of the entity. It is also relevant to note that the entity will have to re-present the prior year financial statements for comparability reasons in accordance with IFRS 5:34.

References

Business Benefits Group (2019). Due diligence in mergers and acquisitions. www.bbgbroker.com/due-diligence-in-mergers-and-acquisitions/. (Accessed 15 October 2021).

Corporate Finance Institute (2022). Due Diligence Investigation or audit of a potential deal or investment opportunity. corporatefinanceinstitute.com/resources/knowledge/deals/due-diligence-overview/. (Accessed 18 October 2021).

Corporate Finance Institute (2020). What is a proxy fight? corporatefinanceinstitute.com/resources/knowledge/finance/proxy-fight/. (Accessed 16 October 2021).

Corporate Finance Institute (2022). What is due diligence? corporatefinanceinstitute.com/resources/knowledge/deals/due-diligence-overview/. (Accessed 15 October 2021).

Deloitte (2009). Retention after a merger Keeping your employees from "jumping ship" and your intellectual capital and client relationships "on board".

Deloitte (2017). M&A due diligence workshop, 2017 Engineering and Construction Conference. Available at: https://www2.deloitte.com/content/dam/Deloitte/us/Documents/Real%20Estate/us-engineering-construction-ma-due-diligence.pdf. (Accessed 21 October 2021).

Feldman, E.R. and Hernandez, E. (2020). Synergy in mergers and acquisitions: Typology, lifecycles, and value, *Academy of Management Review*, 47(4). https://doi.org/10.5465/amr.2018.0345.

Graebner, M.E., Heimeriks, K.H., Huy, Q.N. and Vaara, E. (2017). The process of postmerger integration: A review and agenda for future research, *Academy of Management Annals*, 11(1), 1–32.

IAS 28 — Investments in Associates and Joint Ventures (2011). (n.d.). Retrieved 21 August 2022, from https://www.iasplus.com/en/standards/ias/ias28-2011

IFRS 10 — Consolidated Financial Statements. (n.d.). Retrieved 21 August 2022, from https://www.iasplus.com/en/standards/ifrs/ifrs10

IFRS 11 — Joint Arrangements. (n.d.). Retrieved 21 August 2022, from https://www.iasplus.com/en/standards/ifrs/ifrs11

Investopedia (2021). Due Diligence. www.investopedia.com/terms/d/duediligence.asp. (Accessed 16 October 2021).

Karim, S. (2006). Modularity in organizational structure: The reconfiguration of internally developed and acquired business units, *Strategic Management Journal*, 27(9), 799–823.

McKenzie, B. (2017). *Post-Acquisition Integration Handbook: Closing the Deal is Just the Beginning*. Baker & McKenzie LLP: Chicago.

Miller Jr, E.L. and Segall, L.N. (2017). *Mergers and Acquisitions, Website: A Step-by-Step Legal and Practical Guide*. John Wiley & Sons: Hoboken.

Monin, P., Noorderhaven, N., Vaara, E. and Kroon, D. (2013). Giving sense to and making sense of justice in postmerger integration, *Academy of Management Journal*, 56(1), 256–284.

Motis, J. (2007). Mergers and acquisitions motives. Toulouse School of Economics EHESS (GREMAQ) and University of Crete.

Pablo, A.L. (1994). Determinants of acquisition integration level: A decision-making perspective, *Academy of management Journal*, 37(4), 803–836.

Perry, J.S. and Herd, T.J. (2004). Reducing M&A risk through improved due diligence, *Strategy & Leadership*, 14, 1368.

Schweiger, D.M. and Goulet, P.K. (2005). Facilitating acquisition integration through deep-level cultural learning interventions: A longitudinal field experiment, *Organization Studies*, 26(10), 1477–1499.

Steigenberger, N. (2017). The challenge of integration: A review of the M&A integration literature, *International Journal of Management Reviews*, 19(4), 408–431.

Weber, Y., Shenkar, O. and Raveh, A. (1996). National and corporate cultural fit in mergers/acquisitions: An exploratory study, *Management Science*, 42(8), 1215–1227.

https://doi.org/10.1142/9789811260506_bmatter

Index

G

O

P

Q

T

CPSIA information can be obtained
at www.ICGtesting.com
Printed in the USA
JSHW061537010323
38170JS00001B/2